I0815879

REMEMBERING GEORGE CARDINAL PELL

Remembering George Cardinal Pell

Recollections of a Great Man of the Church

Compiled by Tracey Rowland

IGNATIUS PRESS SAN FRANCISCO

Ignatius Press gratefully acknowledges the generous gift of Teresa DeMaria, which made the publication of this book possible.

Cover design by Enrique J. Aguilar

ISBN 978-1-62164-702-7 (HB)
ISBN 978-1-64229-312-8 (eBook)
Library of Congress Control Number 2025933209
Printed in the United States of America ♾

Dedicated to the members of the
Australian Catholic Students Association (ACSA),
past, present, and still in the mind of God

CONTENTS

Appendices: Homilies and a Eulogy
Honoring George Cardinal Pell

INTRODUCTION

George Cardinal Pell the media creation was a very different figure from the man we encountered one-on-one. He rarely showed any emotion in public, though I do remember his smile one Easter Vigil when he completely doused the journalists covering the event with holy water—something he could do without fear of recriminations because sprinkling the congregation with the aspergillum (a large brush dipped into a bucket of holy water) is part of the ritual.

He belonged to the generation brought up to "keep calm and carry on" or simply "get on with it". In his youth public figures were expected to exhibit qualities of character described in classical literature as *gravitas* and *dignitas*, and while this public expectation has long since broken down, he clearly saw it as part of his job description. In private however, his manner was very warm—indeed, paternal with younger people—informal, and nonclerical.

His friends often joked that his ecclesiology or "model of the Church" was that of a football team. Meetings with him were like a chat with the coach. I can remember a young Father Fisher joking with Marcia Riordan, then the director of the Respect Life Office for the Archdiocese of Melbourne, that Archbishop Pell was strongly opposed to abortion because it deprived those whose lives were destroyed of the opportunity to enjoy football! A more serious understanding of the cardinal's ecclesial vision, however, is offered by the Honourable Joseph Santamaria, K.C., in his contribution to this volume.

When I approached Ignatius Press with the idea of this collection of memoirs from people who knew the cardinal well, and who might reasonably be described as "friends", the response was, "Yes, but we don't want submissions to the Congregation for the Causes of the Saints; we want something more like a series of personal reflections that showcase the breadth of the man's humanity, not a hagiography."

It has been difficult to follow these guidelines since so many contributors felt compelled to offer words of homage. The person who in my judgement best followed these instructions was Timothy Cardinal Dolan of New York, whose story about the "rodeo" wins my prize for the best anecdote.

The memoirs appear in alphabetical order by the contributor's surname. Some are from those who knew him in public life; some from priests who were seminarians when he was their archbishop; a few from journalists and scholars; a couple from the world of finance, where he was trying to sort out the corruption in the Vatican; a couple from his Ballarat days, first as the son of the Royal Oak publican, then as a young priest; a few from his brother cardinals and bishops; and an assortment from religious who worked closely with him. A recurring theme is his use of direct and unvarnished speech. He didn't "beat about the bush". A number of the contributors associate this trait with a childhood spent chatting with people in his father's pub and playing very competitive football.

In addition to the memoirs, I received copies of homilies delivered at Masses said for the cardinal by Gerhard Cardinal Müller, Archbishop Anthony Fisher, and Monsignor Charles Portelli. I have created a separate section for them at the very end of the collection, along with the eulogy delivered at St Mary's Cathedral in Sydney by the former Australian prime minister Mr. Tony Abbott.

The first time I met George Pell, I was a young academic, and most of my colleagues were some species of Marxist. It was 1988, and we were both at an event to celebrate one thousand years of Christianity in Ukraine. He walked up to me and said, "I hear you are the right-winger in the Politics Department!" All I knew of him was that he was an auxiliary bishop, and there were plenty of those who would regard being "right-wing" or simply not a Marxist, or not enthusiastic about liberation theology, as a problem. I gave him a Paddington Bear stare and said, "I think of myself as a post-modern Christian humanist".[1] He looked confused and disappointed. If I had said "guilty as charged, my lord" or "my compliments to your intelligence service", we would have become instant friends. Instead, that relationship was to be delayed for a few years until I married someone who could tutor me in the art of boyish banter. Years later there was a moment in the courtyard at Domus Australia when he asked me what I made of someone who had recently been appointed to a high office. I replied, "He's not my beer, Your Eminence", and he laughed a lot, and I felt as though I had finally mastered his Royal Oak patois.

My earliest encounter with a bishop of any kind was in my childhood in Rockhampton. My primary school was located behind the cathedral. Bishop Francis Rush would sometimes leave his presbytery and come across to our playground. He kicked footballs to the boys and mostly chatted with us girls. He visited the Mater Hospital run by the Sisters of Mercy almost every day. He anointed the dying and congratulated the mothers in the maternity ward. He was famous for remembering the names of children in the

[1] I had come across this label reading a book by a Russian Christian who used it to mean someone who refused to accept the Kantian separation of faith and reason—that is, someone who was "post" or "beyond" being intellectually crippled by Kantian precepts.

large Catholic families. He drove a posh grey car (I think a Mercedes) that was easily identifiable since no one else in Rockhampton owned one. The car had been a gift to him from the Catholic people of Central Queensland and the "outer Barcoo" when he became their bishop.[2] His successor caused waves of despondency to descend over the diocese by asking for a Mazda! His successor wanted a "people's car". Bishop Rush was in touch with his people through his daily visits to the hospital and through his random visits to our school playground; nonetheless, he was also a local dignitary, and his car was a symbol of his civic dignitary status. The Catholic people were proud of him and proud that their bishop, their social leader, had the best car in town.

Cardinal Pell similarly had this capacity to be both "with the people" and a civic dignitary. I remember one night in Rome when he was dining with a bunch of Australians, mostly seminarians, at an outdoor café in Trastevere. A group of Indian street traders came along. These traders descend upon tourist areas to sell what most people regard as junk, except for their umbrellas, which are useful for rescuing tourists caught in rain showers. The seminarians wanted to get rid of the hawkers as quickly as possible, but the cardinal engaged them in conversation, took an interest in who they were and how they got to be street traders in Rome, and bought one of their toys: a mechanical dog that danced and sang a song. The lyrics included "I don't just want you for the weekend. I want you for the whole of my life." The cardinal defended his purchase by saying, "I'm the prefect for the economy. I have to stimulate the economy." He then gave the toy dog to me and told me

[2] The Diocese of Rockhampton stretches from towns located on the Pacific coast of Central Queensland westward into outback Queensland, through which meanders the Barcoo River that was mentioned in the famous "Bush Christening" poem of Banjo Paterson. The poem begins with the words "On the outer Barcoo, where churches are few, and men of religion are scanty".

to bring it home as a present for his friend Bishop Peter Elliott, known for his love of *cats*. I sometimes use this story as a way of explaining to students the meaning of *noblesse oblige*. The cardinal did not need a singing dog, but the hawker probably needed to sell a few singing dogs to keep body and soul together. The cardinal was being gracious. He cared about the street traders, while most people who live in Rome regard them as a nuisance.

The Archdioceses of Melbourne and Sydney are much larger than 1970s Rockhampton or the tourist traps of Rome. Like all the metropolitan archdioceses across the world, they tend to be managed by a class of bureaucrats, often with little, if any, theological or spiritual formation, beyond whatever they picked up in a Catholic school, which is likely to be not much in the period of the past fifty years. As with all bureaucracies there is a tendency for the personal element to be sacrificed on the altar of administrative efficiency.

One aspect of the child-abuse tragedy is that the victims, as they came forward, had to jump through legal hoops and processes governed by protocols. A certain amount of this is inevitable because unless legal tests are set, anyone can come forward with untrue allegations in an effort to make money or simply to destroy someone's reputation for good character. Balancing the legal with the pastoral is extremely difficult. I feel deeply sorry for those whose experience of the process was far from healing—those who found themselves contending with Catholic Inc. rather than the Church as their mother. I long for the day when dioceses are much smaller, allowing bishops to have personal contact with those for whom they are responsible—allowing them the time to kick footballs in playgrounds and visit the sick in hospitals—in general, allowing them to get to know the people for whom they are to be shepherds, as was the case in my rural Queensland childhood.

That said, over the years I saw Cardinal Pell in many contexts with Catholic students, and he took a personal interest in their well-being. He spent around a million dollars a year on university chaplaincy work, making sure that the Catholic students at the universities in Sydney could attend lectures and courses on theological topics at a level that was at least on par with whatever they were studying at their university. He completely understood the need for laypeople to receive an intellectual formation that was Catholic, and he was aware that the Catholic school system was failing in this regard. He worked hard to foster religious education programs that had some intellectual content, but unless teachers themselves have received a strong theological formation, they are not in any position to give it to children. He was also generous with the gift of scholarships, and he was proud when Australian Catholics were successful on the stage of the nation and even sometimes on the stage of the world. He did not suffer any kind of cultural cringe. He thought that Australian Catholics had a contribution to make, and his vision was global without his being a globalist in the negative sense of that term.

My own experience of his "no cultural cringe" disposition occurred in the late 1990s. There was a Catholic bioethics conference in Cambridge attended by then-Archbishop Pell and about a dozen young Australians from the world of medicine and academic life. Archbishop Mario Conti from Glasgow had the job of introducing Archbishop Pell to the conference. He began his speech by saying that he, Conti, had travelled from Glasgow to Cambridge with two assistants, but from the number of Australian accents in the breakfast queue, it was clear that Archbishop Pell had filled an entire Qantas jumbo jet with his entourage. Quite simply, Archbishop Pell had rounded up as many young pro-life academics and medical types as he could find and helped fund their trip to the conference. Archbishop Conti confessed to having walked along the breakfast queue asking the Australians for their best "Pell story", and he retold a number of these in his introduction, adding to +Pell's larger-than-life reputation. Archbishop Pell later told us that we had been "very indiscreet", but the indiscretion was born of pride in having an archbishop who was not another boring bureaucrat. We all knew that our man was at least interesting. We all basked in his reflected glory. In the late 1990s he made it chic to be an Australian Catholic—not by intending this outcome, but just by the fact that he was a return to the model of the bishop as the social leader of the Catholic team. At the time I was a student in Cambridge, and at Fisher House (the Catholic chaplaincy), the two most talked about clerics were George Pell and Francis George. The American students would speak of "our George and your George".

Of course, Catholics of the 1960s generation sometimes found this larger-than-life international fame embarrassing. They didn't want to be led by someone they regarded as a social dinosaur—a sort of new model or revamped Daniel Mannix. Archbishop Mannix had been a polarising figure in Melbourne society. For the best part of five decades he fostered the upward social mobility of the Irish and later Italian working class. Once the glass ceilings were broken, however, the generation who "made it" wanted to consolidate and protect their social gains. They were not keen on starting a new culture war with decidedly post-Christian elites. Nonetheless, the younger generation of Catholic leaders who had been the guinea pigs in the pastoral experiments of the 1960s and '70s—experiments renowned for putting all their pedagogical eggs into the basket of human feelings and completely neglecting any kind of intellectual formation—cheered for the bishop who was demanding more intellectual rigor and fidelity to Catholic teachings, however socially unfashionable.[3] Several memoirs in this collection attest to the cardinal's support for the intellectual formation of young Catholics and the paternal encouragement he gave to young intellectual types.

Physically, Cardinal Pell resembled a bear, and he even sometimes sounded like a bear. His "ums" were often quite guttural, or in the description of one contributor, "gravelly". Nonetheless, the animals with whom the cardinal was most often associated were the kangaroo and the lion. His enemies in Italy who thwarted his attempts to clean up the financial corruption within the Curia called him "the kangaroo", while his friends concurred with Archbishop Fisher's comparison of the cardinal with the English king Richard Cœur de Lion.

Speaking of lions and kangaroos, the only place on the planet where one can find an ambo supported by kangaroos (rather than a lion or two) is in the chapel of Domus Australia, a hotel near the central station in Rome. Domus Australia was one of the cardinal's big projects. His idea was to have a hotel in Rome where Australian pilgrims would feel at home. At breakfast guests can read the front page of

[3] Religious education programs in Catholic schools in the 1950s had a focus on dogmatic theology, on the rote learning of doctrinal propositions. This had the merit of intellectual rigor, but it was very lopsided and left out many other aspects of faith formation. After the Second Vatican Council, there was a swing towards religious education programs focused on affectivity. At the same time, "sacro-pop" music replaced solemn chant and polyphony. This cultural moment is sometimes summarized by the description of people who went through Catholic schools in the late 1960s and '70s as members of the "Kumbaya" generation. The standard caricature of the religious education of this generation is a coffee table covered in a batik cloth and set with multicolored candles, around which students sit in a circle and share their deepest, most personal spiritual experiences. As they do so, some teacher, often a nun, strums "Kumbaya" or some other "sacro-pop" song on a guitar. It was infantile, philistine, and a great invasion of personal privacy.

the day's *Australian* and spread their toast with vegemite. Unlike most Italian hotels that notoriously have showers the size of broom cupboards, the showers at Domus Australia, upon the cardinal's insistence, were large enough to accommodate the Australian male in comfort. Like Australia itself, the rooms at Domus are spacious. The chapel, however, is the prize of the establishment. In addition to kangaroos supporting the ambo there are oil paintings of saints, each with a close connection to the Church in Australia, mounted above the side altars. When it came to the grand opening of the hotel, the cardinal somehow managed to talk Pope Benedict into cutting the ribbon. It was no doubt the only time in the life of Pope Benedict that he was invited to open a hotel, and it was a boy from a Ballarat pub who made it happen.

Another aspect of the cardinal's personality to which contributors have attested was his ability to remain friends with people who didn't agree with him 100 percent of the time. In his memoir the Honourable Tony Abbott mentioned that he and the cardinal took differing positions on the Australian Constitutional Referendum in 1999. The issue was whether to retain the monarchy or move to a republic. The cardinal famously threw in his support for the republican campaign. At the time I was working in the Victorian office of the "No Case" (retain the monarchy) campaign, and so many of the cardinal's closest friends were not just on the monarchist side of the debate but were substantial financial donors to the monarchist team. At the time Archbishop Pell was sharing a house with Bishop Peter Elliott, and the entire Elliott clan are God, King, and Country types. Another contributor, Anna Krohn, is the niece of the late Michael Parker, who was a close friend of Prince Philip, as everyone who has watched *The Crown* on Netflix knows. (Whether the depiction of Lieutenant-Commander

Parker as a bad influence on Prince Philip—indeed, as an Australian larrikin—is fair is another matter.) Another of Anna's famous uncles was Paul Fitzgerald, the portrait artist renowned for his painting of Queen Elizabeth. Yet another contributor, British journalist Joanna Bogle, a daughter of an officer in the Royal Artillery, is a cradle monarchist. In her teenage years Joanna was a proud Queen's Guide. The list of the cardinal's friends who are staunch monarchists, and even members of Catholic royal families, could fill a book of its own. Suffice it to say that none of us found ourselves dropped or cancelled for not supporting him on this issue. (In my own case I was a double dissenter—both a monarchist and a European-style paleoconservative rather than an American-style neoconservative.[4])

My strongest association with the cardinal was through ACSA—the Australian Catholic Students Association—of which we were copatrons. ACSA was founded at the turn of the twenty-first century. In my undergraduate years the national Catholic student association was called TCFA—the Tertiary Catholic Federation of Australia. TCFA was not merely on the liberal end of the theological spectrum; some of the ideas it promoted were simply wacky. My strongest memory in this regard is of a TCFA newsletter promoting "Sophia" as the fourth Person of the Godhead. Archbishop Fisher remembers being invited to attend a TCFA swimming pool Mass! The idea of receiving Communion in a bikini is quite a neuron-pathway blocker, but such was the enthusiasm for "inculturation" in the 1980s.

[4] Paleocons and neocons have a different understanding of the causes of secularism, and they take a different stance on the liberal tradition. Paleocons do not accept that Thomas Aquinas was a Whig, or indeed, any kind of luminary of the liberal tradition. Paleocons have more in common with the British Tory tradition than with the British Whig tradition that has been influential in Catholic circles in the United States.

Father Gregory Jordan, S.J., was then the rector of John Fisher College at the University of Tasmania, and he became tired of this problem of the subjection of his students to theological garbage. The result was the foundation of ACSA, with Father Jordan serving as chaplain until his death in 2015.

"Jordo", like Cardinal Pell, had a great capacity to father people. He was an old-style Jesuit who mentored youth on everything from what shoes to wear to social events to what kind of girl or boy to marry. He often joked that his vocation was to introduce good Catholic boys to good Catholic girls and vice versa. In Brisbane he built up his own ecclesial community, a parish full of people he had mentored through their university years, at whose weddings he had officiated, and whose babies he had later baptised. Father Jordan and all those families he influenced were loyal supporters of Cardinal Pell.

During the days when the cardinal was in prison many institutions closely associated with him were pressured to remove his name from their honour boards and to remove all plaques testifying to his assistance in bringing about this or that foundation. The ACSA students never gave in to this pressure. The cardinal's name and coat of arms remained in a position of prominence on their website. They continued to pray for him and defended his name in the public space. The moment he was free, they invited him to be the keynote speaker at their next conference. For this reason, this collection of personal memories is dedicated to the members of ACSA, past, present, and still in the mind of God.

—Tracey Rowland

I

Head of the Australian Catholic Tribe

George Pell first came into my life by reputation. It was hard to visit the Jesuits' Campion Hall in Oxford, which I did regularly in the early 1980s because of my friendship with the legendary American Paul Mankowski, without hearing of the formidable Australian, likely to go places in the Church, who had done a doctorate there some years before. A few years later, I finally met him. By then he was an auxiliary bishop in Melbourne. A small group had dinner together at one of the Greek restaurants located on Sydney's Elizabeth Street. By then I'd lost any vocation to the priesthood but not my faith or my admiration for the Church at its best, and Pell was someone I instantly warmed to—thoughtful, combative about the right things, engaging but not too gushy—exactly the kind of leader I would have liked to be myself, had my time at the seminary not petered out with the dawning understanding that I lacked the patience, the ability to be celibate, and the depth of faith needed to be a credible priest.

I resolved to stay in contact with him and cheered when he was made archbishop of Melbourne. And it seemed to me that his funeral sermon for B.A. Santamaria, which was more of a rallying cry than a eulogy, had placed him at the head of the Australian Catholic tribe—that is to say, all those who regarded themselves as Catholic and respected the work of the Church without necessarily being exemplary in their practice of the faith. By that time, I would try to see him a couple of times a year, especially to discuss with him the issues where faith and public life seemed especially to intersect, such as the private member's bill overturning the Northern Territory's euthanasia laws, which Kevin Andrews shepherded through the Parliament; the bill on using "spare" embryos for medical experimentation; and the bill to strip the health minister (at the time, me) of any role in the approval of the abortion drug RU486.

Pell was an appointed delegate to the 1998 constitutional convention. It was the only time I ever disagreed with him on a serious issue. Given his habitual respect for tradition and mistrust of innovation, I still wonder whether his support for a republic might have been a bone thrown to the *Zeitgeist* to atone for all he despised in it. It was during a meeting there, involving his Brisbane Anglican counterpart and fellow delegate Peter Hollingworth, who addressed Pell familiarly, that I called him "George" rather than "Your Grace" or "Eminence" for the first and only time. Of all the people I've known well as an adult, he's the only one I never felt comfortable addressing by his first name—perhaps because he felt more like a second father to me than an older friend or colleague.

Soon enough, there was no one I respected more or whose counsel I more highly valued. Not long before the 2004 election, I came into possession of some information bearing on public life that I felt couldn't just be filed away. But if I told any of my political colleagues, that would make it their problem, not mine. So after early morning Mass at St Mary's Cathedral (he'd been appointed to Sydney by then), I visited Pell in the presbytery. After seeking reassurances that there was no criminal conduct involved, he advised me to let the electorate take care of the matter (which it did). Entirely coincidentally, a week later the cardinal (as he'd by then become) publicly criticised Labor's election policy to defund some Catholic schools. A week or so after that, ABC's *Lateline* host accused me of putting him up to it, because someone had seen me leaving Pell's presbytery, as if it were impossible for two prominent Catholics to meet except as part of a giant right-wing conspiracy. My exasperated suggestion that I might have been going to confession didn't impress anyone who thought smoke must always mean fire.

As it happened, I did make my rare confessions to him. Contrary to his unfailing public orthodoxy, and a public manner that sometimes bordered on the imperious, he was an entirely pastoral priest, usually meeting this sometimes-ambivalent penitent halfway. He had the gift of encouraging candour and offering spiritual advice without exuding judgement, and I always came away from such encounters sure that I could do better.

Just before he went to Rome to take up his position as prefect for the economy, I hosted a dinner for him in the prime minister's office with senior members of the government and some of those close to him. Beforehand, he presented me with an original *Punch* cartoon of Churchill, by then in his second prime ministership, augustly looking down on his colleagues, who were wrecking the nursery. Perhaps he had a premonition of what was to come. Perhaps he simply recalled that Churchill was a hero to me, as he should be to all would-be conservative MPs. In any event, it was a typically thoughtful touch, and pondering again the exhortation that came with it brings on an aching sense of loss.

Perhaps there was nothing sinister in the coincidence of the "Get Pell" campaign by then gathering steam in Melbourne with his uncovering of a web of self-serving and injudicious ecclesiastical financial entanglements in Rome. As might be expected, Pell bore the calumny of the well-placed official leaks with more stoicism than exasperation. I phoned him the afternoon the news broke that his second trial had produced a guilty verdict. His wintry humour included being entirely reconciled to the likelihood of being "a guest of Her Majesty" by the following day; he knew that justice might remain an ideal merely hoped for in this world.

I'm not sure how I would or should have reacted to the conviction, had I thought for a moment that he could have been guilty. Child abuse is a particularly repellent crime. But even before the facts were widely known, the alleged crime was so utterly out of character for the man I knew as to be not just implausible but impossible, at least to my mind—but not, it seems, to a vast swathe of the public who were only too ready to believe a priest guilty of sexual misdeeds and to believe that someone must pay for the sins of the Church. I can't recall ever generating as much real public outrage as I did when I told an interviewer, who persisted in asking, that, yes, I had been in touch with the cardinal immediately after his conviction. In my unsuccessful campaign to hold Warringah in the 2019 election, it was a toss-up as to what had annoyed local voters more: an obstinate refusal to regard climate change as the most critical issue we faced, or a refusal to renounce my friendship with "a convicted paedophile".

If being subject to a living martyrdom, a modern-day version of crucifixion, led him sometimes to exclaim, "My God, my God, why hast thou forsaken me", he never really showed it. He must have known that many doubted his innocence or suspected that he'd somehow participated in the cover-up of crimes—even though he was actually the first major prelate who regarded clerical deviants as criminals to be reported to police rather than sinners to be given a second chance in another parish. It was so unfair that Pell, of all people, should have been targeted in this way. Yet there's no doubt that when I visited him in jail, in December 2019 ("I was simply visiting a friend", I told the subsequent media ambush outside), he was much buoyed by Justice Weinberg's withering dissent in his first appeal, a dissent that was triumphantly vindicated by the 7–0 High Court verdict.

Naturally, given the animus against him, there was no immediate peace even after his release from jail in April 2020. The only time he ever showed any real frustration (at least to me) was when media vehicles quite literally pursued him up the highway from Melbourne back to Sydney. My call to the then–NSW police minister asking for some intervention to stop this harassment brought no obvious relief. The only protection he ever had was from a group of Maronite Christians, who gathered outside the seminary where he was to live and forcefully told the media vultures that they weren't welcome.

We caught up regularly for meals after his release from prison. Unsurprisingly, an account of the dinner meeting, at the Australian Club, of three contentious individuals found its way into the media, notwithstanding the club's privacy rules. A frequent topic was the West's contemporary self-forgetfulness and enervation and my anxiety that, for the Church, it would be "back to the catacombs". As he occasionally referenced this observation, only to disagree with it, I think my friend misunderstood me as meaning that there should be a *retreat* to the catacombs, when actually I meant that this was where the *Zeitgeist* would seek to drive us. One thing for sure was that no one ever cowed George Pell. Never was the motto Be Not Afraid more truly lived. Almost to his last moment, this mighty warrior was striving for his vision of a more faithful Church and a better world. I don't believe I've ever known a finer man.

Along with Archbishop Daniel Mannix and Santamaria, Pell is undoubtedly amongst the very greatest Catholic figures that Australia has thus far produced. And more so than those of the other two, as the very exemplar of being hated, excluded, insulted, and scorned for the sake of the Son of Man, Pell's story has resonated far and wide in the universal Church.

In his Santamaria eulogy, Pell observed, "It is the mark of the false prophet that all men speak well of him." He then theatrically paused before declaring, "Bob magnificently avoided this fate." Even more so could the same be said of the late cardinal. His prison journals should gladden our hearts and lift our minds till we meet again in the new world he so believed in.

—The Honourable Anthony John (Tony) Abbott

2

Lamingtons at Domus Australia

In 2014 the canonisation of Saint John Paul II and Saint John XXIII coincided with the annual Australian and New Zealand Army Corps (ANZAC) Day commemoration for Australians.

The men of the heroic Australian and New Zealand Army Corps are remembered every year on April 25, as this was the day they landed at Gallipoli in 1915. Their losses were tragic, their courage was of an extraordinarily high level, and their place in Australian and New Zealand history is central. In 2014 large numbers of Australians were gathered in Rome for the canonisation ceremonies. It was unthinkable that they would not also, as a matter of course, mark ANZAC Day, and the leading Australian cardinal would obviously be at the core of some commemoration.

George Cardinal Pell more than lived up to the task. In an unforgettable sermon in Rome's unique Australian church—the establishment of which owed much to the vigour and dedication of this remarkable Australian prelate—he preached at a beautiful and moving Mass, which created in its own way a moment of Australian history. There is always something powerful about people gathering together for something important when they are far from their own land: There is a special feeling of unity and comradeship, sharing a togetherness precisely because they are far from their own familiar territory. Cardinal Pell spoke into this mood and gave it something far beyond national feeling or sentimentality.

Gallipoli, he reminded the packed church, was where the Australian idea of "mateship" really evolved: relying on one another, trusting one another, facing hardship and even fear with a sense of not being alone. He gave this familiar idea a richer meaning and placed it firmly in the hands of God, putting it well beyond any clichés or popular slogans. To be in communion with one another is to be as God made us. The "me" thing doesn't work.

There were probably many other occasions when George Pell gave voice to the best of what Australia is, and could be, all about—but for me this was the most unforgettable. Growing up in Britain in the 1960s, I had always known in a vaguely legendary way of what we, and the West generally, owed to Australia in two world wars, but here there was an everyday, practical sort of commemoration of it, without pretension, in the rich Australian voice of a strong Australian bishop.

Afterwards we all gathered at Domus Australia for lamingtons and much talk and lively togetherness.[1] And of course Cardinal Pell was there at the heart of it, easy and open as he invariably was on such occasions—a pastor with his flock. It was an exciting time to be in Rome, and he was so very much part of it—and all the more so because he didn't do this in any sort of grandstanding way but somehow as the

[1] A lamington is a square sponge cake covered in chocolate or sometimes raspberry icing and dipped in desiccated coconut. It was first concocted in Queensland and named after the governor of Queensland, then Lord Lamington. It is said that his chef created them when there was a shortage of ingredients. Lord Lamington is reported to have referred to the cakes as "those bloody poofy woolly biscuits". In 2006 the lamington was inducted into the National Trust of Queensland's list of Heritage Icons, and each year on July 21, Australians celebrate National Lamington Day. Lamington drives were once a popular form of fundraising. People would buy lamingtons by the dozen.

warmhearted host to people who had an absolute right to be there and were as much a part of everything as he was.

I had first met him many years before, when he was a tall, burly priest guest at a gathering of the Catholic Women's League in rural Australia where I was the lunchtime speaker. He was, I think, representing, as vicar-general, the bishop at this gathering—but his approach was to make everyone feel that the whole thing had an importance and value in its own right: He was a pastor amongst his flock, making the whole thing go well. He was known even then as a firm upholder of the truths of the faith, a man on whom people could rely: a presence with a message of dependability.

Then, over different meetings and encounters over the years, there were talks that ranged from the deeply serious—discussions about the Church, young people, education, problems—to the cheery and even absurd. At a memorable lunch in London, he arrived in good humour, having accidentally created some confusion at the Chinese Consulate where, because of a misunderstanding about the address, he had initially been taken by an enthusiastic taxi driver. It was very typical of him to admit that, although a little puzzled, he had for a moment thought that perhaps a lunch had for some reason been arranged there, that the consulate had been lent as a convenient address. He was perfectly happy to be blamed for any confusion.

Much later, talk turned to the plight of the Church in the West, where open affirmation of the Church's teachings, especially on marriage and family issues, could lead to trouble for the speaker. "If I'm put in prison for being a Catholic journalist", I joked to him, "will you come and visit me?" "Oh, I might manage a postcard or a food parcel" was his laconic and cheery response.

Oh goodness, how completely unthinking I was at that time. So easy to joke, and then the grim reality came for this heroic pastor. Even now, writing about it makes me wince.

His was a true and gritty heroism. His last visits to London saw him greatly and rightly honoured—but his style remained always just the same. There was something very Australian about it: downbeat and lacking in pretension. Pell's voice was gravelly and measured: He didn't chatter or gossip, much less ramble or pontificate. I remember him surrounded by young people at St Patrick's in Soho—all eager to talk to him, to listen to him, just to be near him to let him know how much they valued his witness, his courage, his faithfulness. Tall as ever but now rather stooped with age, he listened and conversed as always, open and friendly. Here he was a pastor amongst his flock.

—Dame Joanna Bogle

3

Frustration in the Foxhole

In some other language there will be a better word for what joined me so curiously to George Pell. The closest in English is "frustration"—but that misses the affection from which our relationship, I hope, sprung.

Take the last time I heard his voice, two years ago. I was in my library, by the fire, when my phone rang. It was the cardinal, in Rome, and he had an urgent question: Had I heard the call?

I'm frustrated right now, not remembering his exact words. And maybe my memory has failed me twice over, because I have always remembered—or imagined—a crackling on the line, as if Pell were speaking from some distant realm or planet.

In a way, he was. How astonishing, that a cardinal so senior in the Vatican should ring some godless journalist on the other side of the world in the hope of hearing—at last—he'd heard God's call and found the faith that so enriched Pell's own life.

Just to underline that: I had met Pell just a dozen times. If he'd shown this concern for me, how many others had he worried over?

My memory may be fickle, but I haven't forgotten my instant shame at feeling I'd failed him again—yes, frustrated him.

He'd sent me an unimpressive book, supposedly by philosopher Antony Flew, to hasten the conversion he felt was imminent, especially after I'd told him of reading accounts of conversions by William James to understand how others had done it.

I was so disappointed. In fact, I in turn was frustrated that Pell—with all his ferocious intellect and his love of skewering secular frauds—could have been so impressed by such a worthless account of Flew's own conversion from atheism. His book was actually written in large part by some paint-by-numbers publishing-house ghostwriter for an evangelical ghostwriter exploiting the aging Flew, who'd barely read the result himself.

How odd, that this learned cardinal should have put so much faith in something so slight and even meretricious.

Yet how touched I was that Pell cared so much for me and my soul, and how ashamed I felt to confess I was still waiting for that knock on my door.

Yes, I felt ashamed. I felt somehow lazy, prideful, and willfully stubborn not to believe as Pell did, especially since he'd tried to bring me to God from our very first meeting a quarter of a century earlier.

Let me tell you about that too because it helps explain why I feel that the many other journalists who mocked him and crucified him never understood this most important public thing about him.

Indeed, one of his most pitiless and malevolent critics even wrote a book, *The Prince*, which the publisher promoted as "a portrait of hypocrisy and ambition" of "a cleric at ease with power", without ever allowing that Pell was a man of reverential faith—a faith he felt commanded to share.

This is the man I saw from my first meeting—a man who near the end of his life showed himself in full to the rest of the world in his wonderful *Prison Journal*.

I first met Pell when he was archbishop of Melbourne, wresting his Church from the grip of the anti-orthodox Left, to the fury of Melbourne's establishment media in that stiflingly Leftist city.

I'd just started my own equally deplored career as a conservative columnist, just as the so-called culture wars took off, and it was on that battlefield that we shared a lonely foxhole.

In reality, we met in his red-carpeted office, where Pell dispensed with any chitchat and—smiling—boomed that I, being godless, was "living on the fat of Christianity", which I instantly recognised as true.

But what could I do about it? How could I reason myself into beliefs that come through faith alone?

I fear I set Pell a challenge. He tried to help me, knowing I was serious about that, yet never succeeded.

Perhaps, being also a political churchman, he gave me some extra attention, but converting me was not actually in his interests. He agreed that an agnostic defender was more useful to his Church than a "he would say that" believer, yet it always rankled with him that I never could quite hear God's call. Like I said, it frustrated him.

And so he presented me with a copy of his sermons on Luke, his favourite disciple. He even got me to launch his book with the title *Be Not Afraid*, his favourite Biblical text. In doing so, I declared my own favourite was "Come unto me."

Looking back, our choice of passages summed up our essential difference—the preacher and the searcher.

But perhaps the difference wasn't always that stark. My last anecdote is from my visit to his temporary apartment in the Vatican, after he'd spent a week in the witness box on video-link to a royal commission looking to make him a scapegoat for the sins of his Church.

The hearing had been a ghastly business, resembling something between the Salem witch hunt and the bloodlust of the hearings in France's Terror. The proceedings stank of malice, and the hearing room at Rome's Hotel Quirinale was packed with journalists almost begging for Pell to be flayed alive.

His ordeal over—or so we thought—his very closest friends put on a lunch for him. Pell arrived late, and for the only time in my life, I saw him in tears.

He hadn't cried during the hearing. He never flinched later as he was made to walk through a screaming Melbourne mob to his show trial on farcical charges of child sex abuse.

He showed no tears when he was wrongly jailed for a crime that he could not possibly have committed.

Nor did I see him cry when he was finally released from jail, after the High Court threw out the remaining charges against him. Through all that he lived by his motto, Be Not Afraid.

Yet I saw tears fall down his face as he told us in that Rome apartment that he'd just met some of his accusers who had flown in from Australia to tell journalists he was a monster.

He wept because they'd hugged him. This bulky man almost floated into the room. He was joyful.

"Come unto me."

I have told of Pell's gentle frustration with me. But there was also mine with him.

I have felt acutely that I did not have his deep learning, but I do know something of the vicious rules of the media and public opinion.

I advised him early on, at a meeting organised by his chief counsel in his troubles, to show the public his heart—to show he really got the tragedy and the scandal of the Church's betrayal of too many children.

He wouldn't. Or couldn't. He ignored me as he'd ignored his counsel. I guess he felt he was a leader of the Church, and not the mob's puppet. Be Not Afraid.

In frustration, I asked him in one interview in Rome why he did not join in smashing his Church for its sins, instead of being too coolly measured for a media pack demanding contrition and some blood.

But once again, he would not save himself. He represented the Church, he said, and not himself.

Frustrated? I was beside myself as I saw this stubborn man then torn down for want of some self-preservation.

No doubt, he was following the example of his Lord, who refused to bow before his own accusers and deny their lies: "Thou sayest it."

How I miss him.

How glad I was to know a man who to the end—to our last call—cared most of all that he should help others know the Lord he loved.

How I feel I frustrated this godly man.

—Andrew Bolt

4

Under the Hedgehog's Armour

George Cardinal Pell reminded me of my late father. He was a man of a particular generation. Physically large. Emotionally contained. He stood firmly in his beliefs. He was certainly noticeable in any room where he stood. You could easily spot him towering above the crowd, head bent forward to listen to those standing a foot below him.

Whether it was his size or stature in the Church and Australian public life, some found him intimidating. My experience was contrary to this. I found the cardinal to be gregarious, warm, and welcoming. Perhaps a little too welcoming at times. I remember attending a gathering at the Union, University & Schools Club on Bent Street in Sydney in 2011. I was running late from another engagement and was trying to slip into the large event unnoticed, as the formalities had already commenced. From his place at the speaker's podium, the cardinal announced in a booming voice, "Ah, here's *our* Jacinta." There was no going unnoticed.

This endearing, informal welcome by the cardinal to a packed crowd was an acknowledgement not of my political standing but of my belonging to the Church as one of the faithful. In *our* cardinal's eyes, I may have been a senator, but I was a believer first. The cardinal's sense of community was often underappreciated.

I could sympathise with the cardinal on the way he was portrayed by his critics and opponents. As a politician and a person of faith, I was at times called out by journalists or political opponents as a "Catholic crusader" for my position on moral and ethical issues. I recall Penny Wong commenting about my persona in *The Australian* after I was appointed as a cabinet minister in the Rudd government in 2013. Penny said that it's easy for politicians to be stereotyped and that my public caricature stood at odds with the woman she knew. The same could be said of George Pell. The man I knew was different from the caricature by which he was portrayed. He likely didn't recognise the character depicted in much of the commentary written about him.

The cardinal was presented as an ideological and cultural warrior. He was seen as a stalwart defender and protector of orthodoxy in the Church, a conservative. He was accused of protecting the Church to the point of covering up or denying justice for those who had been abused or harmed. He was sometimes seen, even by those in the Church, as something of a lone warrior going out early with the Melbourne Response to investigate and respond to complaints of child sexual abuse in the Archdiocese of Melbourne.

While it's not always easy to separate the myth from the facts, the man I knew had a genuine desire to reform the Church and to respond to the needs of the marginalised, the vulnerable, and the disadvantaged.

Though the cardinal and I were both born and bred in Victoria, he did not reach out to me while he was archbishop of Melbourne. It wasn't until he was archbishop of Sydney that I first engaged with him following the embryonic stem cell debate. Despite seeking advice from the cardinal and other religious leaders at the time, then–Prime Minister John Howard lifted a national ban on stem cell research using "surplus" IVF embryos. It wasn't the only time the cardinal fervently opposed a Coalition's policy position, even though some thought he had significant influence over conservative leaders like Howard and Tony Abbott. Another example was the cardinal's strident opposition to WorkChoices, which eventually sounded the death knell for the Howard government.

The man I knew put his theological and moral beliefs ahead of political relationships. The cardinal's reputation as a calculating political operative was not accurate according to my experience, as someone who had skin in the game. Sure, the cardinal could assert himself on the playing field as he would have as a ruckman in his AFL (Australian Football League) playing days, but he, like a declining number of us, was doing his best to promote a life-affirming approach to complex ethical and moral issues in an increasingly liberalised society.

It was following this debate that I had lunch with the cardinal, who was still archbishop at the time, out of my curiosity to understand the Melbourne Response. As a Catholic and a politician from Victoria, I'd certainly heard a range of views on it, but I wanted to get an understanding from the man himself.

While the subsequent Royal Commission raised several issues with the Melbourne Response, we need to see it in the context of the time it was introduced. There was no national redress scheme. There was no real understanding of the extent of abuse and no transparent process in place to investigate claims. Each individual diocese, and other organisations, had been managing cases behind closed doors or through the courts up to that point.

The Melbourne Response was the first of its kind. It was the first attempt to address the matter with a set of standards that subsequently evolved, and necessarily improved, over time. Time has not been kind to the Melbourne Response, or to many responses by institutions dealing with child protection in that period, but it's easy to judge history in retrospect when you are nearly three decades down the road. There is an ongoing imperative to improve our efforts in safeguarding and child safety in all arenas of life. For example, we have yet to achieve a national Working with Children Check despite efforts over decades.

The cardinal was renowned for his understanding of the transformative power of education. I recall a dinner event hosted by the cardinal, at the Union, Universities & Schools Club, that I attended with quite a number of more senior federal politicians from both sides. I thought I should use the opportunity to engage with people I didn't know and proceeded to sit down at a table in the middle of the room with my back to the speaker.

Surprisingly, the cardinal sat next to me, despite his minders' obvious plans for him to be seated at a more prominent table in line with his hosting duties. With the single focus he is known for, and in no relation to the topic at hand, the cardinal had a lengthy discussion with me on the needs of students with profound disability in his schools and the lack of funding available for special schools to support them better. Up until that point I had no idea how passionate he was about school education. The conversation that evening, which I later relayed to Julia Gillard as education minister, was the catalyst for a funding formula to further support students in special nongovernment schools. The Eileen O'Connor Catholic College in Lewisham was founded under these new arrangements.

It was examples like this, of unexpectedly sitting next to a midlevel politician instead of my more senior colleagues, that revealed either a single-minded doggedness to "get the job done" when the opportunity presented itself or the will to put his convictions ahead of his connections. Perhaps he just enjoyed my company.

Not long before his death, I had three further meals with the cardinal, one in Sydney and two in Rome. In Sydney, the cardinal insisted on walking me back to my car, and as we left the restaurant, he dropped his glasses. We didn't notice right away, but a passerby returned them to the restaurant. It was this act of human kindness that struck me, whether the passerby knew it or not, as humanising the cardinal after he had been dehumanised so publicly during his trial and had endured 404 days of imprisonment before being exonerated.

In his prison journals, the cardinal demonstrated his incredible forbearance and, in the Christian tradition, offered up his suffering as a redemptive sacrifice, finding respite in prayer and reflection.

> On many occasions I have explained that so much depends on Jesus having both a divine and human nature in the one person. If Jesus is divine, then his death and Resurrection can be seen properly as transforming the brute matter of evil and suffering into all-powerful, transforming, and healing spiritual energy.
>
> All human suffering is transformed if it can be associated for some good human purpose with Jesus' redemptive activity. Naturally I am offering my difficulties for a successful appeal, for the Church, for all victims, but also for a good friend, that her cancer may continue in remission, and for a young couple, that they may be able to have their own children. The prospect of a reward of heavenly happiness brings another beautiful dimension to the stoic and dignified endurance of human misfortune.[1]

[1] George Cardinal Pell, *Prison Journal*, vol. 1, *The Cardinal Makes His Appeal* (Ignatius Press, 2020), 172.

Nor was he aloof with his fellow prisoners, showing warmth and pastoral support when he engaged with them.

The second lunch was after his final return to Rome, when we attended a conference hosted by the University of Notre Dame Australia and Australian Catholic University called "Catholic Schools and Religious Liberty: A Global Perspective". I had been asked to respond to the cardinal's address "Religious Liberty and the Catholic School", which was one of his final public addresses.

Diverging from my prepared script, I decided to take an informal approach, and we had a lively discussion following the cardinal's talk. He referred to philosopher Isaiah Berlin's essay *The Hedgehog and the Fox*,[2] arguing that with all the challenges facing Catholic schools, they needed to "form more Christian hedgehogs with considerable armour". The cardinal said we need to develop people to be more robust—to know what they believe in and to stand for what they believe in. In the final weeks of his life, this opportunity to share in an enlivening, engaged conversation with a group of Catholic education leaders around the future of the Church was a gift to the cardinal.

For all the words that have been written and will be written about him, I don't think they will be able to capture accurately or express fully the man or the soul of George Pell.

In many ways, the cardinal was a hedgehog. Berlin's notion is that hedgehogs view the world through a single idea—in our case, the promise of eternal life through Christ's Resurrection. To the foxes—who see the world through many experiences and perspectives—the hedgehog may seem slow and protectionist. However, there is a vulnerability under the hedgehog's armour.

[2] Isaiah Berlin, *The Hedgehog and the Fox* (Weidenfeld and Nicolson, 1953).

The cardinal also had that vulnerable side, which I encountered in many of my engagements with him. And as with my father, and many men of his generation, it was often overlooked because, being stoic, he didn't like to show it.

—The Honourable Jacinta Collins

5

From Shadows and Illusions into the Truth

In the latter part of the fourth century John Cassian, the author of the great Christian spiritual classic the *Conferences*, sought wisdom concerning life, and especially life in Christ, and he found it amongst the monks in Egypt. As he visited these holy men, a theme that often came up was the importance of discretion—an accurate assessment of reality and the ability to see through the illusions that are so frequently generated by the world, the flesh, and the devil.

We all incline towards illusion, because the acknowledgement of reality can be painful, especially when our sin and ignorance are revealed.

Napoleon Bonaparte, the antithesis of a monk in the desert, made a similar observation: The chief requirement for a great general is to be able to read accurately the reality of the situation in front of him. This is a principle that Napoleon successfully followed until, blinded by success, he invaded Russia.

These insights from the past come to my mind as I reflect on Cardinal Pell, who always impressed me not only as a man of deep faith, hope, and practical love and as an exemplary bishop, truly with "the smell of the sheep", but as a man who could read with precise accuracy the situation in which we find ourselves. He could see what was real, and he could see through the destructive illusions that abound in modern society and sometimes seep into the Church. He could do that not only because of his great intelligence and learning (for many who are intelligent and learned are all the more easily deceived) but because of a clarity of vision that was founded on his humble faith in Christ crucified. Whenever we come upon a feel-good, sentimental Christianity, it is essential to remember that the sign of our faith is not a happy face but the Cross of Christ. Cardinal Pell was grounded in the ultimate reality of the providence of God, made manifest in the revelation of Jesus Christ, who did not cling to his equality with God but lived amidst the reality of our fallen humanity, accepting even the brutal horror of death on the Cross. No illusion there.

The epitaph of John Henry Newman reminds us that ultimately we come to that clarity of vision when we die: *ex umbris et imaginibus in veritatem*—from shadows and illusions into the truth. Outside and inside the Christian community there is much superficial thinking, full of shadows and illusions, often arising out of a desire to escape the challenges, especially moral, of natural law and of the Gospel. It is more comfortable, though ultimately disastrous, to go along with the illusory ideologies of the spirit of the age. It is vital that we move from shadows and illusions into the truth of objective reality while there is still time. Cardinal Pell could see that reality clearly and helps us do the same. He was a straightforward, honourable man who said what he thought and meant what he said. That is refreshing in a world of smoke and mirrors, in the secular world and also in the Church.

He was called by the pope to help straighten out the tangled mess of the finances of the Holy See. He famously said that, through steady efforts to reveal the reality of the financial situation and to shine more light upon the actual state of affairs, his goal was to replace the exciting but immensely destructive scandals, which discourage the faithful people of God, with the boredom of a financial system that does not make the news because it is transparent, honest, and functioning well. Scoundrels seeking personal advancement love the shadows and the complexity of illusion. Simple openness, shining light on the actual state of affairs, is a major advance in purging the financial system of corruption. Church finances must be marked by faithful stewardship of the material goods, which, after all, ultimately come from the hard-working faithful. The cardinal did much to ensure financial integrity, though against much opposition.

Cardinal Pell, like all of us in these last several decades, confronted the grave evil of sexual abuse committed by some clergy. He did so honestly and courageously, leading the way to reform many years ago. This devastating evil also festers in darkness; the fundamental scandal is not that such behaviour is revealed, despite whatever embarrassment that causes to the Church, but that it happens at all. He himself was entrapped in the injustice of false accusation, so bizarre as to be incomprehensible, used in an attempt to destroy him by those who could not abide his faith or the vigour with which he proclaimed it. He responded with compassionate understanding to the legitimate anger of the survivors of abuse by clergy, survivors who had indeed suffered grievously but who wrongly focused that anger on him. Knowing his innocence and trusting in God, he could endure wrongful imprisonment with a serenity astonishing to those without faith, and in his prison experience he lived without recrimination a fruitful life of faith, hope, and love.

As priest and bishop, with significant pastoral experience in Australia and later in his assignment at the Holy See, Cardinal Pell offered a bracing countercultural exposition of the reality of the Gospel of Jesus Christ. In a desert of sterile ideological mirages, he showed the way to the real oases on our journey in life from which we can draw water joyfully from the wells of salvation. Like that great bishop of equally tumultuous times, Saint Francis de Sales, he spoke and wrote with clarity and charity. It was the clarity that the servants of illusion, the honorary chaplains to the *Zeitgeist*, could not abide.

With his learning and an intelligence grounded in profound faith, he could cut like a hot knife through the empty inanities that can flourish in popular culture, in the media, in the dried-out groves of academe, and also in the Church. The brightly coloured train of words rolls along, but too often there is no content in the boxcars, or, even worse, what is there is toxic.

Cardinal Pell was immensely learned, and that learning was always illuminated by his simple dedication to the reality of Christ, God with us, whom we encounter in word and sacrament. He was profoundly aware that we are stewards, not masters, of the mysteries of faith. No one on earth has the authority to alter the enduring revelation of God, found in the Sacred Scriptures, especially in the New Testament of Our Lord Jesus. The magisterium, the teaching office of the bishops and pope, is not a freshly inspired oracle of God that can change the teaching received from Christ, the way secular dictatorships regularly change the party line. I recall Cardinal Pell remarking at one synod, as some delegates seemed to dissolve the Gospel call to holiness into a wordy and worldly blur, that we seemed to be ending up in a Hegelian flux. The Dogmatic Constitution on Divine Revelation of Vatican II reminds us of the normative standard of the revelation of Jesus, the Word of God; we Christians await no new revelation, in which the spirit of the age replaces the Holy Spirit. As the old saying goes, when you marry the spirit of the age, you are soon a widow or widower. And when you throw doctrine out the window, people do not come through the doors. As Newman observed, religion without doctrine is like filial love without a father.

We are sent to evangelise, not to be colonised by current intellectual trends, no matter how dominant they are in government, media, or academia, and Cardinal Pell vigorously addressed this danger, especially in what turned out to be his final writings. Newman is often invoked by those who want to change the substance of the faith by calling their proposals the development of doctrine (hiding that change through the manipulation of language, so that it seems to be no change at all). But most of Newman's book on that topic outlines the dangers of distortion and the need for careful tests to be sure that the doctrine of the faith is legitimately and organically developed, not distorted. An acorn develops into an oak, not a tulip.

Cardinal Pell could also see through the currently prevalent distortion of Newman's concept of conscience, which turns the clear voice of the aboriginal vicar of Christ into an echo of whatever we desire, as long as we spend an appropriate amount of time and effort in rationalization. It is remarkable how often the will of God that emerges from a process of discernment turns out to be indistinguishable from our own will.

As Chesterton said, original sin is the one doctrine that we can clearly prove, for its effects are evident all around us. That is certainly true in the realm of behaviour, but also in the realm of thought. The Church operates in a fallen world, and its bishops and theologians can be as prone as anyone to replace the bracing encounter with reality with the deadly but comfortable experience of illusion. Into that world of academic ecclesial bafflegab, sometimes encountered even in Church documents and Church assemblies, so soothing to the ear but so thin in substance, Cardinal Pell would intervene with the clear articulation of faith and reason, revealing the splendour of truth. I think he realised that studied vagueness about doctrine in faith and morals could be not only vapid but also spiritually deadly to the holy people of God, especially to those amongst us who are struggling. Many a deadly crocodile lurks amongst the reeds of the swamp of ambiguity. Chaos and confusion are not fruitful but rather are most dangerous to those who are vulnerable; one of the first things God does on the first page of the Bible is to overcome chaos by bringing order to creation.

Cardinal Pell expressed the faith of the Gospel of Jesus Christ with unambiguous clarity—so refreshing, so necessary if we are all to respond to the universal call to holiness emphasised by Vatican II. It is not a universal call to mediocrity, in which the challenge of the Gospel is merely an ideal to be honoured with our lips but considered to be, in practice, beyond the capacity of anyone actually to live. But God does not play with us by proposing a Gospel that cannot actually be lived; for all our frailty and our frequent failure, remedied through his mercy, he gives us the grace actually to live the demanding Gospel call to holiness.

Compassion is love rooted in truth, and it is the mark of a disciple living in the imitation of Christ, who on the Cross showed that love for us. Its illusory substitute is sentimentality, a desire to make people feel good, to feel accepted, at least for the moment, but not in the context of Gospel truth. Jesus welcomed everyone, but he did not stop there; he called us to repent, for the kingdom of God is near at hand. He accompanied the disciples on the road to Emmaus, but he did not simply accompany them. They recalled later how their hearts burned within them when he confronted them on the road with the normative truth of the Word of God and led them to turn around, no longer stumbling further into the darkness, but racing back to Jerusalem to proclaim the risen Lord.

Many years ago I participated in the installation of a bishop. Dozens of bishops were present, all of us resplendent in mitres, pectoral crosses, and episcopal rings. The preacher stated that while we all looked like bishops, what mattered was for us actually to be bishops. Cardinal Pell was indeed a bishop, not merely through validity of ordination but through a life of integrity and apostolic zeal, grounded in the reality revealed by faith and reason and able to lead us to recognise that reality, to act accordingly, and to keep clear of the illusions generated by the trendy ideologies that swirl around us.

It is hard to accept that the vibrant voice of Cardinal Pell is no longer to be heard, interjecting a salutary realism into our discussions of the path forward for the disciples of Jesus through this valley of tears on our way home to the heavenly city Jerusalem. And so it is up to all of us, and perhaps in a particular way to the bishops of the Church, to learn from his wisdom and to imitate his courageous witness to the Lord Jesus.

—His Eminence Thomas Christopher
Cardinal Collins

6

A Rodeo in a China Shop

It was March 12, 2013. How could I forget it? The College of Cardinals had solemnly processed into the Sistine Chapel for the start of the conclave to elect a successor to the retired Pope Benedict XVI. We had quietly entered, taken our oaths one by one, repeating them in Latin as the cameras rolled. Then came the dramatic moment for the papal master of ceremonies, the very somber and mild-mannered Guido Marini, to bellow out the required words *extra omnes*, the mandate for all but the cardinals of the conclave to exit and the heavy doors of the chapel to be slammed shut.

I was next to my friend George Pell because his *sotto voce* commentary was always worth hearing. Monsignor Marini's "*extra omnes*" came out in a soft whisper, almost like a plea rather than a command, to which the Australian AFL footballer commented, "What was that all about? Where I come from, those Latin words would be translated, 'Get the hell out of here!' "[1]

[1] Cardinal Dolan had written "Australian rugby player", but the editor changed this to "AFL footballer". AFL stands for the Australian Football League, and it was this form of ball chasing that Cardinal Pell, coming from the state of Victoria, played. He was in fact chosen to play this form of football in his youth at the highest "A Grade" level. Instead of following this lucrative "pop-star" career, he entered a seminary. Rugby is another form of ball chasing typically played by boys from elite private schools and much more popular in the states of New South Wales and Queensland than in the cardinal's home state of Victoria. Rugby is the better-known game internationally.

That episode comes to mind as I reflect gratefully upon George Cardinal Pell. He was witty, blunt, and hard-boiled, occasionally with the vocabulary of a sailor. Yet he was fearless, loyal, obedient, and a friend with traces of tenderness.

He indeed had his own viewpoints, to which he tenaciously clung. In the days leading up to that conclave, and certainly during the twenty-four hours we were locked in, he was clear about his leanings for the next successor of Saint Peter and not afraid to let us know.

I, for one, appreciated that, because I happened to concur with many of his prescriptions for the Church, to be sure. But, even more importantly, I realized that George Pell *loved the Church*!

We Catholics are, of course, all summoned to love the Church. That sentiment is heightened for a priest, who is so united to Christ by ordination that he, the priest, shares the Lord's nuptial bond with his bride, the Church, to borrow the poetry of Saint Paul. Notch it up more for a bishop and a cardinal. "Love for Jesus and His Church must be the passion of your life!" Pope Saint John Paul II would preach to priests and bishops, a quote the Australian often repeated.

George Pell was head-over-heels in love with the Church. Like any other husband, he could be preoccupied with flaws or harmful habits he noticed in his bride. While heartily supportive of the genuine reforms of the Second Vatican Council, he worried about dangerous trends in its implementation, with an unfortunate resultant dilution of her evangelical energy and a toxic movement in the Church to ape the secular, progressive culture of Western Europe and North America found even in his beloved homeland.

Commentators have observed, and I would concur, that George Pell became for Australia what John Cardinal O'Connor, the archbishop of New York, was for the

United States: a courageous, compelling, credible witness to the truth of the human person, the sanctity of human life, and the integrity of Church teaching. Both these men admired Pope Saint John Paul II, the pontiff who appointed them bishops, and his bold proclamation of a confident, faithful Catholicism, where Jesus Christ was the answer to the question posed by every human life.

I once asked George if he was bothered by the many who, while arguing with his approach, considered him a "bull in a china shop". He replied, "I don't agree at all! I'm a bloody rodeo in a china shop!"

Yet he was not a bully, as some concluded. Sure, he'd hector me relentlessly to sign a letter or speak out on a particular issue, but while he would express disappointment when I would not, he would assure me he trusted my prudential judgment. Except for the time I told him I was not going to World Youth Day in Australia because it was too long a journey. "Sure," he came back, "you northerners expect us to travel endlessly to your events but won't come to ours." I changed my mind!

No wonder Pope Saint John Paul II, Pope Benedict XVI, and Pope Francis trusted him for delicate roles: in the Congregation for Divine Worship, in the consultation for the nominations of bishops, and, especially, in the reform of the Holy See's finances, where he actually received threats from those opposed to his exhaustive audits. He was a loyal soldier ready to serve wherever asked.

His muscular orthodoxy and legendary bluntness produced a lot of enemies. Perhaps his most effective service to the Church and the people he loved came from his years in prison over charges contrived by these opponents and later found groundless. As his inspirational books on those rough years displayed, he never flagged in his faith and hope. But those years took their toll.

People rarely saw his soft side. I did. Never will I forget his phone calls when he knew I was under pressure or when my mother passed. And his hospitality in Rome was legendary.

I was with him for *cena* only days before he entered the hospital for what was to be routine orthopedic surgery. He looked worn and exhausted but strong enough to resist my invitation to come back here to New York for the surgery.

We miss him, a giant physically, spiritually, morally.

—His Eminence Timothy Michael Cardinal Dolan

7

Keep Boxing!

"Those of you who know the faith need to be a voice for the Church in the public square. I am speaking to all of you, but I am especially speaking to you young women. We need young women speaking publicly for the Church, but you have to know what you're on about. So that means if you've got your first and second degree, you should keep studying. And make sure you learn something about economics, because Catholics are always criticised for not knowing their sums. I think that's a card that's overplayed, but it is best if you know something about the economy as well."

This isn't an exact quote, but I recall Cardinal Pell saying something along these lines at a Theology on Tap meeting in early 2008. I was twenty-five or twenty-six at the time, and while it was not the first time I had heard the cardinal speak, it was the first time I really listened to him. I was then a corporate lawyer and had never really thought about any public expression of my faith outside of Sunday Mass. But his exhortation to defend the faith through further study resonated with me, and I promptly enrolled in a master's of bioethics and a diploma of finance. I wasn't exactly sure what I would do with these qualifications, but I trusted them to be a response to the cardinal's call to arms and that the Lord would use them one day, if he so pleased.

I heard the cardinal speak publicly many times during that World Youth Day year, but it was a talk he gave to a much smaller audience a year later, at a celebration of its first anniversary, that next really held my attention.

Cardinal Pell had given an address to young adults gathered at St Mary's Cathedral, and a time of Q and A followed. A young woman raised her hand and asked whether the cardinal had ever met the pope.

Everyone laughed. The very reason for the gathering at the cathedral was that it had been a year since the pope's visit to Sydney: Of course the cardinal had met him.

"I've been privileged to meet the pope many times", the cardinal answered. "And let me tell you a few stories about him." He captivated us all for the next several minutes with personal stories of Pope Benedict XVI.

By the end, no one was laughing at this young woman. Her simple question had gifted us some insights into the relationship between Cardinal Pell and the pope that we would not have otherwise heard.

The cardinal could have just said yes and moved on to the next question, but he didn't. I remember thinking at the time that it was kind and clever of him to save this young woman the embarrassment by using her question to share some anecdotes about the pope. From that day, I became a fan of Cardinal Pell, admiring both his courage and boldness in defence of the faith, but also his ability to be gentle with those who were right in front of him.

It would be a number of years until I properly encountered Cardinal Pell.

I joined the Archdiocese of Sydney's communications team in early 2014. While Cardinal Pell was still the archbishop at the time, his move to Rome as the first-ever prefect of the Secretariat for the Economy was announced just weeks after I started in my role, so I never got to meet him properly while he was in Sydney.

Over the next couple of years, I focused most of my attention on writing about the Royal Commission into Institutional Responses to Child Sexual Abuse and providing some context and clarity to Catholics looking for something other than the media sensationalism that surrounded the public hearings. His Eminence had evidently read some of my work, and so, when I was in Rome making a pilgrimage for the Jubilee Year of Mercy in February 2016, he kindly invited me to his office for a cup of tea and a chat.

He was gracious and kind and spent a full hour asking about my background and my hopes for the future and encouraging me in the work that I was doing. Being invited to a one-on-one meeting in his office inside the walls of the Vatican remains one of the most surreal and beautiful experiences of my life.

It would be only several months before we had cause to speak again—this time, under more difficult circumstances.

Our next conversation was on the evening of Wednesday, July 27, 2016, when the Australian Broadcasting Corporation's (ABC) *7.30 Report* aired—for the first time—allegations against the cardinal of a history of child sexual abuse.

It was the middle of World Youth Day week in Kraków, and so a good number of staff members at the Archdiocese of Sydney, including the senior members of the communications team, were in Poland. I was a relatively junior member of the communications staff but was the only one available in Sydney to assist in the media frenzy.

At 10:00 A.M., I was advised that the program would air that evening and that I would be responsible for ensuring the statements from Cardinal Pell and Archbishop Fisher were delivered to the media and published on our website and social media channels that night.

The day was spent reviewing and commenting on statements that could only be prepared in draft: They would not be finalised until we had seen the program and heard the full details of the allegations.

The ABC livestream was not available to be viewed overseas, so it was decided that the cardinal would listen to the program by phone.

As 7:30 P.M. approached, the cardinal's private secretary in Rome—Father Mark Withoos—phoned me and asked me to put my phone on speaker, close to the television, and to turn the volume of the television up as loud as it could go.

I did as I was told and watched the program, knowing that the cardinal was listening in on the other end of my phone. The thirty-minute program seemed to go on for hours, and we heard awful allegations of indecent assault in a Ballarat swimming pool, of indecent exposure in a Torquay swimming pool changing room, and of sexual assault in a Melbourne cathedral.

When the credits began to roll, I stared at my phone and froze. What was I going to say to the cardinal? What *could* I say?

I picked up the phone, hands and voice shaking, and said, "Your Eminence, I don't know what to say to you right now."

He was very matter-of-fact about the whole thing, telling me the volume was too low and he had heard the program only in part.

I told him I would get to work on typing up a transcript straight away so that he could read the text.

He apologised for the trouble. "I know it's late and you've had a long day, and there are still a few hours of work ahead of you. I'm sorry for the hassle", he said.

I assured him that I was happy to do it, because getting to work was the only way I could show him my support in that moment.

Katrina Lee, the formidable archdiocesan communications director, was overseas, but we spoke frequently in the hours that ensued.

The transcript was prepared and the statements were written and rewritten, approved, and sent to the media.

It was about 2:00 A.M. by the time it was all finished, and I made my way home in a taxi. While I was still on the way home, Katrina phoned me again to check in. I told her the statements had gone to the media and were published online as instructed and assured her that I would be back in the office early the next day to deal with the morning media inquiries.

"But are *you* okay?" she asked.

She told me that Cardinal Pell had insisted she call to check on my welfare because he thought I had sounded terribly upset on the phone.

I don't know if this was the worst day of the cardinal's life up until that point, but it had to be a contender. Not eight hours before, he had been accused on national television of the same heinous crimes that he had spent the better part of two decades trying to address. His reputation had been destroyed, the media were camped outside his residence and office, and he was staring down the barrel of a criminal investigation.

No one would have blamed him for thinking completely of himself that night, but he didn't. His Eminence thought of—and took the time to check on—the junior communications staffer back in Sydney whom he had met maybe once or twice.

In the years that followed, the cardinal continued to provide me with encouragement, support, and practical guidance.

He would occasionally send an email or a text to tell me he enjoyed an article I had written and to exhort me to “keep boxing”.

He would sometimes phone or email to offer tips on how a particular talk I had given could be improved, especially if he thought I sounded too negative about the culture wars. “You can’t lead people if your content just depresses them. You have to inspire them and give them hope.”

He even told me that I should drink warm water before giving a talk because cold water would make me cough.

My experience of the cardinal in the few years that I knew him was that no one escaped his attention or his concern. No one. He was generous and warm and sincerely interested in the improvement of everyone, even me.

He was a good man. God rest him.

—Monica Doumit

8

Catholic Herbs and Spices

Cardinal Pell was the most unpretentious man I have ever met. No matter what, he never wanted any fuss. This attitude seemed to imbue his outlook on everything.

I have fond memories of when he would come to the convent for Holy Hour and dinner. He was his down-to-earth and relaxed self and loved to chat and share jokes. I remember one evening when he came over. After an engaging chat by the fire, we headed into the chapel for Holy Hour. The cardinal was suffering significant knee pain at the time, so we had set up a comfortable chair for him at the back of the chapel. He swiftly observed that he would need a chair with arms. It took me a few minutes to go upstairs and return with one, but the cardinal had beaten me to it. To my amusement he had sourced one of our roller chairs from the office, but unfortunately the one that had quite a wobble to it. An exchange at that point was out of the question, since he was already sitting in the chapel in that chair, deep in prayer; it was he and the Lord, and I wasn't about to disturb him. I couldn't help worry during prayers whenever he moved, though, because his chair would roll slightly. I prayed that it would hold!

One time we got to talking about his health and how he was feeling, given his upcoming trial. He expressed that it was all in God's hands and that justice would prevail in the end. His complete trust in God's providence was edifying. One time when it was remarked how unfair the unrelenting attacks against him were, he smiled pensively and said, "Yes, but someone we know suffered all this before us first, didn't he?"

Cardinal Pell loved Australia and Australian history. He was always interested in how the university students were engaging with the Church (or not) and what questions or concerns they might have. He also enjoyed hearing how the Catholic chaplaincies were going and showed keen interest in the inter-chaplaincy debates on "hot topic" issues. Developing a generation of critical thinkers was very close to his heart. I recounted to him how one of my students, not a believer, had commented in class that the medieval philosopher we were studying at the time had too many Catholic "herbs and spices" sprinkled into his theory and that he simply couldn't buy it. The cardinal laughed with genuine delight at the phrase and expressed how refreshing it was for a student to speak up like that. That was exactly the kind of engagement he encouraged in others.

Just a couple of weeks after he was released from prison, he came over for dinner again. I wasn't sure how he would be, given his experiences, but in a matter of minutes he set the tone with his usual humour and geniality. I couldn't believe how peaceful he was; there was a quality about him that seemed otherworldly and untouchable, undoubtedly born from his prayer and suffering, yet he was still very much himself. It reminded me of the reticence certain people have who have suffered greatly and yet remain very positive. He was cracking jokes with more wit than ever.

During the last lunch with us before he left for Rome, the cardinal again expressed a desire to help young people return to the Church and wanted to know what kinds of questions they had. He desired to know what more could be done for them, especially those who had rejected the faith altogether. He wanted them to encounter Our Lord and experience a richer life in faith. Sadly, we never came to realise this project in any formal way. But I have often wondered whether our beloved cardinal has been speaking to the Lord about how to get the people of Australia back to the Church. I wonder whether he has been interceding for the next Eucharistic Congress to be held in Sydney. I have another memory of him now, speaking at a youth event months after World Youth Day in Sydney. In his inimitable way, he retold the story of the Good Thief who never gave up hope and got into Heaven on his cross at the very last minute by the power of Christ's love. The cardinal then looked at all of us with a smile and a twinkle in his eye and said, "All right, then, it's your turn now; go and do good. On your bike and get going."

We miss you, dear champion of the truth, defender of the faith, soldier of Christ.

May you rest in peace.

—Mary Julian Ekman

9

Friends

In 1967 I went up to Oxford for Michaelmas term and met a tall young Australian priest. In the previous year, Father George Pell had been ordained in Rome. His mentor, James O'Collins, bishop of Ballarat, had sent George on to Oxford for doctoral studies. His topic was Saint Cyprian and the early Church in North Africa. I was "reading theology" in preparation for Anglican ministry. We immediately became friends, and I soon learnt how much he valued friends and enjoyed their company.

Although he was devoted to the memory of Dr. Daniel Mannix, George loved all things English. His father's people were originally English. He was particularly fascinated by the High Church Anglicanism I showed him in St Stephen's House. In return, at Campion Hall, where he lived, he introduced me to various Jesuits, some very eccentric. More importantly, I shared his enthusiasm for the Second Vatican Council, which had unfolded while he was studying in Rome.

Then came my crisis, which had been building up for some years. I knew I could no longer remain an Anglican. George was one of the first in whom I confided. Typically blunt, he said, "I will stand by you, and I will be your sponsor." But he never put pressure on me. It had to be a free decision. George Pell always respected conscience. So he was my sponsor on June 24, 1968, when I was reconciled to the Church. On December 8, he was my Confirmation sponsor.

Many years later, a lady with no sense of humour gushed, "Oh, Your Eminence, I believe you were sponsor to Bishop Elliott when he became a Catholic." Not given to flattery, to her horror he replied, "Yes, and it was the worst thing I have ever done to the Church!"

He continued doctoral research in Oxford, and I returned to Melbourne to enter Corpus Christi Seminary. When he returned as assistant priest at Swan Hill, he invited me to give a short seminar at Nyah West, even though I was only a seminarian. He knew his friend's capacities even if that friend was uncertain.

This ability to discern the skills of friends extended throughout his life, for example with the Redemptorist sociologist Michael Mason and with Aldo Rebeschini, rector of the reformed seminary. He tapped into their expertise, encouraging those who worked with him, but he never exploited them. Friendship meant mutual trust.

After he went on to direct Catholic teacher training in Ballarat, he was present when I was ordained a priest at the Fortieth Eucharistic Congress in 1973. Again, that encouragement of friends came to the fore when he invited me to give some evening classes at Aquinas College.

Hospitality and dining out with friends were priorities. Four young priests would save up to go to a fine restaurant: George Pell, Denis Hart, Gerry Diamond, and Peter Elliott, a veritable "gang of four". Dressed in clerical mode, we were just enjoying one another's company—and the food. But we were being watched by others who dined there regularly, key officials in the Catholic Education Office, hostile because we refused to genuflect to the official "life situation" method of teaching catechetics, which George dismissed as "fairy floss".

They spread it around that the four of us were plotting to take over the Church! Forty years later that gang of four comprised a cardinal, an archbishop, a bishop, and a monsignor. While George facilitated the careers of the other three when he could, there was no plotting in smart restaurants, only taking time to relax.

Was George Pell a "bully", as has been alleged? He was a formidable ruckman, the most aggressive position in Australian Rules football. Yet off the football field he was a gentle man, protecting younger boys who were being bullied at St Patrick's College in Ballarat.

On a personal level he could be forceful if he believed you were not living up to his expectations, whether he was coaching a junior football team or telling me to "snap out of it" and not retreat into a traditionalist cocoon in 1978, that gloomy final year of the reign of Pope Saint Paul VI.

Later, when he brought me from Vatican service to edit the Melbourne Religious Education Texts, he called me in one day and demanded to know why I "had only spent one shilling and sixpence" on this major project. So I spent without limit and learnt how he would generously fund whatever project he envisaged as of value for the future of the Church he loved. He argued that the money always came back.

He was rector of the seminary in Melbourne, which he reformed and rejuvenated, forcibly at first. Then he became an auxiliary bishop just before I went to work in the Vatican in 1987. Not particularly in tune with his archbishop, Sir Frank Little, he had time to work beyond Melbourne. Vatican departments entrusted him with projects for justice and peace, and he was appointed visitator to struggling seminaries in developing countries. He often stayed with me when he came through Rome.

On one occasion when he arrived in Rome to report after visiting Cambodia, I saw that he was strained and on edge. He was deeply distressed by the atrocities of the Khmer Rouge. He sat with me recounting what he saw, and there were tears in his eyes. We both rejected Marxism and were friends of Bob Santamaria. Now we saw how cruel communism could be, and we felt real sorrow for the victims.

In Oxford we had already clashed with the Left in the form of "Catholic-Marxist dialogue" or *Slant*. Some vocal Dominicans were key players. George and I went to a *Slant* meeting and asked the "wrong" questions. They were furious and called George "the big Australian bastard", while I was "the little Australian bastard" (provoking them by wearing a red tie).

Later I worked out that we had a better knowledge of Marxism, albeit critical, than these armchair "Catholic Marxists". But that was twenty years before the Berlin Wall came tumbling down and the Soviet paradise imploded.

George regarded children as friends, "youngsters" to be treated like adults. When he called me back from Rome, I lived with him in the archbishop's house in Kew. My brother Paul and sister-in-law Gillian asked whether their children Vanessa and Nicholas could stay overnight with us. George agreed and welcomed my niece and nephew to breakfast the next morning.

He engaged them in a loaded conversation by asking Vanessa, age twelve, who her hero was. "Elizabeth I", she primly replied. So he provoked her: "But, Vanessa, she had a sour old Protestant face." He winked at me when she hit back with a sermon on the glories of the Virgin Queen. Finally, Nicholas, age eight, cut in: "And Queen Mary burnt all those people."

However, George not only enjoyed the company of precocious children; he also delighted in some naughty children, such as a young Santamaria who crouched behind the front hedge and sang out "silly buggers!" at passersby. But he could be severe with rebellious adolescents, such as one sent to him to be "smartened up" when he was parish priest of Buninyong. I witnessed George putting the sulky youth through a tough boot camp. The young man later turned out well.

He did not always agree with his friends. I was a monarchist. He was a republican. As such, he participated in the Canberra consultation before the referendum of 1999, when he befriended the maverick Archbishop John Hepworth, a staunch monarchist.

George took the extreme republican position, for a popularly elected president. But our disagreement was polite. He also disagreed with my analysis of Australian society as secularist, claiming that religion continued beneath a sceptical facade. The resurrection of ANZAC Day later vindicated him. But we agreed that Sydney was more "religious" than Melbourne.

When Pope Francis called him to the Vatican to clean up the money, he was immediately in danger, as his sister, Margaret, perceived: "George, they will shoot you in the back!"

He was not welcome in the Vatican. At the time, a retired Italian official who worked in the Secretariat of State ranted in my face, "Your Pell does not understand our way of doing things!" He soon became the cardinal who knew too much about "our way of doing things". So he had to go. Then unfolded the saga of his being framed, tried, and jailed.

Unlike some clergy, he related well with women, starting with his beloved sister, Margaret. Catholic intellectuals were favoured: Clara Geoghegan, Anna Krohn, Tracey Rowland, and others. He believed women should play a more prominent role in the Church, but he never favoured women's ordination.

He worked patiently with his difficult housekeeper in Kew, until her football team was playing against his team, Richmond, when breakfast the following morning was a frosty affair. However, as others have noted, he never lost the "common touch". Raised in a Ballarat pub, he could join in any conversation with anyone.

The pub no doubt inspired in him a love of open fires. In his houses at Mentone and Kew a wood-burning fireplace was installed and used in the winter. A house became a home when people could gather around a warm hearth.

When it came to liturgy, George was dignified but relaxed, disdaining the complexities favoured by Hart and Elliott. "I never know where to put my hands..." He lacked the confidence to sing the Mass in English, but he had a good voice, as I learnt when he sang Gilbert and Sullivan around the piano at John and Christine McCarthy's house in Sydney after a John XXIII Fellowship Conference.

From time to time he celebrated the Traditional Latin Mass. When restrictions were placed on it, I telephoned him in anger and anxiety. His immediate response was "No, this is good. It will force traditionalists to stand up and fight."

One liturgical topic his friends learnt to avoid was his renovation of the sanctuary in St Mary's Cathedral, Sydney. Consecrated by Pope Benedict in 2008, the white marble altar displays a horizontal bas-relief of the Holy Shroud of Turin. I could not grasp the symbolism, but I never asked.

However, St Mary's was a regrettable exception. In close association with his master of ceremonies and loyal friend, Charles Portelli, George has left us a series of beautiful projects. Once again, money was to be spent freely.

George completed the restoration and new sanctuary in St Patrick's Cathedral, Melbourne. With extraordinary vision, he reinvigorated the dull cathedral grounds: the fountain of life flowing down from the cathedral, statues of

Saint Francis and Saint Catherine, busts of modern saints, and the grand bronze statue of Daniel Mannix at the cathedral entrance.

Other projects directed by Charles Portelli included the magnificent seminary chapel in Melbourne, the Benedict XVI Centre's basilica near Sydney, and his own private chapel. But his greatest project, supervised by Charles Portelli, was Domus Australia in Rome. The restored church contains fine paintings by Paul Newton, including a tribute to George's hero and friend Cardinal Thuan. The first side altar awaits the canonisation of this Vietnamese witness to the faith.

I see George's generous patronage of art and artists as a kind of sacrament of his vision for the future. George was a historian, but he always looked to the future. However, he was not always a man of the present. I tried to teach him how to use a TV remote without success. "I press this?" "No. You don't, please!" He could not type, and he left computers to others. He wrote with a strong hand, in black ink from a fountain pen.

George was naturally ecumenical, as I saw in Oxford in 1969 when he welcomed my father, Les, an Anglican vicar, and my mother, June. Somehow, she thought he was a Jesuit, to his amusement. But his ecumenism was not conventional. In Sydney he soon became a friend of the strictly Evangelical Anglican archbishop, Peter Jensen, and his wife, Christine. But he bewailed the occasion when he presented them with a bottle of fine wine and then had to bring it home.

Others may pay tribute to his mark on the Australian Church, undoubtedly as a great leader. I prefer to recall George Pell as the gifted man I knew: human, urbane, holy but not pious, a Christian gentleman who followed Christ as a faithful disciple.

I hope my personal recollections may throw light on obscure corners of George Pell's life, dispel some myths and calumnies, and assist us all towards that journey he has already taken. Heaven is not inhuman. Friendships continue in eternity; after all, Our Lord said, "I no longer call you servants, but friends."

—Most Rev. Peter J. Elliott

10

A Big Man with a Big Heart and Big Dreams to Match

I first met the relatively recently bishopped George Pell in 1988. He had heard about me and especially my work in bioethics, which was fast becoming a fashionable field in Australian culture and which we both thought the Church must keep on top of. He rang me up asking me to give him some tutorials on bioethics. I was just a seminarian at the time and he was a bishop, so it was an intimidating request. But so began a friendship that would significantly shape the course of my life.

The first thing that most people noticed about George Pell when meeting him for the first time—or indeed subsequently—was just how big he was. He was a towering presence with broad shoulders; add a mitre and crozier and he dominated even the biggest cathedral. So, too, in meetings of the cardinals he stood out, literally head and shoulders above the crowd. Sometimes there was a stony, serious look. At other times an impish smile. One way or another, you noticed him.

Whether at formal meetings or social occasions, media interviews or chance encounters in the street, there was a kind of gravitational attraction. It was not just the sight of him. His deep, booming voice was almost hypnotic and radiated authority. And he didn't mind dominating the conversation!

But this wasn't just about his physical scale. He was a highly intelligent and erudite man, with an Urbanianum licentiate, Monash master's, and Oxford doctorate. He was a ravenous reader and proud of his library, and his interests were not limited to the ecclesial: Though there was plenty of theology, there were also biographies, philosophies, histories, geographies, social commentaries. Many of the books have underlining and scribbled comments in them. He knew a lot about a lot and was never shy about sharing his thoughts, no matter how unfashionable his position or how polarising the subject.

At the farewell to Pope Benedict and acknowledgement of volunteers at the end of Sydney's World Youth Day in 2008, I remarked that the cardinal had been our leader and inspiration at every stage of the bidding, planning, preparation, and execution of that World Youth Day. I said, "He is a big man, Your Holiness, with a big heart and big dreams to match." The pope reminded me of those words years later. He had asked me to call on him in his retirement so he could inquire after his friend the cardinal, for by then a media, political, and police witch hunt had landed him in jail for crimes he could not possibly have committed. Benedict gave me a message to convey to George in prison, which I did the next time I visited him there. We spoke in a coded way about "I" and "XI", lest our conservation appear the next day in *The Age*. The former pope was confident that George's big heart would carry him through and that he would be exonerated, in this life or the next.

Mention of his time as "a guest of Her Majesty"—what he called his "enforced spiritual retreat", though one in which he was denied the opportunity to celebrate Mass—invites all sorts of remembrances, but in this context I'd just notice that imprisonment didn't diminish his spirit one iota.

I had sent the cardinal a photo of the image he had commissioned for Domus Australia in Rome of his friend Cardinal Francis-Xavier Nguyen Van Thuan, who was detained by the Vietnamese communist government in a reeducation camp for thirteen years, nine of them in solitary confinement. On one of my visits to George in the Melbourne Detention Centre, we discussed Thuan's courage, which he was determined to emulate, along with that of Saint John Fisher, the bishop of Rochester imprisoned and ultimately beheaded under Henry VIII; George was a devotee of Fisher's life and writings. Though he was genuinely shocked at the injustice of it all—George could be almost naïve about how good Australia's legal system was—he was not embittered by his 404 days in solitary confinement. If anything, he emerged gentler and more forgiving. Few of us would, I suspect, have endured such a thing in as good a spirit. I am convinced it was his solid prayer life, above all, that carried him through. If ever I was looking for him and could not find him in his study, I'd usually locate him in the chapel. The big man remained big-minded, big-hearted, and big-spirited to the end.

Considering his rather imperial scale and (some thought) imperious demeanour, one might expect his style of episcopal management to have been very hierarchical and those he consulted to have been few and grave. Yet that wasn't his modus operandi at all. He surrounded himself with capable people and was unintimidated by any of them shining in his sky. He had various "kitchen cabinets" and breakfast meetings of diverse advisers—all ages and backgrounds—that paralleled the formal structures of consultation. He wanted their ideas. And he was good at delegating.

As one of his auxiliary bishops, I was a victim of his generous delegation. I once said to him that I was on twenty-four committees and struggling to do justice to them all. He responded that if I had the time to count how many committees I was on, I had time to be appointed to more! Another time he asked me what I thought of World Youth Day. I said that although I hadn't been to one myself, I thought it was a genius pastoral strategy of Pope John Paul II and that I had not met a single young person who had attended who had not been the better for it. He asked how much of the archdiocese's patrimony and energy he should risk on it. I said he should risk a very great deal—if need be, all: that there was no point having assets if there was no one to leave them to. He knew I was exaggerating and said he would not let me near the cheque book. I didn't think too much about his queries besides the fact that he was obviously seeking my counsel as someone with experience of Catholic young people. What I was unaware of at the time, however, was that Pell was playing chess while I was merely playing draughts.

The next time I heard about World Youth Day was at a meeting of the Council of Priests some months later. There was elation all round when the cardinal announced that Sydney would be bidding for the event. He then said, almost in passing, that Bishop Fisher would be leading the bid and, if we got it, coordinating the entire thing. Those present saw my jaw hit the table. It would be the biggest job of my life, but till then I knew nothing about it. By the grace of God and the big archbishop, WYD-SYD08 turned out to be the largest religious gathering (indeed, the largest gathering for any purpose) in the history of Australia and of Oceania. It was also surely the happiest week in our history. And it was to have a transformative effect on thousands of young Australians that is still bearing fruit to this day.

George Pell had a real gift when it came to ministry to young people. In an era of doctrinal and cultural confusion, he offered them beliefs and ideals, direction and security.

He let them see his ordinariness: On pilgrimages he wore a daggy cloth hat, shirt, and shorts; rode camels; and took part in activities however ungainly. Many have stories to tell of how down-to-earth he was with them, and how pastoral. An Aboriginal man testified to how the cardinal had assured him of his human dignity and God's love at a time when he was filled with self-hatred and doubts. His commitment to improving the lives of young people was at the heart of his great educational project: advocating for sound teaching and fair funding for Catholic schools, directing Aquinas College Ballarat, radically increasing resourcing for university chaplaincy and youth ministry, and helping establish and grow four tertiary institutions (Australian Catholic University, the John Paul II Institute for Marriage and the Family, the Sydney campus of the University of Notre Dame Australia, and Campion College).

If school and university education and ministry to young people were to consume a great deal of his energy, so, too, did the seminaries and seminarians. After serving for some years in Ballarat parishes, he was appointed rector of Corpus Christi Seminary in Melbourne. As rector and then as archbishop, he reformed the existing seminaries in Melbourne and Sydney and established a Redemptoris Mater seminary in Sydney. He was also the pope's inspector of seminaries in the Pacific. He was a genuine father to seminarians and priests, many of whom testify to how he inspired or assisted them. In fact, like the "John Paul II generation" and "Benedict generation" of priests, there is a "Pell generation" who would say they owe their vocation in large part to him.

In 2005 Cardinal Pell was made a companion of the Order of Australia for service to the Church in Australia and internationally, for his contribution to ethical and spiritual debates, and for his services to education and social justice—for example, in Aboriginal Catholic ministry and as chair of

Caritas. In fact, leaders of many Church agencies, ecclesial movements and lay associations, and chivalrous and service orders testify to his leadership and encouragement. I remember him going each year to say Mass for the homeless and marginalised at David's Place in inner-city Sydney, and how at home he was with the street people and how concerned he was for their welfare. He was generous to a tee, helping many of the needy and encouraging the same generosity in those who worked with him.

He was, of course, famously committed to Catholic orthodoxy. He was wary of the slide into secular agnosticism in much of the world, especially Northern Europe, and he put the brakes on the Church in Australia following suit. He was very much on board with the call of the popes, from Pope Saint Paul VI onwards, to a "new evangelisation" of individuals, families, institutions, and cultures. He cared deeply for that Western civilisation that had for so long borne the Gospel to the world, and he worried about the animus of the "politically correct" or "woke" towards both that civilisation and the religion that inspired it. He was convinced that without the protection of the Gospel, the unborn and the elderly, the prisoners and the mentally ill, the indigenous and the poor would be even further disadvantaged. In promoting these themes he became a lecturer on the international circuit, a newspaper columnist, and a regular media interviewee. He readily engaged in public debates, including with liberal Jesuits on contraception, women's ordination, and conscience on ABC's *Four Corners* in 1993; with Richard Dawkins over religious belief in 2012; with climate catastrophists; and with others. He believed the Church must be out there contributing in the public square, and not just locked away in the sacristy, as Pope Francis has also insisted, and his public stances made him the best-known Australian churchman in history.

There have been various reports of the cardinal's supposed dissatisfaction with some Vatican policies towards the end of his life. Undoubtedly, he was a critic of, for instance, the China policy and of some appointments and approaches that he did not think would advance Church teaching. But he was always confident in Christ's ultimate stewardship of the Church and loyal to the institution of the papacy, especially the three popes with whom he worked closely: Saint John Paul the Great, Benedict XVI, and Francis. By them he was appointed auxiliary bishop and then archbishop, first of Melbourne, then of Sydney, then cardinal. At one time or another he had a role in the Vatican dicasteries for Bishops, Divine Worship, Doctrine of the Faith, Evangelisation of Peoples, the Family, Healthcare, Justice and Peace, Migrants, the New Evangelisation, Pontifical Mission Societies, and Vox Clara. Pope Francis also appointed him to his inner Council of Cardinal Advisers. These many roles gave him ample opportunity to get to know all three popes, and he had many stories to tell about each.

In 2013 Pope Francis asked him to be inaugural prefect of the Secretariat for the Economy, a position many then ranked third highest in the Church, and charged him with investigating the Vatican finances and righting them. The cardinal accepted immediately, even though he knew this meant leaving behind his beloved family and friends in Australia, along with the many pastoral satisfactions of being archbishop of Sydney. He knew he would encounter opposition. But he was determined, he understood money, and he knew the Vatican finances needed a major cleanup. He persevered, even when obstructed by men at the top who should have respected his mandate and goals. He uncovered considerable maladministration and even corruption and years later has been thoroughly vindicated in this. But it cost him a great deal. Some would even connect the accusations of child abuse that were made against him and the shameful legal process that followed with those who were determined to block his efforts on behalf of Pope Francis.

I said that a big cost of accepting Pope Francis' commission was that he would have to leave his relatives and friends behind in Australia. He was especially close to his sister, Margaret: They were best friends from childhood. But he loved his brother, David, and his family also and holidayed with them all each year. And there was an endless stream of friends and colleagues at his table and events. Now they would be far away. Of course, there were occasional discreet returns to his homeland, and some of his dearest visited him in Rome. As in the decades before, he demonstrated there that he was an extrovert, raconteur, and host, welcoming each and all who came near.

He loved history and the arts. He renovated Domus Australia in Rome, the Benedict XVI Centre in Gross Vale, and the John Paul the Great Chaplaincy at the University of Sydney all to a high standard, commissioning many new artworks and obtaining older ones. There was a consciousness that each generation must add to the Church's artistic patrimony. He was a devotee of classical music and a regular at symphony concerts. Sir James MacMillan wrote a motet on very short notice for the cardinal's funeral based on his episcopal motto, Be Not Afraid. He loved sports, first as a player and later as a spectator, and tried to keep fit himself: I remember him determinedly power walking round and round the balcony of Cathedral House when wet weather prevented other outdoor exercise. But his scale and the sport in early life left him with crippling joint issues, and so affected was his mobility that he eventually sought hip surgery in Rome in early 2023.

He died in the recovery room after that operation. His Requiem Mass in Saint Peter's Basilica in Rome drew the biggest crowd for a retired cardinal in living memory. Cardinals of every ecclesiological hue have since said to me that they regarded him as one of the great figures of the modern Church and a martyr for the faith. His Funeral Mass in St Mary's Cathedral in Sydney also drew an extraordinary crowd of admirers and interceders, as well as a few hecklers. Former prime minister Tony Abbott readily agreed to offer some words of remembrance after Communion, and he amusingly quipped that the demonstrators chanting "Pell, Pell, go to Hell" were the cardinal's first miracle, because he had convinced them of the reality of the afterlife!

I was fortunate enough to be sent by the bishops of Australia to represent them at the funeral for Pope Benedict XVI in early 2023. I spent most of my extra time that week, including several meals, with the cardinal. He was in a chipper mood, full of wit and wisdom. Neither of us dreamed this would be the last week of his life. But now I trust that he is meeting merrily with his friends Popes John Paul and Benedict, Cardinals John Fisher and Thuan, and many others in that Heaven, where we can all hope to see him again one day.

—Most Rev. Anthony C. Fisher, O.P.

11

Faithful to the Primacy of Peter

I met His Eminence George Cardinal Pell for the first time in 2014 while I was a member of COSEA, the Pontifical Commission for Reference on the Organisation of the Economic-Administrative Structure of the Holy See, created by Pope Francis in July 2013. Its purpose was to undertake several audits, at the request of His Holiness, of the financial and administrative affairs of the Holy See. Cardinal Pell became involved halfway through our work, and we had many opportunities to discuss COSEA's findings with him. He was amongst the cardinals who had repeatedly asked for more transparency, accountability, and adherence to international ways and practices in those areas prior to 2013. One of the strong recommendations of COSEA in terms of governance, so as to avoid repetition of some of the problems experienced in the past, was to create a Secretariat for the Economy. It would report to a Council for the Economy that would act as a supervisory body. In March of that year, Cardinal Pell was named the first prefect of this newly created Secretariat for the Economy, and he held that position until he returned from Australia after his acquittal. Some weeks after his nomination, Cardinal Pell suggested to His Holiness that I be appointed chair of the Board of Directors of the *Istituto per le Opere di Religione* (IOR)—that is, the

Vatican Bank—at a time when its entire board was about to be replaced.

I took on this responsibility in July 2014, and the new board that would lead the complete overhaul of this institute was then named. Although the IOR has never had any formal relationship with the Secretariat for the Economy, His Eminence and I would meet from time to time to compare notes on some of the critical problems we were each encountering in trying to reform the administration and finances of the Holy See. These meetings continued until he chose to return to Australia to face the false accusations against him.

In 2016 my wife and I invited His Eminence and some other Australian friends to our home in Brussels for a couple of days. During his stay we visited the battlefields of the First World War in Picardy, France, where so many young Australians gave their lives for the freedom of France. I shall never forget the emotion we all felt in Ypres, Belgium, at the Menin Gate at the end of our journey, when we heard at 8:00 P.M. the Last Post, the traditional final salute in honor of the memory of the soldiers of the former British Empire and its allies who fell during World War I.

Upon our return, when we were all together, our conversation touched on some of the challenges of the ongoing administrative and financial reform process in the Vatican. His Eminence stated, "I have always been and will always be a papist, and I shall always be faithful to the successor of Peter. I believe in one faith, one Church, one pope." But, he added, "that does not mean that I will always agree with some of the decisions of the pope. And when I disagree on matters that I consider of high importance, I will express it without hiding and always respectfully. But I shall always be obedient." He was particularly eager to make sure that our children, who had been part of the conversation and with whom he had an affectionate connection, understood this point.

While visiting him in jail in Melbourne some years later, a few months before he won his final appeal in the High Court of Australia, I was struck not only by his inner peace and trust in God but also by how he continued to be well informed about and interested in the developments in the Vatican: The Church was the love and passion of his life. During these 404 days he regularly prayed for the Holy Father and the burden that he must bear.

As I was asking for his blessing before leaving the jail, he said, with a touch of his usual humor, "My days here are in many ways not as harsh as what I had to endure since I took the position as prefect of the Secretariat for the Economy." He was referring to the systematic opposition he had to face in carrying out the necessary and reasonable economic and financial reforms in the Vatican. This opposition is best illustrated by the comments of a well-known cardinal who, during the consistory of cardinals in 2015, publicly compared the plans that had been laid out for those reforms to those of the Russian Comintern. In addition, His Eminence was under no illusions about the dark forces in the Vatican that had worked against him and directly contributed to his woes, and he spoke of them on many occasions once he was back in Rome.

One of his great joys when he returned to the Vatican after those 404 days in jail was to be granted an audience with Pope Francis. The words that His Holiness publicly stated about the work that His Eminence had done and how much the Church owed him for his sacrifice surely meant a great deal to him.

—Jean-Baptiste Douville de Franssu

12

"Hey George!"

"Hey George!" were the words called out by my five-year-old son as he ran across the entrance hall of Cathedral House in Sydney, chasing the big strides of a newly appointed Cardinal Pell. I reprimanded him because before we visited, I had made sure to instruct the children about the correct way of addressing a cardinal.

Cardinal Pell turned and admonished me with "He is speaking to me, not to you." He then turned towards the child and asked, "Yes, Tim?"

Recently reflecting on that incident, the same son, now twenty-six, commented, "The person we knew was certainly not the one portrayed in the media."

Back in 1985, I was befriended by the then-Father Pell when he was appointed rector of Corpus Christi Seminary, Melbourne, and I was an undergraduate student of theology. In addition to studying, I was employed as the national secretary of the Australian Family Association based in the offices of B. A. (Bob) Santamaria's National Civic Council. Bob was writing his biography of Archbishop Daniel Mannix, and as I lived near the seminary, he had asked me to deliver the manuscript to Father Pell, who had agreed to read it prior to publication. I was asked to do that on two occasions, and each time, Father Pell invited me into his office and made me coffee. I then had no reason to call on him again. But one evening, as I was walking from the library to the car park, I heard a big booming voice behind me: "Clara, you have abandoned me. Come and have a coffee sometime." I then took the liberty of visiting for coffee every four weeks or so.

He subsequently lectured me in Church history, and in 1987, the year he was appointed auxiliary bishop of Melbourne, he was one of my research supervisors—a role he continued after his appointment. We became friends. There was no subject I did not feel comfortable discussing with him. He had an easy relationship with young people and was mentor to many, including other contributors to this collection. I introduced him to some of my friends and he asked for introductions to others. I would often visit his house for my supervision sessions, and one day I asked him how the role of bishop was suiting him. He was candid. "They don't tell me anything. I am basically the chief altar server", was his reply. In light of later events and questioning by the Royal Commission, this is revealing.

In January 2001 I had an interesting meeting that shed much light on the rise and rise of Bishop Pell's reputation in Rome. I was in Rome undertaking some research at the archives of Propaganda Fide. Bishop Peter Elliott, a mutual friend of mine and Cardinal Pell's, suggested I call in on Father Joseph McCabe, a Maryknoll Missionary and friend of Bishop Elliott's. Father McCabe was at the time secretary to Jozef Cardinal Tomko, prefect of the Congregation for the Evangelisation of Peoples. It was an interesting meeting. Father McCabe asked me many questions about the Australian Church and asked whether I knew Archbishop Pell of Melbourne. I confessed that I did.

"We want him in Rome", said Father McCabe.

"You can't have him", was my spontaneous reply. I gave him reasons for my objections, which may or may not have been in the interest of the universal Church.

Father McCabe went on to tell of his first meeting with Pell, years earlier, as they were transiting through the Hong Kong airport. Pell was travelling from Australia to Rome, and Father McCabe and Cardinal Tomko were heading back to Rome after business elsewhere in Asia. When they arrived in Rome, Cardinal Tomko instructed Father McCabe to take the bishop's bags, and they dropped him off at his accommodation. Father McCabe had an idea. There had been some issues with the seminary in New Zealand, and he thought that Bishop Pell might be an appropriate Vatican envoy because of Australia's proximity to New Zealand and also because "they would understand each other's accents." The New Zealanders were not particularly happy with the proposal, and Father McCabe admitted he was totally ignorant of Pell's reputation. As it happened, Pell was able to resolve whatever impasse had been troubling the Church in New Zealand, and the Congregation subsequently looked to Pell to resolve issues in Southeast Asia and Oceania. He also did important work for Caritas in those regions. Some of these missions are outlined in Tess Livingstone's biography of Cardinal Pell.

It appears that before each mission, Father McCabe or an official of the Congregation would contact Archbishop Little and ask to borrow Bishop Pell. It seems that Archbishop Little was very accommodating in facilitating Pell's absence from Melbourne. Unbeknownst to Archbishop Little, as he liberated himself from Pell's presence, Pell's reputation in Rome was undergoing a meteoric rise. Not surprising, then, that when Archbishop Little wrote to Rome requesting a coadjutor, Rome accepted his resignation and appointed Pell his successor.

On the last Sunday of January 2021, a Mass to celebrate Australia Day was celebrated at the Urbaniana in Rome. Most of the priests and students living or studying in Rome were present, and I had been asked to do one of the readings.

Archbishop Pell, then of Melbourne, was the principal celebrant. Apparently he was a last-minute fill-in for Cardinal Cassidy. I was speaking to him after the Mass, and he mentioned that he knew my husband had been offered a job at the Melbourne archdiocese. I replied that my husband was not happy with the conditions being offered, to which he responded, in typical irreverent Pell fashion, "Tell him the Big Bastard will look after him."[1] (I was a little uncomfortable with the knowledge I had gleaned from Father McCabe a few days earlier, and indeed, there had been constant rumours, fearful amongst his friends and joyfully anticipatory amongst others, that Pell would go to Rome.)

"That's good while you are there. What happens if you go?" I challenged him, meeting his eyes.

"Denis will look after him", came the unflinching reply. Denis Hart was his vicar-general and his successor as archbishop of Melbourne.

This exchange was enough to convince me that Pell was not long for Melbourne. Two months later, he was appointed archbishop of Sydney. I could fool myself into believing that I had convinced the Roman Curia that he should not go to Rome—at least on that occasion. The Roman appointment would come years later, when Pope Francis appointed him secretary for the economy.

Pell was a player on the big field—the international circuit—but to us, he was a family friend. He mentored me and continued that role with my children. He constantly teased my sons for rowing for Ballarat High School, the nemesis of his alma mater, St Patrick's College. He laughed when my daughter reported that she had told the principal

[1] "The Big Bastard" reference goes back to Pell's time in Oxford, where he met and became friendly with the then-Anglican Peter Elliott. The two Australians were referred to as "the Big Bastard" and "the Little Bastard".

of Sancta Sophia College at the University of Sydney, where she resided, that she knew the cardinal because they were both old girls of Loreto College in Ballarat. (Loreto College is currently a secondary school for girls, but in Cardinal Pell's day the sisters also ran a primary school attended by the young George Pell.) When my daughter and her school friend chanced by him in Rome, he took them out to dinner. My daughter's friend became one of his staunchest defenders during the dark days of his trial. My son continued to refer to him as George. I picked my son up at the airport on Christmas Eve in 2018. The court cases were over. The sentence would not be handed down until March 2019. The first words he said upon entering the car were "So what is happening with George?" It was not public, but we knew.

George Pell was a loyal friend to thousands, not just my little family. He touched so many. In 2019 I had a chance encounter with a woman I had known in my student days. She knew I was friends with Cardinal Pell and told me of her distress at his being sentenced to jail. I suggested she write to him in prison. She began to do so regularly, and he replied to one of her letters. That letter, she told me, is one of her most treasured possessions. Our conversations about the cardinal renewed our old friendship. On the spur of the moment she decided to fly from Melbourne to Sydney for the funeral and was astonished that she managed to get into the cathedral. This response was from just one average Catholic laywoman.

One of the most moving scenes in St Mary's Cathedral during the vigil prior to the cardinal's funeral was the sight of a young priest, a large, tall man, possibly the same stature as the young George Pell, in tears beside the casket. Cardinal Pell's death took us by surprise, but yesterday I was speaking with someone who did not consider herself his friend, although he gave financial support to some of her projects. She offered the view that the ordeal of facing the baying mob each day as he entered the court and his time in prison could well have weakened his heart. For a while I liked to entertain more sinister explanations, but she may well be right.

—Clara Geoghegan

13

Boffins, Bastards, and Birth Rates

I knew Pell well enough for him to write a foreword to my memoirs, *Ordinary Bloke, Extraordinary Life*, published in 2022.

In the late 1960s when he was in Oxford, he was friendly with an old Jesuit, born in the north of England. Pell recalled him as a skinny man with thick glasses and a prominent Adam's apple whom they knew affectionately as "the Boffin". A specialist in eighteenth-century unbelief, he read the *Daily Telegraph* each morning but could not manage the older texts. So Pell, and a number of others, would read him long slabs of David Hume, the Scottish philosopher. The Boffin, Pell recounted, liked Australians, and one day Pell explained to him that in Australia the word "bastard" could be a term of endearment.[1] The Boffin was pleased with himself as he replied that he could understand this. In his foreword to my memoirs Pell went on to explain that I, a businessman-professor, was "a bit of an old bastard, with a heart of gold". It is not every day one gets called an "old bastard" by a prince of the Church!

[1] When Prince (now King) Charles was a student at Geelong Grammar in the Australian state of Victoria, his classmates affectionately called him a "Pommy bastard".—Editor's comment

Pell, a tall and well-built man, was a very good Aussie Rules footballer, and had he not responded to the call to the priesthood, he could have had a good career in that arena.

I first met Pell in 2000, when I was executive director of an organisation I had founded, the Business/Higher Education Council, which comprised university vice-chancellors and leading business executives for the purpose of enhancing collaboration between business and higher education. He was then archbishop of Melbourne. I invited him to address the Council on a topic of his choosing. Much to my surprise, he chose to speak on population trends. Perhaps I should not have been surprised because for several years he had publicly expressed fears that Australia could not hope to hold this island continent with only nineteen million people. As he pointed out, to the north, we had gigantic Asian neighbours. Some have had limited success in curbing their birth rate, and several have no desire to do so.

He then addressed the issue of declining birth rates in the Western world and the likely effect this decline will have on society and the world economy. As we all know, birth rates have continued to decline, and many countries are experiencing the difficulties of an aging demographic. Pell argued that the declining birth rate has dire implications, not only for the Australian society and economy, but also for the world. He bolstered his arguments with detailed statistics.

He used the Japanese Island of Oshima as a stark and graphic example of likely futures. Oshima is a small Japanese island, twenty miles long, cradled between the large islands of Honshu, Shikoku, and Kyushu. Pell said we can confront the future there. He said we might call this the price of our success—perhaps even the wages of sin. Along with Germany, Japan has the most quickly aging population in the world because the Japanese are living longer and having fewer and fewer children. Their fertility rate has fallen to 1.39; a rate of 2.1 children per woman is necessary to keep the population stable. Oshima is the Island of the Old, with the most aged population of all. Pell said the barber with the cut-throat razor was eighty-four years of age, as was the papergirl. The taxi driver was only eighty-three years old, and the policeman a sprightly sixty-year-old. Pell went on to point out in the town of Towa, at the eastern end of the island, octogenarians outnumber teenagers by more than three to one and septuagenarians by seven to one, and half the population was over sixty-five. Towa had a population of 20,600 in 1945; fifty-five years later, the population is 5,500. Pell argued that Oshima was not a social aberration, a development that goes against the current. He said that following present patterns, Japan's population will be halved by the end of the twenty-first century—and so will Western Europe's!

Pell's prophecy has proved accurate. On January 1, 2006, Towa, along with the towns of Ishidoriya and Ohasama, were merged into the expanded city of Hanamaki, and Towa no longer exists as an independent municipality.

Pell outlined the scenario with which we are confronted: In 1950 the developed world accounted for 24 percent of the world's population. In 2050, he predicted, it will account for no more than 10 percent. In that year not a single European state, including Russia, will match the Philippines in total population. If this happens as predicted, it will represent an enormous shift in the balance of global power. Falling fertility rates and increasing longevity, he said, would provoke continual and radical change in our economies.

Pell was very concerned by the impact this would have on the basic unit of society—the family. He highlighted the distressing outcome that if the trends in those countries with the lowest fertility rates—Italy, for example—continued, then within two generations more than three of every five children will have neither brothers and sisters nor aunts, uncles, or cousins.

The important message Pell was articulating was the very real link between children and hope. For in children and hope lies the future of families and the nation.

It was one of the most informative addresses I have ever heard, and it really made me contemplate a possible, very different future.

As usual, George left me with plenty to think about.

—Professor Ashley Goldsworthy

14

Teaching Youth to Distinguish the Lamb from the Wolves

Closing my eyes, I can still see the newly minted archbishop settling into an armchair just beside the base of the stage after addressing the hundreds of young people crammed into the opening night of the Thomas More Summer School. With a trace of a smile, he would turn attentively to the open microphone, waiting for his favourite moment—question time with the young people of Melbourne. He absolutely loved it. He enjoyed every minute listening to our questions, concerns, complaints, and overzealous initiatives. He was an avid and anything-but-passive listener. For upstarts like me, he would challenge us midsentence to reframe arguments more clearly or stretch our ideas to consider the complexities involved in making our initiatives a reality. What surprised, honoured, and enthused us most was how seriously he took us.

He actually wanted to know what we thought and set about addressing it, backing our initiatives with his confidence, his leadership, and whatever support we needed. On one of those open-mic evenings, after thanking him for his clear teaching, I wondered aloud why those well-meaning people leading youth groups were not trained to hand on the faith. He asked us all for advice and then went on that very year to enlist Anna Krohn, O.A.M., to develop an archdiocesan-accredited youth leadership formation program. Later, I received a meeting request. A little worried that I might have spoken too boldly, I slipped into St Patrick's Cathedral before the meeting to ask the Lord's help. It turned out all three young people invited to the meeting had made the same detour. Afterwards, we found ourselves in the office of the archbishop, and it was astonishing the confidence he had in us. He threw us an idea about developing an archdiocesan Office for Youth and left us to thrash out the details. He took that eventual framework with him to Sydney, along with our beloved Steve Lawrence and many other people who were blessed to have his friendship and are still actively serving the Church today.

It has been impossible to describe to others what it was like to be a young Catholic university student in Melbourne during the time of Archbishop Pell. I have never experienced anything like it anywhere else. His installation was like an Easter Vigil "Lumen Christi" moment in the Church when all of a sudden, the cathedral is filled with the warm light of faith. In the space of a few years, we witnessed the construction of a new seminary (the old one was now too small), the establishment of the John Paul II Institute, the rollout of a K–12 religious education program, the establishment of Catholic youth ministry at an archdiocesan level, and the beginning of Australia's World Youth Day adventures. He drew in vibrant, intelligent Catholic speakers and teachers to form us to engage with the world of ideas and the richness of our Catholic intellectual heritage. I remember how proudly he introduced us to Cardinal Scola, beaming at the cardinal's assessment that this truly was a wonderful place to launch the John Paul II Institute. On the lighter side, we loved watching how much he enjoyed stopping traffic—having the police make way for the hundreds of young people making the Stations of the Cross down the centre of Melbourne during local World Youth Days.

He knew us not only by name but also by vocation. He would follow what God was doing in us and, like John the Baptist, would equip us to distinguish the Lamb from the wolves. He always spoke the truth, which made us seek his advice and follow it. He was keenly interested in each of us and remained so all his life. The theme of a lot of our conversations was catechesis. He wanted to know what the kids who struggled with faith were asking so that he could address their questions. He insisted that four faith statements be printed in bold on the back of the *To Know, Worship and Love* religious education textbooks so that, as he said, "at least if they reject the faith, they know what they are rejecting." Actually, the last time I saw him, which was after his release from prison, he was discussing those statements and decided he wanted another added: "Suffering need not be useless. United to Christ's suffering in the passion, it can be changed into grace, spiritual energy."

—Sister Mary Helen Hill, O.P.

15

Informal but Not Shabby

I first met Father George Pell in October 1984 when I had my interview to be accepted into Corpus Christi Seminary, Melbourne. I belonged at the time to the Diocese of Wagga Wagga under Bishop William Brennan. Normally I would have been sent to the seminary in Sydney, in my own state of New South Wales, but once the appointment of Father Pell as the new rector of the Melbourne seminary (in the state of Victoria) was announced, Bishop Brennan decided I would go there instead. He knew of Father Pell in various ways, amongst which were two pamphlets written by him and published by the Australian Catholic Truth Society: *Bread, Stones or Fairy Floss: Religious Education Today* (1977) and *Are Our Secondary Schools Really Catholic?* (1979). In Australia the academic year and the calendar year go together, so a college or seminary year is from February to November, and the summer vacation is in December and January. Father Pell conducted an interview with each prospective candidate before actually beginning as seminary rector in February 1985.

I entered the seminary in 1985. Father Pell's strong leadership and presence had a big impact on the seminary. As relayed to me by the older seminarians, the climate of confusion, as well as the persecution of conservative seminarians, suddenly came to an end.

At Corpus Christi, staff and students had their meals together with no assigned seating. Father Pell was ready to talk (or spar) with any student or staff member who happened to be at the table. Once, one of the staff, the late Father Joe McMahon, concluded a little dispute with Father Pell by saying, "We've got to hang our hat on Vatican II." Father Pell replied, "We've got to hang our hat on the *Gospels*."

Cardinal Pell could take cheek as well as give it. He could make a joke and take a joke. He would talk to you man to man. While being fatherly and dignified, he never stood on his dignity. He could talk to anyone naturally regardless of age, position, or education. He was genuinely interested in people and what they had to say. Priests and laypeople came to see him in private to consult him about personal issues or larger issues for which they got no help from their own local authority.

Cardinal Pell appointed me Sydney chaplain to Courage (the organisation for people with same-sex attraction). After he was released from jail, I invited him to attend a meeting of my monthly Courage group of men. He gave a little talk and said he would answer any questions. One of the men asked him, "Cardinal Pell, why did you not testify at your trial?" He answered, "At one time I wanted to and thought it would be a good idea, even though my lawyer did not. But when I saw how the prosecutor was treating all my witnesses with disdain and calling into question everything they said as if they were liars, I feared that if I was treated by him in that way, I would get irritated and I might react and do harm to my own case." At the end of the meeting, he stayed behind to talk to the men individually, and he happily obliged many of them who asked for a photo with him.

In Rome one time in 1998, two young Australian diocesan priests were with him on an outing to a shrine. As they were walking along the streets of Rome, he observed the strict traditional clerical dress of one of them and the casual dress of the other. He said in jovial exasperation, "On my left, I am accompanied by a pox doctor's clerk, and on the other, by a would-be hippy Franciscan. Can we just have some balance amongst the modern clergy?"

As a priest, bishop, and later archbishop, Cardinal Pell would sometimes wear a black clerical shirt and sometimes a grey, blue, or white one. When visiting him in his episcopal residence in Melbourne, I asked him, "Your Grace, how do you decide what colour shirt you are going to wear each day? Do you consult your crystals first thing in the morning and work out your identity for the day and then choose the corresponding colour—or how do you do it?" His old friend Monsignor (now Bishop) Peter Elliott facetiously corrected me, "Don't be ridiculous, Peter. There is no secret about it. Bishop Brian Heenan [in Rockhampton, a thousand miles away, and regarded as rather liberal] at the start of each month sends out a fax to all the bishops across Australia to tell them what colour they are to wear each day. It's as simple as that." Pell rebuked us, "A pox on both your houses!"

Before a dinner that Archbishop Pell was to attend with many of my family and relatives, I asked him, "What colour clerical dress will you be wearing?" "Black, of course," he replied. "I wouldn't dare wear any other colour with your family!"

Bishop Pell, auxiliary bishop of Melbourne, came to Wagga Wagga in 1992 for the occasion of my priestly ordination. The night before the ordination, he phoned my family home and asked Dad, "Anything happening there tonight?" Dad said, "Yes, there is, come on up." "Formal or informal?" asked Bishop Pell. "Informal, of course", said Dad. Ten minutes later, the doorbell rang. Dad opened the door, and there was Bishop Pell, dressed ever so casually.

Dad cheekily greeted him with the words, "I said informal, not shabby!"—to which Pell replied, "I took you at your word—now let me in!"

Cardinal Pell personally replied to many people, young and old, who wrote to him in jail. From both Melbourne's and Sydney's chancery, Archbishop Pell answered every letter he received. Of course, drafts were often prepared for him by his staff, but he went through every letter and made any necessary changes before sending it.

Cardinal Pell often sent a draft of an important article or speech to three or more people for their observations and suggestions, and he accepted corrections and took on board what people said. He told me in 1985 when I was a seminarian that a commentator, writing about religious education, had once sent him a draft of his article for comment. Father Pell remarked to me, "You know, I went through his article carefully and made several comments and suggestions and amendments—and he did not adopt a single one of them." For his major speech on Islam, after the events of September 11, 2001, Pell consulted his good friend the Australian Biblical and Islamic scholar Father Paul Stenhouse, M.S.C. (1935–2019). When Cardinal Pell sent me the text of his upcoming book of sermons on Luke's Gospel, *Contemplating Christ with Luke* (2012), I went through it all and corrected little things and made suggestions to improve some of the ideas and remove ambiguities. He said to me some time later, "I'm embarrassed to say I accepted nearly all your corrections!" Bishop Anthony Fisher, now archbishop of Sydney, was present, so I remarked to him, "Of course, I left a few mistakes in so that people would know it's his own work."

Pell was invited to write a weekly column for Sydney's *Sunday Telegraph*, a popular easy-to-read newspaper, and did so for thirteen years. They were simple but thoughtful pieces on any topic at all—human, cultural, ethical, social, religious, and even some on sports. Addressing a Catholic crowd at the Catholic Adult Education Center of Sydney, Pell said, "You might think those columns are a bit weak or wishy-washy. The reason is that I am not writing for you good people, already committed to Christ and the Church. I'm writing there for the great mass of unwashed pagans who don't have much or any religion. I'm trying to do what Saint Ignatius advised about entering through their door but taking them out by yours."

At the Catholic Institute of Sydney, where the Sydney seminarians do their theology studies, the Sacrament of Holy Orders was covered only somewhat in a course called Ministry. Cardinal Pell contacted the Institute directly and said that course was to be replaced by a course called Theology of the Priesthood, which he himself would teach, starting in 2008. Knowing that he could not always be available for all fourteen weeks of classes, he asked me to be his replacement for the weeks he could not teach because of meetings in Rome and other unavoidable commitments. He asked me to prepare an outline for the course, and knowing my bent for scholastic theology, he said, "You prepare the doctrine, and I'll humanise it!" He was not a scholastic thinker himself; his own bent was historical and cultural. Of one scholastic theologian, under whom he studied in Rome as a seminarian at Propaganda Fide College, he said, "Brilliant man ... hopelessly out of date." Pell read broadly on historical, biographical, and cultural issues. He had an extensive library and regularly bought new books. However, when he became a bishop in 1987, he acknowledged that he had to reread or revisit theological works to keep himself well informed on Catholic doctrine. After episcopal ordination he asked a priest in Melbourne to give him a list of recommended theology books. In 1990 he was appointed a member of the Vatican's Congregation for the Doctrine of the Faith, headed by Cardinal Ratzinger. That, too, gave him an impetus to learn more theology! Pell greatly admired Cardinal Ratzinger and his supremely masterly intellect (and other virtues).

Cardinal Pell was no traditionalist himself, but he vehemently opposed any measure to sideline or exclude traditionalists. He said, "Every mad group is made to feel welcome in the Church; why can't traditionalists be made to feel welcome?" For that reason he was very glad to say the Traditional Mass on occasion, and he was opposed to the 2021 document *Traditionis custodes* (officially "Guardians of Tradition" but often translated as "Jailers of Tradition"), which put tight restrictions on the Traditional Latin Mass. He said in 2022, "That document won't last beyond this papacy. It'll be like *Veterum sapientia*—it will just become a dead letter. No one will bother to enforce it." (*Veterum sapientia* was issued in 1962 by Pope John XXIII to revitalize and restore the use of Latin in Church life. Amongst other provisions was the insistence that "seminary studies are to be taught in Latin".)

From its beginning Pell was very much opposed to the cause of the canonisation of Pope Paul VI. "His papacy was a disaster! We would have been much better off if Cardinal Siri had got elected." He expressed that opinion a number of times.

The ill-informed used to say that Cardinal Pell was autocratic and nonconsultative as an archbishop. The truth is that he was never a micromanager and was far more tolerant than his reputation allowed. When people like me with Lebanese background suggested certain measures be employed upon dissidents, he replied, "We can't have Lebanese solutions to every problem!"

Cardinal Pell used to say, "The Jesuits have replaced Jesus with social justice." When a Jesuit headmaster of a school wrote an article in *The Australian* (the major national newspaper) on "Jesuit Education", there was not one mention in it of God or Christ or revelation. Of course, justice got a good mention. Cardinal Pell made the comment to me—and said he must write to the Jesuit headmaster to tell him—that "going by this article, Jesuit education has nothing to do with Jesus!"

When one Jesuit complained to Cardinal Pell about Opus Dei, Pell replied, "Don't you complain about Opus Dei; they are doing what the Jesuits used to do and should be doing: going for people high up to convert them and to live the spiritual life."

Pell loved opera and classical music and liked to invite friends to accompany him to performances at the Sydney Opera House. Once I was there with him, and the retired politician Tom Uren (1921–2015), a socialist, greeted him as we walked past: "Hello, Cardinal Pell!" Tom Uren was one of those of whom Cardinal Pell's friend Catholic political activist Bob Santamaria (1915–1998) said, "You could look at a man like that and know what you have got: an enemy you can respect. When you look at others, you don't know what you have got"—referring to others whom Santamaria called "nihilists". A well-known socialist figure (I am not sure who, but probably not Tom Uren) said to Bob Santamaria once, "I'm a *pre–Vatican II* atheist."

Pell admired Santamaria but thought he was sometimes too negative. Pell said at different times, "You've got to give people hope. You can't just talk about how bad things are without providing hope." He never gave a sermon or a speech just lamenting the state of things. He was always encouraging, both in private and in public.

When Pell mentioned sin or Hell or Purgatory in sermons, he was never intense about them but simply matter-of-fact. Even that did not stop liberal clerics from complaining though. At a clergy meeting he said, in his usual mild and indirect fashion, "I don't think we should be preaching as if we can presume everyone is automatically going to Heaven." That was too much for one of them, who immediately remarked to his confrère, "What a fundamentalist!" To anyone who knows the meaning of the word, Pell could never be called a fundamentalist. He was not an expert on Biblical matters and was sometimes unclear on them, but he was certainly not a fundamentalist. In a TV debate with Australian Father Paul Collins, M.S.C. (who not surprisingly later left the priesthood), Pell remarked, "I won't be called a fundamentalist just because I adhere to a few necessary fundamentals." Collins had been claiming the priesthood was unknown for the first few Christian centuries, and Pell rebuked him, "Don't try to fool me with claims about the early Church; I have a doctorate from Oxford in early Church history."

Cardinal Pell's funeral was unique in one respect. It must be the first time in history that as a casket was taken outside a church, there were people across the road shouting out abuse at the body in the coffin in front of grieving family members: "Cardinal Pell, go to Hell!" Not even serial killers or violent gangsters have had such protests and abuse aimed at them at their funeral. In fact, the verbal abuse began before the funeral and could be faintly heard for a time from within St Mary's Cathedral. So Tony Abbott, former Australian prime minister, in his eulogy at the funeral, said, "As I heard the chant 'Cardinal Pell should go to Hell', I thought, Aha! At least they now believe in the afterlife! Perhaps this is Saint George Pell's first miracle."

—Rev. Dr. Peter Joseph

16

Seeing the Present Through the Lens of History

As we had arranged, I met Cardinal Pell at St Anne's Gate at the entrance to the Vatican at 1:30 P.M. on Friday, June 23, 2017. He was in an affable mood from the start. He took me on the short walk to his apartment, where the table was set for lunch for two, prepared by a charming sister who was in attendance.

The apartment was comfortable and a decent size, with a large bookcase. Pell told me he had once prided himself on having read all the books in his library, but that was many years ago, and such a boast was no longer valid. We had a glass of water each and started the conversation. I reminded him of the terms: It was strictly off-the-record and he would not be quoted, but I was at liberty to use the material, unattributed, that he provided. It became one of the more remarkable lunches of my life.

I made detailed notes later. Given Pell's death, I am entitled to reveal what he said, yet its gravity is such that I still intend to keep the bulk of his remarks confidential.

We talked about the Catholic Church, Pope Francis, the cardinal's dealings with the pope, and the crisis of Vatican finances. He was plainspoken in a very Australian manner—down-to-earth, direct, no beating about the bush, yet unemotional, no phoney dramas, no exaggerations. "I don't think we have had a pope like this who wants to open up debate about issues of doctrine and dogma", he said. "This is a dangerous situation for the Church."

Pell had strong opinions. He didn't conceal them; he wasn't embarrassed by them. He understood nuance, but he didn't fudge. He didn't play both sides of the street. He struck me as an Australian formed by the 1950s when you knew your principles, stood up for what you believed, and enjoyed your mates. He was a muscular priest.

The cardinal was a brilliant person to converse with because of these characteristics and because of the remarkable context—he was a man of God who understood the world, an Australian yet an internationalist via his high position in the Church. He understood his history.

Pell was concerned by the pope's lack of any administrative sense and apparent inability to manage things in an ordered way. I sensed a cultural issue here: Pell was steeped in the Australian-based British tradition of institutional financial management in contrast to the Italian-orientated Vatican practice and a pope with a Latin American mindset. Was this ever likely to play out smoothly?

Pell saw Pope Francis as a complex man who enjoyed making decisions but was ineffective at follow-through and often reluctant to face the consequences of his decisions and preferences. He said Francis had a gift in his ability to relate to people; the personal dimension was palpable. He described being present when Francis had a meeting with a group of disabled people—the pope had embraced them one by one. The human impact was very great. The people were deeply moved. "This is what the pope does well", Pell said.

We canvassed the plight of the Church—the divisions over doctrinal issues, the pope's promotion of climate change action, his scepticism about capitalism, the warning to Francis from four cardinals of a "grave disorientation and great confusion" amongst many faithful. Pell felt that the origins of Francis in a Latin American Church and society were highly relevant in these tensions.

Yet Pell's sense of fortitude was on display throughout the lunch. He saw the present through the lens of history. His grasp of the Church's long history of surge and vicissitude seemed to vest him with a philosophical faith and confidence in its capacity to surmount the contemporary turmoil.

While he didn't speak directly in these terms, Pell was conscious of his own extraordinary role in these critical events. He felt corruption had been entrenched in Vatican practice—reports had been made in the past—and he speculated, without knowing, about the forces that had led Pope Benedict to step aside. He explained in detail about the backlash and sabotage being directed at the people now attempting to purge the financial corruption. The Vatican's opponents of reform seemed to be able to enlist the power of the Italian state in their resistance.

Given his responsibility in restoring the finances, Pell was at the heart of these issues. He had a meeting each fortnight with the pope conducted in Italian. While the pope was supportive of Pell, he had little understanding of the financial issues or economics, and, by the time of my lunch with Pell, any sense of the pope's support was being eroded.

We had an excellent lunch—pasta for the first course, followed by chicken and carrots. Pell had a glass of red wine, and I had a glass of white. He talked about Rome, reflecting that "Rome has always been important, in every century, at every time."

Towards the end he turned the discussion to Australia. He asked me how the hell the Turnbull Government had got itself into such a mess with the Catholic Church in Australia, notably over school funding. We discussed the influence of the growing Muslim population in Australia and its future political and religious impact.

Pell told me he would need to return to Australia in a couple of weeks' time to face charges. He had a letter of support from the pope. It was his intention to return home, stand trial, have the matter resolved ASAP, and return to his position in Rome. He was concerned that his absence would weaken the financial reform effort. He was sceptical of the Vatican's ability to purge corruption from within.

I gave Pell a cautious warning about the forces being aligned against him. Maybe he knew or suspected. Those forces, in fact, turned out to be more virulent and, in an Australian way, corrupt than I had imagined. I told Pell I would do what I could to support him during the coming campaign by our legal, media, and governing institutions to convict and imprison him. He showed not the slightest sign of self-pity or a persecution complex. Indeed, he was thinking not of himself but of others. He walked me back to St Anne's Gate. It was 3:35 P.M.

After a gap of more than five years, I lunched again with Pell in Rome on October 5, 2022, in a different apartment in the Vatican area—it was an event of tribute and celebration. There was a group of five of us, and Pell had been keen to catch up when he heard we were in Rome. Once again, his hospitality was generous.

But given the events he had lived through—his humiliations, his conviction, the failed appeals, his long imprisonment, and finally the unanimous exoneration of the High Court—this lunch bookended a period that I doubt any of us could have imagined.

When we sat down at the table, Pell made it clear he wanted to pay a tribute to the *Australian* newspaper for the support it had given him throughout this period, and then, in a wider sense, to News Corporation. He spoke warmly and with much appreciation. I said that as a newspaperman, there are times and issues when you are called upon to take a stand, and this was such a moment. Rarely in history, I said, have virtually all the instruments of secular power been deployed, backed by a public mood laced with vengeance and a legal system falsely purporting to deliver justice. *The Australian* had been deeply proud of the sustained and unremitting position it took.

It was a warm lunch amongst friends. We discussed, inevitably, the Catholic Church, the pope, the possible succession, the tribulations of the West, and the condition of Australia. It seemed, though, that Pell's vindication had created a ray of hope—it was as though his prevailing in the teeth of such hostile power offered fresh hopes and possibilities for all of us in an age of deepening gloom. Here was something to celebrate. It showed the tide could be turned. He was an example to the rest of us.

Pell talked about his fate briefly, and what was striking was his generosity, his lack of ill will. To be honest, I found it extraordinary. There was no sense of resentment, no trace of bitterness, no complaints about judges or politicians, no obsessions about an outrageous injustice. On the contrary Pell shared anecdotes about his time in prison, even told jokes. He had an appreciation for the sufferings of those who had accused him. He had offered up his ordeal in prison for the sins committed against young people by the Church.

Towards the end of the lunch, on behalf of our group, I made a few comments. I talked of our admiration for the way Pell had conducted himself through the trials, conviction, and imprisonment. He was a model of respect for others amidst a grave misjustice being committed against him. Unlike Pell, I made some critical, but justified, remarks about our public and private institutions and the way many of their leaders had betrayed their personal and professional standards by taking part in the mob mentality.

It was C. S. Lewis who said, "We make men without chests and expect of them virtue and enterprise. We laugh at honour and are shocked to find traitors in our midst."[1] That was the Australian experience in the Pell saga.

We never knew our October lunch would be the last time we saw Cardinal Pell. In retrospect, it was the best farewell.

—Paul Kelly

[1] C. S. Lewis, *The Abolition of Man* (MacMillan, 1947), 16.

17

Beer and *Bookkeeping for Dummies*

I have the immense privilege of having known the cardinal since I was nine years old. In my first year as a chorister in St Mary's Cathedral Choir, I sang at his installation Mass as the eighth archbishop of Sydney, in May 2001.

Apart from his down-to-earth nature, his keen interest in people, and his genuine concern for the marginalised, the characteristic I appreciated most in the cardinal was his capacity for humour. He could make people laugh, especially by highlighting the ironic dimensions of any situation, and he had the capacity to take a joke directed at him.

One of my earliest memories of his capacity for humour was of a day when some of us young choristers asked him whether he wanted to hear a hymn we were working on. He obliged us, and we began the first verse of the hymn "I Am the Bread of Life" by Sister Suzanne Toolan. When we reached the chorus, which we managed to sing in harmony, we began to slap our cheeks in a percussive manner each time we sang the line "I will raise him up." We were, of course, making fun of what the cardinal called "happy clappy" liturgy—something rarely on offer in St Mary's Cathedral, renowned for having the best cathedral choir in Australia. The cardinal was highly amused and laughed out loud before encouraging us in our musical education.

I recall another time in 2012, just after I was accepted to join the cardinal's archdiocesan seminary. My mother approached the cardinal after Sunday Mass, and instead of thanking him for accepting me, she lamented the fact that I would be moving away from home, abandoning the nest, as it were. The cardinal didn't look the slightest bit concerned or contrite and responded, "At least you haven't lost him to a woman!"

Seminary life, like military life and other forms of highly regulated social interaction, requires the occasional deviation from formality to lift the *esprit de corps*. In 2014, on the cusp of his move to Rome to become the prefect of the Secretariat for the Economy, the cardinal came to a farewell dinner at the seminary. At the dinner two seminarians, Thomas Hunter and Ronnie Maree, now a priest, presented the cardinal with a box of items they hoped would be useful for the tasks that awaited him. The collection of treasure included *Bookkeeping for Dummies*, a few Australian flags, a few cans of beer, some paper money, cash receipt books, and a money box. At the time none of us could have imagined the mendacity that was awaiting him in Rome. Rather than *Bookkeeping for Dummies*, he needed something like an *Oxford Handbook of Money Laundering* and a DK guide to the Italian mafia.

During the awful period of his trials before his imprisonment, we were blessed to have him reside with us at the seminary. I would always make it a point to visit him after breakfast to see how he was and whether he needed anything. Ronnie did the same, helping the cardinal in printing out emails, articles, and the like. He never really mastered computers or smartphones! One morning the cardinal told Ronnie and me that his successor, Archbishop Anthony Fisher, would be visiting him that evening for dinner, so Ronnie and I decided to assist in crafting the menu for them. We went to the local supermarket and thought of an entrée, main, and dessert. Uncle Tobys Le Snak [crackers with prepackaged cheese dip] would be a good opener, to be followed by canned chicken (always a reliable source of protein), and then a cardinal-red M&M's chocolate block for dessert. I'm not sure whether these items made an appearance at dinner that night, but I do remember the cardinal saying weeks later that he didn't mind the Le Snak biscuits and dip!

On another occasion I visited him and noticed a statue on his living room table. The cardinal explained that it was Saint Patrick lighting the Easter fire. I replied that it looked more like Saint Patrick attempting to dance, for which he scolded me, even if it was a playful scolding! The cardinal was of Irish descent on only one side of his family, but the Irish genes had a habit of dominating. The saint who most often comes to mind in the context of the cardinal is not, however, Ireland's Patrick but England's George—the fellow who is usually depicted in iconography thrusting his sword down the throat of a dragon. When the cardinal was living at the seminary, Richard Sofatzis, then a seminarian and now a priest, informed me of a large stuffed toy dragon who resided at his family home with no purpose. The reason he approached me is because I had "prior convictions" when it came to importing stuffed toys into the seminary. A few years earlier I had found a large abandoned bear by the side of the road and brought him inside, and I would move him to various locations throughout the seminary that were common places for people to gather. The rector, Danny Meagher, now a bishop, eventually ordered the bear's eviction. So when Richard sourced a dragon, we brought him in and named him George. One morning I brought George over to meet the cardinal. His initial response was to bellow, "Get that out of here!" but after a bit of advocacy on behalf of George the dragon, he relented and asked whether I could leave it with him for a short visit.

During his time in jail many people wrote to the cardinal, and, to try to cheer him up, Ronnie and I wrote a letter that contained this postscript: "Whilst watching the Bulldogs play last week on your Foxtel connection in Freeman house, it seems that we finished all the mint slice and pink lady apple juice. We'll ask Della [the seminary secretary] to restock the fridge again ASAP." Freeman was the house the cardinal lived in during his seminary stay, and he had a liking for mint slice and apple juice, simple delights denied him in prison.

The second time I visited the cardinal in jail, it was with the newly ordained priests Fathers Ronnie Maree and Joseph Murphy. For this visit we sat together around a table in a common area. The cardinal walked in dressed in his green prison overalls. Father Joseph blurted out, "Good to see you dressed for the occasion, Eminence." Even from jail the cardinal appreciated such humour.

In reflecting on the life of the great Cardinal Pell, I hope these instances paint the picture of a man who, whilst taking his ecclesial responsibilities very seriously, had the lightness of spirit to joke with his friends and to be on the receiving end of the jokes of those who were very much his subordinates. Our cardinal did well at both.

—Rev. Fr. Roberto Joseph Keryakos

18

The Educator *Sans Frontières*

"We are not offering one holiday package from an equally valid set of alternatives; nor are we offering a philosophy, another way of life. We are calling our students to faith in the Son of God, a faith lived out in the Catholic Church."[1]

These simple and slightly sardonic remarks were given by George Cardinal Pell towards the end of a homily at a Mass at St Mary's Cathedral Sydney in 2006. The homily was delivered in the manner we all remember, with his distinctive and deliberately articulated Australian descant. The congregation was a large gathering of educational professionals and academics at a National Catholic Education Conference.

The homily laid bare his desire to be clear and down-to-earth, his impatience with "trendy" relativism, and his straightforward commitment to an evangelical compass in Catholic schools. For some people, such blunt-cut remarks (and his commanding physical presence) hid the true personality, learning, and cultural vision of the man.

For some, particularly his fierce critics in the headline-craving, polarised secular Australian media, such insistence on the polestar of orthodoxy fed what were too often the cartoonish and defamatory "Pell" tropes of the press. No

[1] George Cardinal Pell, *Test Everything: Hold Fast to What Is Good*, ed. Tess Livingstone (Ignatius Press, 2015), 283.

doubt present at that Mass were some education bureaucrats, educated in Catholic institutions but versed in the latest pedagogical fads, who rolled their eyes at such "primitivism". There might have been a swathe of others in the cathedral who were zoned out but polite. The cardinal was a realist about that likelihood too. Also in the pews would have been bright-eyed people, probably in the younger age bracket, for whom the homily and the cardinal's clarity struck a chord.

In the years since the shock of the cardinal's sudden death, many people, young and not so young, though aware of this type of mixed reception, have spoken of the importance of his presence to them personally and vocationally. Some of these have been students or young apprentices in trade or business who, when passing from adolescence and early adulthood, were mightily encouraged by his interest in and conversation with them. There were many opportunities hosted by the cardinal himself: World Youth Day events, student retreats, cultural and devotional events. Some knew of the cardinal from afar. It is striking how many thousands of people around the world from many different classes and ethnic and even religious backgrounds took the time to attend devotions for his release or wrote to him during his imprisonment in solitary confinement. Some sought to assure him of supporting prayers, some to share outrage, and some to ask for his prayers.

But it was always more than his words. The man was a medium who was more than his message. It is true that in his speaking or demeanour, he sometimes fumbled the ball of his good intentions by an excess of stoic pith or Aussie wit. But he never lost his relish for really listening to people, especially the young and those who were still forming their intellectual landscapes. In conversation he was attentive to those who authentically differed in various ways from his own Catholic conviction. He was not so patient with the pernickety, the officious, or those he sensed were staging an ideological campaign.

Conversazione

George Pell had an enormous gift for lasting friendship and a largesse that invited what he called in Italian *conversazione.* This expressive word comes from the Latin root *converso*, which evokes his approach to so many—a turning towards another, a spending time and conversation "by" or "with" them. It was perhaps George Pell's favoured cultural and pedagogical method.

Very often, *conversazione* in true Italian style took place at a well-catered table around which ideas about history, ethics, faith, and the state of the world would be chewed on along with generous food and good wine.

I remember being a relatively young and idealistic student attending such a *conversazione.* I came with a friend of my own age who shared my interest in the nexus between theology and the world. We sat nervously aware of the greats and notables around the table. At some point there was a thought-provoking introduction by the impressive author who was the special guest for the night. Then the auxiliary bishop (as he was then) George Pell as host asked each guest in turn for a brief response to the topic at hand. It was dinner turned into an Oxford tutorial.

Then his gaze came to my friend and me. We took a collective deep breath and tried to capture what we genuinely thought without tripping over our inexperience. I sensed a few backs stiffening at the table but felt buoyed up by the warm, crinkling interest and humour in the bishop's eyes. It was clear he was not poking fun at us but enjoying the festival of ideas.

It has been said that the young George was steeped in this laconic openness to others while serving in his father's pub, the Royal Oak, which still operates in his birth town of Ballarat. It explains a great deal. He took this openness and the informality into many different settings.

My father-in-law, a humble but intelligent retired Catholic layman who had worked in the chemical engineering lab at Melbourne University, was attending a public talk about archaeology at the university. He said that a large and (even then) well-known figure, dressed in a tweed sports coat and clerical collar, slipped into a spare seat beside him and leaned over to him with an extended hand: "Hello—I'm George Pell." That convivial greeting and the catholicity of the conversation that followed was typical and impressive.

Institutions

The cardinal spent his life encouraging the gaining of knowledge as the growth in responsible "wisdom", and he did this over a wide swathe of areas, both formally and informally. He was rooted in both the Latin and the Greek origins of the concept of education in its broader senses. If the Latin linguistic origins derive from the root term for "drawing out"—*educere*—cognate with leading along, this George Pell did as both a leader and a mentor. The cardinal wrote, "Knowledge of itself is not enough for faith or for living a good life, but it is one essential constituent if an educated person is to continue as a believer."[2]

Many of his efforts in establishing formal educational institutions in Australia have been documented well elsewhere. While many of his friends had begun to despair of

[2] Archbishop George Pell, *Issues of Faith and Morals* (Ignatius Press, 1996), viii–ix.

the enterprise, George Pell still devised ways to reinforce the institutions established by the religious orders in the first fifty years of Catholic Australia or to reform them—hence his work as president of the Teachers' College (Aquinas College, Ballarat) and in Catholic universities (Australian Catholic University and the University of Notre Dame Australia). He was also a pioneer in his support for liberal arts (Campion College Australia) and in seminary reform. He shouldered the expansive mission of Pope Saint John Paul II and his successor, Pope Benedict XVI, through new directions in youth ministry and building chaplaincies, in promoting the *Catechism of the Catholic Church*, in supporting the establishment of Diocesan Offices of Life, Marriage and Family, and in becoming the founding president of the John Paul II Institute for Marriage and Family (Melbourne Session).

In his homily cited earlier he noted, "The Holy Father [Pope Benedict XVI] acknowledges that this reverence for reason was taken into Revelation, into John's Gospel from Greek philosophy, and this was a providential conjunction."[3]

It is education as *paideia*, the Greek notion of applying "logos" to "ethos", that Cardinal Pell extolled here. He continued, "Here lies one of the secrets of European and Western civilization. Here lies the reason for our Catholic schools, for our reverence for education, why Catholics should never be fundamentalists and can never be postmodernists who reject the idea of truth."[4]

Education in this sense is not limited to the institutional structures of the "official" and bureaucratic processes, nor to a limited period of a person's life. Formation "in the faith" informs and nurtures the intellect, the heart and soul, and even the body. It is lifelong and personal. It steeps the baptised or

[3] Ibid., 281.
[4] Ibid., 281–82.

those attracted to Christ in sports, music, art, history, and liturgy in lifelong pilgrimage to love and truth. It should engage the politician and the football player, the mother at home and the scientist, the young and their grandparents.

Exemplars

The cardinal was a patron of many budding Catholic movements and associations in which he invested resources—his time and most valuably his friendship and presence to them. In these settings the cardinal taught by his presence, *conversazione*, and the example of the saints. He preached about the saints frequently. He often chose striking visual forms to bring these saints to life, and he was a very engaged patron of the arts. As befitted his heroic proportions, he had a lively and generous interest in monumental yet dynamic and realist sculpture. He rightly saw that such works left a lasting and powerful "lesson" in bronze for the Church and for society.

As archbishop of Sydney, George Pell donated on behalf of the Catholic Church a large bronze statue of a seated Saint Thomas More by the Dutch-born Australian sculptor Louis Laumen.[5] The statue was placed in the gardens of the Parliament House of New South Wales in 1997 to mark 150 years of responsible government in that Australian state.

Saint Thomas More (c. 1477–1535), the great figure of the English Renaissance—the statesman, chancellor, lawyer, scholar, writer, and beheaded Catholic martyr—was a favourite saint of the cardinal for reasons that are not difficult to see. Thomas More may not have always been

[5] Laumen is a Melbourne-based master sculptor whose work is in high demand and popular with the public. He captures the character of his subjects—sportsmen and military figures, along with saints—with close attention to human anatomy, facial accuracy, and movement.

understood or received by the state or the public world; he was a Catholic humanist, a jovial host, a loving and prayerful man, and a sign of contradiction in his own time.

At the dedication of the Thomas More statue, the cardinal declared, "I congratulate the sculptor Louis Laumen on capturing More's spirit. I believe that this beautiful piece will always be a silent but powerful reminder in this place of the need for high principles, service to the truth and, above all, moral courage."[6]

Within the first years of the establishment of the Thomas More Centre in Melbourne with its expanding annual Summer Schools and talks, George Pell, as bishop and then archbishop of Melbourne, was introduced to the centre. The Thomas More Centre was a formational initiative aimed at fostering "Christian principles" such as those of Catholic social teaching, anthropology and ethics—a centre of Catholic social formation and *paideia*. It was devised by Dr. Joseph N. Santamaria and his brother B. A. Santamaria and was visited and supported by international scholars and public figures such as Professors Ralph McInerny, William May, and John Finnis.

George Pell honoured the Santamaria family in his later prison diaries: "B. A. Santamaria (Bob) was of course one of the great Australians, whom I admired since I was a teenager and consulted as a friend and as an admirer when I was a bishop."[7]

In a short time George Pell became the leading patron and regular star speaker at Thomas More Centre events, gaining a following amongst its young participants. It was during his lively and sometimes provocative engagement that he was able to explore the curiosity of the young—their

[6] Ibid., 250.

[7] George Cardinal Pell, *Prison Journal*, vol. 1, *The Cardinal Makes His Appeal* (Ignatius Press, 2020), 332.

enthusiasms as well as their deficits after the contemporary education they had received in either the Catholic system or through the cultural lens of the times.

George Pell indicated in his 1997 book, *Issues of Faith and Morals*, that these Thomas More Centre events and their audiences provided him with a valuable and welcoming space in which to explore his conversational approach, "an explicit attempt to marry some contemporary concerns" with a mature understanding of Catholic teaching.[8]

What the cardinal could not have foreseen when he supported societies under the patronage of Saint Thomas More, or as he unveiled his public monuments, was that he would not only return often to read the masterpiece of spiritual writing that is the *Last Letters of Thomas More* but also taste just something of that great statesman and saint's fate.

As George Weigel wrote in the preface to the cardinal's prison writings, "He could not have known then that he, too, would suffer calumny, public vilification, and unjust imprisonment. But, like More and Fisher, George Cardinal Pell took his stand on the truth, confident that the truth is liberating in the deepest meaning of human freedom."[9]

The cardinal's calm forgiveness, the softening of his monumental profile after his suffering in prison, and the unanimous vindication by the Australian High Court made him a fine and lasting exemplar of Christian faith.

—Anna Maria Krohn, O.A.M.

[8] Archbishop George Pell, *Issues of Faith and Morals* (Ignatius Press, 1997), viii.

[9] George Weigel, introduction to *Prison Journal*, vol. 1, *The Cardinal Makes His Appeal*, by Pell, 11.

19

An Integrated Personality

I visited Cardinal Pell in the Melbourne Detention Centre on June 3, 2019, totally confident of the falseness of the accusations levelled against him, and found him to be, as was typical, in good humour, cheeky ("You're looking a bit fat"), and invariably interested in the people and projects of my life. He was entirely devoid of self-pity, and, as always, I experienced him as father, priest, and close friend. The experience elevated me, and I delighted in sharing it with people who I knew supported him.

I had first met a young Bishop George Pell thirty years earlier, in April 1990. I had been impressed while attending the Walk for Mary, linking the Anglican and Catholic cathedrals of Melbourne, and sought him out when my two brothers and I were seeking advice for our fledgling parish ministry. I was twenty years old at the time and playing professional football for Hawthorn in the Australian Football League. The supportiveness of the bishop, and the personal friendship that grew, led him to sit and cheer alongside my girlfriend, Annie, when my Hawks won the 1991 premiership—even though he barracked for Richmond. Football was one of many common points of interest between us. He subsequently celebrated our wedding fifteen months later, came for dinner many times over the years, and opened numerous important horizons for me.

It was he who invited me to take up the role of director of Catholic youth ministry in 1996, while I was still playing football, and from him I learnt many things about leadership, evangelisation, and fatherhood. "Put Christ at the centre!" and "Do what's important!" are phrases from him that still resonate. It was under his leadership that I undertook the organisation of the Jubilee Year 2000 World Youth Day pilgrimage of four hundred pilgrims from the Archdiocese of Melbourne to the Holy Land and Rome. He took a back seat in the bus, literally, and spent valuable time mingling and joking with the young pilgrims, who delighted in getting to know him personally. On one occasion, after a guide had finished explaining the rubble remains of Chorazin and Bethsaida, which had previously been cursed by the Lord, he asked to speak, and with a twinkle in his eyes he said, "Don't mess with Jesus!" and left it at that. During the same pilgrimage he delighted the youth by taking them to a waterslide in Galilee! I was very touched at the Sydney World Youth Day in 2008, in my role as director of evangelisation and catechesis, when at its conclusion he introduced me and Annie to Pope Benedict XVI, graciously saying, "Steve was in charge of ensuring that World Youth Day was a religious and spiritual event"—to which the pope replied, smiling brightly, "And it *vas* a religious and spiritual event!" He always provided broad and clear parameters within which to work and gave me lots of freedom for creativity while offering plenty of support. He instilled in me great self-confidence.

The cardinal had invited me to Sydney in 2003, at the end of our family's three-year stint of living in Rome while I led the Emmanuel School of Mission, in order to develop the role of convenor of chaplaincy at the University of Sydney. Annie was by then pregnant with our fifth child and ready to return to Australia, and the cardinal shrewdly spoke of his proposal to her before mentioning it to me, having a good grasp of the dynamic between us—Annie was the rudder to my sails. Both our fifth and sixth children were subsequently born in Sydney and baptised by him. We kept in close contact with the cardinal in the years after leaving Sydney, and he continued to encourage me in my education and ministry roles, stayed interested and close to us as a married couple, and maintained a fatherly presence in the lives of all our daughters and sons, establishing his own relationship with each of them. They can tell their stories of him offering joyful edification, learning, encouragement, and, when needed, gentle correction.

He has always been a source of wisdom and truth, having introduced me to various important writers and writings. For example, he encouraged me to read the *Confessions* of Saint Augustine, he gave me a copy of *Father Elijah* by Michael O'Brien (I've subsequently devoured every book O'Brien has written), and he and I shared spy novels and other good works of fiction (I'm proud to say he occasionally recommended to me an author that I had been the first to introduce to him, but he had forgotten, such as C.J. Sansom). He would also have me read articles he had written or drafts of documents for synods in which he was participating, for my reflection or comment. From the outset his discernment has been practical and helpful and often blunt—which was good for me as an overly spiritual and unpractical young man—and his down-to-earth advice very concrete. When I was discerning my vocation, for example, he said, "Either find a good girl and get married, or join the seminary. Give yourself a year!" He was immensely human, always appreciative of human fragility, awake to teaching moments, and never afraid to disagree ("That's rubbish!"). I am touched that he always encouraged me to cherish and serve Annie and put our marriage first, often asking me, "What does Annie think?"

On November 3, 2022, I was in Rome travelling with my two youngest sons—Jerome (then nineteen) and Ambrose (then sixteen)—on a European journey of three weeks. We had lunch with the cardinal, and, in typical fashion, he was immensely generous with his time, giving us four hours. It is quite unusual that the highlight for two teenage boys of a three-week holiday in France and Italy would be a slow lunch with a seventy-nine-year-old priest, and yet it was a most wonderful time of good food (the cardinal had no qualms about enjoying good food!), instructive and entertaining conversation across broad-ranging topics, fascination with—and advice about—the particular interests and directions of my sons, and lots of laughter. There was no indication that he would pass from this world less than two months later, so I am immensely grateful to God that we were given that opportunity to spend time with him in person so close to his departure for the eternal glory of the Communion of Saints. For the above reasons I dedicated my recently published book, *The Tiny Book for Giant Men* (Parousia, 2023), to him, a true father of mine.

I conclude with a final observation, one that in the many things said or written about him that I have come across since his death seems insufficiently mentioned. Many have commented on George Cardinal Pell, the erudite scholar, the sportsman, the priest, the leader, the visionary, the great manager, the humanist, the astute businessman, the connector, the defender of the faith, the falsely accused, and so much more. But I want to emphasise that he was an incredibly *masculine* man, with a rare integrated personality. A man of warmth, a good man. A man's man. A giant man!

—Stephen Lawrence

20

"Do Not Be Afraid, My Dear"

An Unexpected Guest

We never really thought he'd write back, let alone show up for dinner. I was eleven years old when this giant churchman stooped through our door for the first time. Then-Archbishop Pell had just arrived in Sydney as our new bishop and surprised us by responding to Mum's friendly invitation. No one teaches you how to host an archbishop. We scrambled a bit. *What do we cook? Maybe now is a good time to repaint the house?* But he seemed right at home around the family table, so much so that he became part of the family—for the next thirteen years.

He was our shepherd, friend, and mentor and an "uncle" to me. I remember sitting as a child, hoping to overhear fascinating conversations about "inside news" in the Church, but to my dismay, all he seemed interested in was *us*. Amidst last-minute cooking, Dad would remind us, "Don't forget to have something ready to tell him." We knew that when he walked in the house, he was there for us, and he left outside affairs aside.

He Dared Me to Dream

The cardinal was interested in, but did not pressure us about, what we wanted to do with our lives. I surprised him one day when, filled with an earnest desire to help him in his work, I casually asked him, "What skill set does your assistant have? And when will she retire?"

I was excited and proud to belong to the Church he was serving. It was a mission that influenced the world. I remember listening to him preach with courage and clarity at Mass and seeing him dine with ease and simplicity in our home. He was a man of the kingdom, with a zealous passion for Christ, yet he was never overwhelmed or openly anxious about what Jesus had entrusted to him.

He was always available. He never said no to a young adult event, unless he was out of the country. I helped organise a monthly event called Theology on Tap, where hundreds of us would gather for a word. I once asked Cardinal Pell to speak on martyrdom. I'll never forget the unexpected word he gave us. He told us that martyrdom may or may not come our way. Regardless, we are to seek not martyrdom but Christ. He believed in the capacity of young people and opened the door to World Youth Day 2008, allowing God to change the face of Aussie ground and countless futures like my own. His witness sowed the seeds for my vocation in inspiring my desire to lay down everything for Christ and his Church.

To my surprise, when I told the cardinal I wanted to enter religious life in New York, he was not entirely enthusiastic. He was a discerning man and well aware of my sometimes-overzealous spirit. He encouraged me to pray, saying, "If it is of God, the desire will grow." It felt like cold marching orders, but I'll be forever grateful for the wisdom of his words. I got out of the driver's seat and surrendered my life to Jesus, and God continued to inflame my desire to respond to him with all of me.

At my farewell Mass, the cardinal said, "I haven't spoken at an occasion like this before, and I don't propose to talk at any great length. I suppose a preliminary thing I should say to you is we're here, but we're not all pleased." We all had a good and much-needed laugh because we knew the cardinal spoke into what we were all thinking. It was a joyous day and he supported my vocation, but it was tinged with the sorrow that comes with saying goodbye. The cardinal had an ability to meet us in the reality of life's joys and sorrows and bring about a laugh when necessary.

He went on, with affection and faith, "This should be a happy occasion because we have a young woman striving and decided to follow God's will ... so we pray that she will identify God's will and follow it. That's the most important thing for all of us, that we're in the niche that God wants of us."

Cardinal Pell never truly farewelled me. He always remained the shepherd of my hometown and "uncle". Although he noted, "I am not a good correspondent; excuse me for this", he faithfully wrote short, poignant letters, which I treasure today.

Captive but Free

It was his handwritten letter from prison that I treasure most, particularly one line that I read during my own little Calvaries: "Doing God's will brings us all a meaning and peace—which many unfortunately never find.... I am well and content with my lot, although I hope." The cardinal united himself with the sufferings of our Saviour, whose final Passion placed him between two thieves. He wrote, regarding his appeal, "I have been robbed twice and am hoping for better" and shared with me the secret to his peace: "You know, God is with us even in the worst of times."

I believe the cardinal's greatest contribution was the proclamation he preached from his prison pulpit. Few heroes endure great public suffering and remain faithful and forgiving. Although the media mocked his every move—and his every move was watched—God let nothing go unseen. I saw firsthand this vivid witness of faith and of the peace that surpasses all understanding (see Phil 4:7).

After the long procedure of approval through the prison systems, God opened the gates for Mum, Dad, and me to visit him in Melbourne Assessment Prison. I had no idea this would be the last time we would see him.

We were taken into a small cubicle, so tiny only one of us could sit, with the other two pressed in close behind. We awaited his arrival silently and nervously. All morning, we had talked about how to make use of our brief time: "Do we ask about anything? Should we avoid topics? Do we tell him things, or will this only make him sad? What if it's awkward?"

All I wanted was to see him, and I hoped that, in some fraction of a way, we'd bring encouragement—for him to know he was not alone or forgotten.

To my amazement, Cardinal Pell did precisely this for *us*. The door opened abruptly, and a guard pointed him in. He was dressed in the green of prisoners, his hair ruffled. But he walked into that cubicle as if he had just walked into our home. Without hesitation and with a gentle smile, he approached the glass as if it were the most normal thing in the world and placed both hands against the window. Without words, we placed ours on the other side, and tears flowed.

He then pulled up his plastic chair, crossed his legs, leaned back as if reclining on our family couch, and said, "Tom's wedding ... tell me all about it."

So we proceeded, with joy, laughter, and memories, to tell him of my brother's marriage just days before. He could have asked about anything. But he didn't think of himself for a moment. He may have been wrongly imprisoned, but he freely chose to remain rightly a priest.

Deprived of almost everything, he never gave up his call to be Christ to every person, on every occasion. His welcome turned a cold and claustrophobic cubicle into a warm and hope-filled place.

He was no lonely Christian in solitary confinement, for he knew no prison bars could keep Christ away. Cardinal Pell believed that God's Word was true of his own situation and precisely in his confined circumstances. God went with him. His prison cell became the sanctuary of his sacrifice. Stripped of the opportunity to celebrate Mass but endowed with the privilege of uniting his own body with Christ, he proclaimed Jesus through his letters, and his daily surrender became his last sermons. Instead of giving in to fear, he chose to give in to grace. He led by following the Lamb wherever he went, even to Calvary.

"I'll Be There"

In 2023 I made my final vows as a Sister of Life. I wanted the cardinal to be there and asked permission to contact him earlier than was typical, hoping extra notice would help the cause. To my delight, his secretary responded within a day: "This is uplifting news! I have put it on the cardinal's desk." It was a joy to know that the invitation had made it to him, although undoubtedly amidst a mountain of timely correspondence. I wasn't sure he'd read it.

Just six days later, on January 10, I returned to my desk after prayer and saw an email at 4:03 P.M. with the subject line "Cardinal George Pell dead at 81". A wave of disbelief, shock, and deep sorrow overwhelmed me. *I won't see him in August. I won't see him again.* I wept long. To lose someone is always an experience of terror. We were made not for death but for life. Within days two sisters and I were en route to Rome to attend his funeral.

We made our way to the small Church of Saint Stephen of the Abyssinians, where his body lay in state. As I walked in, I saw the simple closed wooden coffin with a single red rose placed upon it.

I remained within reach of the casket for hours and witnessed streams of people bid farewell. All corners of my heart cried out, *I am sorry for what you suffered. I'm sorry you died. God, I thank you for his life. I thank you for his witness and all that he endured, all that he gave, even his very self.*

We prayed the Mass at the Altar of the Chair of Saint Peter, where he had been ordained a priest fifty-seven years earlier. The coffin lay under the glorious stained glass window of the Holy Spirit. As we began singing the "Salve Regina", a piercing light shone down upon the sanctuary. He left, borne on the shoulders of men, to standing applause.

One of his caretakers pulled me aside and told me that as the cardinal was getting into the elevator for his surgery, he had turned, pulled a paper from his pocket, and given it to him, saying, "I have known this family for a long time; they're dear to me. Tell her, 'I'll be there.'"

The caretaker placed the paper in my hands. On it was written, in the cardinal's own handwriting, "Dear Sister Grace, as this is a once in a lifetime, I will make a special effort to attend in August. More details later. Love to all. Godspeed. In the Lord, George Cardinal Pell."

Courage

One word resounds in my heart every time I think of Cardinal Pell—"courage". He'd often say to me, "Do not be afraid, my dear." Though he walked a path of persecution, he knew that with God, there is no pointless suffering; nothing is left without meaning. He once wrote to me after a loss, "You have been through a terrible time ... where your faith has sustained you, and I am sure, enriched you personally through this suffering, so you can contribute even more effectively." The love he had for the Church is not wasted or expired but amplified beyond earthly measure in eternal life.

We're experts in underestimation—of God and ourselves. We ask, Is God really that good? Is it really possible to love in this dark, painful, difficult situation I am in?

Cardinal Pell, along with myriad faithful Christians, speaks a resounding yes. God is that good. And love is real. We're quick to give up on the truth of God's imprint engraved in us, as if it can be lost in a wrong move. But we are not casual, meaningless accidents. Life is not cheap. Christ came and keeps coming into us with his breath of life and loves us within our real circumstances, ideal or nonideal. We are part of a much greater story.

Like Cardinal Pell, our story rests on whether you and I let Love into our lives and let our lives be defined by Love. Love is a Person, Jesus Christ. That Person lived inside Cardinal Pell, on the fifth floor, in cell 11, unit 8, and never left him—and he will never leave us.

—Sister Mary Grace, S.V.

21

Concerts, Cricket, and the Gilroy Perspective

Cardinal Pell publicly described me and my family as his "allies"; however, we were not part of his inner circle. His Eminence recognised that the McCarthys were a part of Catholic Sydney and of legal and political Sydney—a social reality that was not dependent on connections with him or his network.

His Eminence came to appreciate that there are Sydney Catholics who, while completely loyal to the Church and fully orthodox in religious belief and practice, have a different political and social philosophy from those who were part of the mid-twentieth-century Melbourne Catholic experience. The legacy of the ALP/DLP split still lingered in the 1980s and 1990s, but the cardinal, whilst a Mannix man, understood there was another perspective. This other perspective, what might be called the "Gilroy perspective" in contrast to the "Mannix perspective", could not be dismissed or denigrated as the rationale of moral cowards. The late "Johnno" Johnson was the exemplar of this perspective amongst Sydney Catholics. Johnno and the cardinal became firm friends in the years following his appointment to Sydney.[1]

[1] For non-Australian readers, this whole paragraph refers to the 1955 split within the Australian Labor Party, caused by the infiltration of the party in some

Cardinal Pell became known to me in 1979 when I heard Father Pell (as he then was) address the John XXIII Fellowship (later the Campion Fellowship) on teaching the Catholic faith. After he became an auxiliary bishop in 1985, his Australian Catholic Bishops Conference appointments brought him regularly to Sydney. On these occasions he often enjoyed having dinner at our home and especially the noisy family concerts that followed. These were led by my wife, Christine, a concert pianist, and accompanied by our six children in various combinations—singing hymns and popular songs and arias from operettas such as *Oklahoma* and *The Pirates of Penzance.*

In 1996 Christine and I were invited to his installation as archbishop of Melbourne. We were then amazed at the swiftness of the Holy See in appointing him to Sydney in 2001. Christine was invited to present a reading at his Inaugural Mass in St Mary's Cathedral, and a suggestion that he commence that historic day with prayers at the tomb of Blessed Mary McKillop (as she then was) in North Sydney was incorporated into his inaugural program.

Thereafter, he was a frequent visitor to our home and built a strong rapport with our sons and daughters, as he always excelled in his relations with young people. I also like to believe that the cardinal developed a more relaxed and confident relationship with the Catholics of Tinsel Town (as some Melbournians derisively referred to Sydney).

---

of its branches by communists. In 1955 some members of the Australian Labor Party left the ALP and formed the Democratic Labor Party (DLP). Cardinal Gilroy, the archbishop of Sydney, and Archbishop Daniel Mannix of Melbourne took different positions on this split. Gilroy favored the typical position of Catholics in New South Wales to remain within the ALP, while many Victorian Catholics, following the leadership of Archbishop Daniel Mannix and the lay intellectual Bartholomew Augustine (Bob) Santamaria, joined or otherwise supported the DLP. The political cultures of Australia's two largest cities are very different.—Editor's comment

The cardinal's greatest project in Sydney was the 2008 World Youth Day. It was a triumph for Pope Benedict and the Church in Australia. It was Cardinal Pell's finest hour. My family were active participants in the World Youth Day events. Deacon (as he then was) James McCarthy read the Gospel at the Mass of Rededication in St Mary's Cathedral; Christine made vestments for various World Youth Day Masses; and Helena and Anthony organised special youth events. The cardinal also arranged for Helena, our youngest daughter, to have a short audience with Benedict.

In 2012 I was appointed Australia's ambassador to the Holy See, following the inimitable Tim Fisher. The cardinal had no influence over the appointment, but he was very pleased with this new role for me and Christine. My appointment to the Holy See occasioned his greatest service to me. On the night before we departed Sydney for Rome, the cardinal arranged to see me at St Mary's for about two hours. He proceeded to brief me about personnel and policies at the Holy See. It was the briefing of a well-informed and active Roman insider. He gave me a sketch of the personnel in the Roman Curia, beginning with Pope Benedict and the then–Secretary of State Cardinal Bertone. All other heads (prefects) of Vatican congregations were covered, as well as the Roman media and religious orders.

The cardinal's briefing was in the aftermath of the Butler Affair in the Holy Father's office, where it was established that important documents had gone astray without detection. Cardinal Pell was furious and criticised the pope's senior advisers for embarrassing the Holy Father in this way, as well as allowing a perceived security risk to emerge in papal administration. Cardinal Pell told me he believed governance in the Holy See was in disarray, and he blamed the Secretariat of State and his secretariat for not supervising the Curia effectively. The cardinal believed Pope

Benedict needed strong support and assistance, and he thought this was not being provided by Cardinal Bertone. Later in the year, Cardinal Pell was flummoxed when my wife and I informed him that Cardinal Bertone was the most charming person we had met in the Vatican and that our driver had told us that Cardinal Bertone was a major football (soccer) commentator with a huge following. As a football commentator, at least, Cardinal Bertone was highly regarded.[2]

In the last part of his briefing of me, Cardinal Pell went on to deal with the Church's overall position in the world both spiritually and politically. It is doubtful whether any diplomat setting out for his posting was as thoroughly briefed as I was at this meeting. Cardinal Pell even offered suggestions for my upcoming engagement with Pope Benedict on the presentation of my diplomatic credentials.

Cardinal Pell very much approved of my intention to present to the Holy Father a map of Aboriginal Australia—that is, of pre-European settlement—showing the various peoples who constituted our First Nations and a letter from former Prime Minister Gough Whitlam commemorating forty years of Australian–Holy See diplomatic relations and recalling this historic milestone as one of his first initiatives as prime minister.

On many occasions, Christine and I had the pleasure of receiving Cardinal Pell at our residence in Rome, particularly

[2] In his book *Beyond the Crises in the Church: The Pontificate of Benedict XVI*, the historian Roberto Regoli remarked: "In the future, an accurate historical evaluation of Benedict XVI's pontificate—one that goes beyond Benedict the individual—must unravel the 'Bertone question.' Historians must examine closely his network of supporters and his opponents. Even if Bertone became Secretary of State directly at the will of the pope, it is equally true that there is hardly any similarity between the two personalities." Roberto Regoli, *Beyond the Crises in the Church: The Pontificate of Benedict XVI*, trans. Daniel B. Gallagher (St. Augustine's Press, 2024), 370.—Editor's comment

after his transfer to the Eternal City upon his appointment by Pope Francis to the position of prefect for the economy. Cardinal Pell always enjoyed Christine's piano playing, and he attended a number of her recitals in Rome.

Cardinal Pell was always available for discussions about the Vatican and world events. He was determined to place the Church in the forefront against human trafficking and modern slavery. He was also an enthusiastic sponsor of the Vatican Cricket Team, which I founded in 2013. He believed St Peter's Cricket Team, as it was also called, was an important initiative in ecumenism and Asian relations.

The death of Cardinal Pell was a great loss and sorrow for many of us. In addition, for me and my family, the year 2023 was the year my beloved wife, Christine, passed away.

May cherished memories of them both be with us for many years, and may we always remember to pray for their eternal rest.

—John McCarthy, K.C.

22

The Crypt and the Atrium

While it is the recent fashion for ordinations to the diaconate in the Archdiocese of Sydney to take place in the local parish that gifted the young men to the diocese, priestly ordinations still take place, as they have for almost two hundred years now, in the cathedral itself.

Sydney priests are generally pretty keen to see, pray for, and welcome their new brothers in the vineyard of the Lord, so there are turnouts of up to two hundred priests at each ordination. Substantial as it is, the cathedral sacristy was quite some time ago found to be too small to accommodate all the Lord's abundant clerical gifts, and so it was decided to set aside the cathedral crypt as the place for the clergy to sign in with their safeguarding card, to vest, to prepare spiritually for the Mass—and possibly to catch a quiet, joyful word with brothers they see less often than they used to.

Amongst the winding of amices, the gentle yet contented hubbub of fraternity, and the occasional confession, a vested priest here and a cleric just off the train there can be seen discreetly making for an unexpected corner of the crypt to take their place, or occasionally queue for a kneeler, for a minute or two in silent and often closed-eyed prayer and reflection. Religious and diocesan, old and young, fat and ripped, liberal and trad, hairy and bald, bearded and clean-shaven, and every hue of skin the Good Lord decided to fashion—there seems to be no defining pattern or distinction other than the fact that they are all priests, intent on one brief but important purpose: to pray at the tomb of George Cardinal Pell.

I was told that this was not to be a hagiography. I've never learnt how to do one of those—and in any case His Eminence would snort at such nonsense. Like all of us, George Pell was a limited, wounded sinner, with his own history, wounds, strengths, and weaknesses. What's more, he knew it. He could be impatient. I didn't always love his language, and he could be pretty rough in a take-down, be it an annoyed or friendly one. He could play too much to the crowd. Like many of his liberal opponents, he wasn't a stickler for canon law. His initial reading of people could sometimes be a good deal off. While a good team player, he often didn't wait for the team to catch up if the ball came towards him but instead grabbed it and ran hard in the right direction, more often than not scoring a sensational try—hang on, that's a strength. Which he would have explained in absurd AFL terms—a most definite Victorian weakness.

He had some pretty sensational strengths though. He was a great encourager. He rang up people all the time to buck them up and get them to have a go. He was clearly a discerning reader—while Dan Brown was "lowbrow", the cardinal thought my columns did "a world of good" and repeatedly urged me to keep writing. He was rock solid—faith-wise, trust-wise, integrity-wise, friend-wise. He trusted his appointees—even if he didn't like them—and intervened only on major stuff. He was a massive believer in reason, humanity, the fundamental goodness of people, making a loud Catholic noise, and the idea that no matter how great the evil, it is always hopelessly outmatched by the good. He was incredibly generous and loyal. He was a hard worker and mastered his brief. He'd always tell you what he really thought, regardless of whether you wanted to hear it—or whether it was the right time. Contrary to many of his critics, he looked to and had hope for the future, always. He loved a good debate and delighted at being bested by young people, for whom he shared with John Paul II a genuine older-brotherly love. He didn't faff around trying to maintain his popularity or blame his staff or the conference or Rome for not getting things done; he just got it done himself and cheerfully took the flak that usually comes from challenging postmodernity and taking a risk and having a courageous go instead of staying safely out of trouble and avoiding change.

So not a hagiography—not a saint's record. I don't know if he was one.

Pretty hard to say that he wasn't a martyr though.

Everyone who knew him will have a particular Pell story that illustrates who he was, what his character was like, and the effect he had on his contemporaries. The following is mine.

I was still a green-eared—or whatever the expression is—first-year at the University of Sydney. A couple of months fresh from the life-changing experience of World Youth Day in Toronto (a very Pell kind of project) at the behest of the newly transformed Catholic chaplaincy (another Pell initiative), I had come back no longer sure what I wanted to do with my life but determined to do what I could to bring the goodness of the Gospel to the campus. Somehow I had been made responsible for the team organising the first Catholic Mission Week at the university, and amongst our complex deliberations we settled on having a lunchtime Q and A with Archbishop (as he was then) George Pell, totally open and promoted to all comers. As Catholics, we thought Jesus' project for humanity was by far the best of the options available, and a simple and open opportunity for students to lob whatever reasoned objection or question they wanted to at the guy responsible for implementing that project in Sydney would be a fair demonstration of whether we had any cred. I thought some of the Maronites overdid it a bit by insisting on accompanying him in a large crowd across the road after Mass from the splendidly named and appallingly designed Chapel of the Resurrection on City Road—now gone—but I understood a little better when I saw the group of unhappy protestors standing with their mouths taped up massed around the entrance to the Stephen Roberts Theatre (also now gone).

They were protesting the Church's oppression of their free speech and activity. I thought at the time that this was probably a fair cop historically—until they were welcomed inside, where they proceeded to speak and shout and interrupt and chant and insult the whole hour, which I thought was less fair, especially given that it so completely contradicted their identification as an oppressed, weak, unpowerful, and voiceless minority. As I have said elsewhere, it was the most appalling, irrational, and dictatorial spectacle I've ever seen at a public forum before or since.

But the archbishop just stood there. He didn't get aggro. He wasn't rude or narky. He remained perfectly calm, taking questions from anyone and everyone, quietly confident, unruffled and patient, acting as if this was just part of his job—that people are owed the truth and that however ill-natured a question, goodness and truth will always do good and set one free. That was George Pell.

Going back through my notes—I had forgotten we had corresponded a few times—I noticed that while all of it is vintage Pell, there is one paragraph, written back in 2010, that opens a window into his heart that his prison diaries have done much to expand upon: "For most of my life

I have found that the cross is not too heavy. While there have been times when it was otherwise, I believe that when we are trying to do our duty and in the right niche (God's choosing, more than ours) God looks after us and does not try us beyond our strength. I hope this will be the case with you and that you will know many times of genuine consolation, if not exaltation."

May it be so for us all!

A few weeks ago I was invited by the principal of one of our parish primary schools to come and see their brand-new atrium. An atrium is the name of the room especially set aside and prepared for the excellent and authentically human program of the Catechesis of the Good Shepherd. As the students began to gather and chatter, I quietly explored the room myself, admiring the orderly and extensive variety of furniture and carefully made objects made available for the learning explorations of the children. There were many kinds and sizes of shelves, tables, lamps, and chairs. As I drew closer to a set of shelves in order to understand better how the number of items stored in there differed one from another, a brief golden rectangle caught my eye—"Gift of the Estate of George Cardinal Pell".

I immediately realised that it would not have been just that shelf—but probably also those two homely carpets. And the large reading lamp lending a comfortable ambience. "And", sister explained, "that little stool that the play tabernacle is sitting on. It was the same stool he set his breviary on whenever he was praying at home. In fact, his breviary was found lying open on that stool in Rome after he died."

And now the seat of his prayer, which he had continued ceaselessly and faithfully throughout the entirety of his solitary confinement in prison, serves as a little table for the play tabernacle for children to discover experientially how

Jesus Christ does pretty much the same thing, in equally solitary fashion, out of love, in every tabernacle in the world. Regardless of whether anyone notices or agrees, it's good and will do good, especially for young people. How totally appropriate. He'd love it.

And the advantage I have as a Christian is that I can also say he loves it. Because we've got good reason to believe he's with the Lord, good reason to learn from his mistakes, as well as glean far more from his generous array of gifts, courage, daring, love, and, above all things, total trust in the Lord, who he believed would never let him down—and believed he never had.

May he rest in peace and help us with our own journeys and fights and crosses and generosity—and above all, may we appreciate the many more countless good things Jesus showers us with in the gift of life, as he always did.

—Rev. Fr. Josh Miechels

23

Firm in Faith and Generous in *Fraternitas*

I had some substantial disagreements with George Cardinal Pell. As a loyal Victorian, he believed that Australian Rules football—a game he had played well and loved—was superior to rugby. As a parochial Queenslander, I held strongly to my conviction that Rugby League (the dominant code of rugby in Australia) was the greatest game of all. Furthermore, in one of our conversations Cardinal Pell revealed a surprising admiration for the Kennedy family and its members' various contributions to American political life. He had met Bobby Kennedy in 1967 on one of his first visits to the United States, and the Kennedy "charm" left its mark on him. I took a more critical stance and argued that the best of the Kennedy clan was the non-Kennedy—Sargent Shriver. I may even have secured some limited concession from the cardinal on the latter point, although I can't be sure. However, of this I can be sure: George Pell loved good discussion and debate.

My contact and friendship with Cardinal Pell extended only over the last two decades of his life. I was not an intimate associate who worked with him on initiatives of major consequence. At the outset I was merely an acquaintance who met him through shared friends. Yet from the beginning I felt we were simpatico, and I was always grateful for the interest and support he extended to me. My appreciation of him grew with each encounter as the years passed. Always in evidence was his deep love for the Church and his desire that Catholics play their part forthrightly and faithfully in public life. Conversations with him inevitably revealed his deep love for Australia, his appreciation for history, his wide-ranging intellectual curiosity, and his wit and insight.

While Cardinal Pell laboured in the Lord's vineyard primarily in Australia and then in Rome, he also had a deep appreciation for the American Church. He had lasting friendships with a number of Americans, especially his longtime collaborator George Weigel, and he visited the United States quite often. In 2004 he went to Chicago to deliver a lecture on a topic dear to his heart—"Newman and Conscience"—for the Lumen Christi Institute and also to visit with his good friend Francis Cardinal George. Cardinal George hosted a luncheon for Pell, and I scored an invitation through the intervention of my good friend Don Briel, the founder of Catholic Studies at the University of St. Thomas. I remember well the interactions of these two great churchmen, the Archbishops of Chicago and Sydney. They were well aware of both the formidable challenges facing the Catholic Church from outside and the painful struggles within it. But they were undaunted. They drew inspiration from then-Pope John Paul II and were unafraid to witness to the truth and to defend it. Each of these great leaders in turn inspired and encouraged others—including me—to battle on whatever the odds. How their leadership is missed.

Cardinal Pell recognised the importance of Catholic education at every level. He had a special concern for Catholic higher education, believing that genuine Catholic institutions were needed to train a new generation of laity to represent the Church in the world—in the professions, in business, and in public life. He played an important part in the formation of the Australian Catholic University. When he saw that institution secularizing, he facilitated the foundation of the Sydney campus of the University of Notre Dame Australia (UNDA). In late 2007 I investigated whether I might play some leadership role at UNDA, and I met with Cardinal Pell as part of that process. We initially gave attention to specific matters regarding UNDA, but we also ranged widely over questions concerning how a Catholic university should fulfill the mission outlined in John Paul II's *Ex corde Ecclesiae*. I explained some of the challenges at "my" Notre Dame—the one in Indiana. He quickly comprehended the issues and stakes involved. He held strongly that a true Catholic university must reject the secularist temptation and instead must operate "from the heart of the Church".

In the end I did not take up an appointment at UNDA and instead continued with my teaching ministry in the United States. Thereafter, Cardinal Pell encouraged my efforts. In one of our last meetings before his unjust imprisonment I gave him some sense of the biography I was writing about Notre Dame's renowned priest-president, Father Ted Hesburgh, C.S.C. That biography, *American Priest*, was published during the cardinal's long period of solitary confinement, but he was able to read reviews of the book, notably one by his friend the late Jesuit priest Paul Mankowski. In the first volume of his *Prison Journal* he revealed his ability to get to the heart of matters when he noted that under Father Hesburgh's leadership the pursuit of truth had been replaced by the pursuit of excellence (as defined by the major secular institutions), with predictable consequences for Notre Dame's Catholicity.

In my biography I suggested that Father Hesburgh's quest to secure the regard of the liberal American establishment for Notre Dame had caused him to do too much "kneeling before the world" (to borrow from Jacques Maritain's *The*

Peasant of Garonne). This was not a charge that could be brought against George Pell. He refused to genuflect before the world, and yet he decidedly did not want to withdraw from the world. He hoped that Catholics generally would act on the Church's social and moral teaching to forge a better world, and he modelled effectively how this could be done, much to the dismay of secular progressives.

Cardinal Pell was never naïve in his political analysis, and he was a realist about the parlous state of the church in the world. He recognised that the decades since the 1960s had seen the erosion of traditional Christian morality as well as increased efforts in Australia and the United States to drive religion from the public square, to neuter it, and to control its institutions. Needless to say, he vigorously opposed such efforts, thereby attracting the venom of his opponents and setting himself up for the vendetta waged against him by elements in the media, especially within the Australian Broadcasting Corporation.

In July 2018 I met Cardinal Pell in Sydney. His first jury trial had failed to reach a verdict, and he was awaiting the second trial, at which he was convicted. Despite the vindictive slander he had endured over the preceding years, his spirits were good and his manner unruffled. We left Cathedral House and walked across Hyde Park to a restaurant on Elizabeth Street. Some folks might have retired from public view during these controversial days, but the cardinal was not one to hide his Christian light under a bushel basket. Far from focusing attention on his own legal travails, the cardinal wanted to discuss the American political scene and the impact of the Trump presidency. I laughed at his question, "Is there any method to Trump's madness?" I can't recall whether we resolved that matter successfully! What I do recall is his quiet strength and his resolute belief that the judicial system would ultimately vindicate him. He knew he was innocent of the awful charges laid against him, and he resolutely hoped the truth would win out in the end.

Sadly, Cardinal Pell's vindication took far longer than it should have, leading to his long days in solitary confinement. And yet his imprisonment brought about one of his most impressive accomplishments. Honest observers can recognise how he fought important battles to defend the Church in the world even while he campaigned against corruption within the Church. His time in prison, however, revealed his capacity to take on that even more difficult personal battle that each of us must fight to ward off the darkness in our own hearts and minds. Cardinal Pell refused to succumb to anger or bitterness against those who had accused him falsely or peddled such accusations. Instead, he took the opportunity to deepen his already strong relationship with Christ and to offer up his suffering for others who were in greater need.

I wrote to Cardinal Pell occasionally during his imprisonment and got reports on his well-being from our mutual friend Michael Casey. At one point I sent him some words extracted from C.S. Lewis' *The Efficacy of Prayer* (1958). In reflecting on them, Cardinal Pell wrote in his journal, "To fall, to complain, to denounce bitterly would further damage the Church, so we pray that God does not miscalculate, does not overestimate our strength, but gives all those in the wrong place at the wrong time the muscle and wisdom to hang on, to muddle through, sustained by the prayers of so many of great faith, both young and old."[1] I want to assert that George Pell did much more than merely muddle through. Sustained by the prayers of

[1] George Cardinal Pell, *Prison Journal*, vol. 3, *The High Court Frees an Innocent Man* (Ignatius Press, 2021), 29.

many, he gave an elegant witness of Christian fortitude. His trust in God never wavered, and his willingness to write of his experience has given us a spiritual testimony that will benefit many. I know it has benefited me. His journals are rich material for all of us who seek to "speak the truth in love" (see Eph 4:15).

I had some limited contact with Cardinal Pell after his release from prison and admired enormously his willingness to reengage the battles of our day. He maintained his firm commitment that the Church must avoid succumbing to what Newman called "the religion of the day". Right to the end, Pell manifested his episcopal motto, Be Not Afraid.

Regardless of whether one is an Australian Rules or a Rugby League fan, one must give thanks for all that Cardinal Pell did on the field for the Church throughout his life. No doubt he will be justly compensated for his efforts by the Lord. May his influence live on in all those who fight the good fight in the Church, in the world, and within themselves.

—Rev. Dr. Wilson D. Miscamble, C.S.C.

24

"A Kind Brute"

Cardinal Pell once recounted to me the story of a dinner he attended. Each of the place cards at the dining table bore a carefully chosen quotation that was said to reflect something of the character of the guest. Beneath the name George Pell were the words "It was Oxford that made me insufferable."

"God knows what they'll say about you, Morgan!" charged the cardinal.

Historically, the ecclesiastical landscape Down Under has been marked by a lingering suspicion towards academia and academics within the priesthood. Hence, it is oft repeated that one must be either a "head priest" or a "heart priest", but never a blend of the two.

Pell, in contrast, was virtually *sui generis* amongst the Australian episcopate in recognising and promoting the inexorable link between the life of the mind and the life of the soul—the unity of head and heart. He repeatedly said to us in the seminary that he wanted his priests to be "men of God and men of the people, but also men who read books!" His vision was clear. The battle for souls in the future would largely depend on the Church's ability to engage in the battle of ideas.

I commenced my own doctoral studies at Oxford almost fifty years after the cardinal commenced his. Even after so many years, I still came across people who remembered him as a student. On one rather serendipitous occasion, I sat next to an elderly don who, to put it mildly, was inhospitable to Pell's moral-spiritual convictions. He vividly remembered Pell, who was aged in his late twenties at Oxford. As such, I asked him, "What was the cardinal like back then?" The don replied with three words: "A kind brute!"

"A kind brute? Isn't that an oxymoron?" I said. The don proceeded to clarify, "When you were with Pell, socially, he could be very convivial and kindhearted. But when you were in debate with him, he would speak with *brute force*."

This blend of kindness with bruteness resonates closely with my own experience of a man I knew for close to twenty years. His bruteness in defence of truth is well-known. His kindness, less so.

The first time I had a proper conversation with Pell was during my interview following my application to the seminary in 2004. After a short (nervous) wait, a skyscraper of a man appeared through the office door and invited me to follow him for a chat. Towards the end of the interview, he said to me, "This is an impressive application, Greg. But I have one concern."

"What is that, Your Eminence?" I asked.

"You're too young!" (I was in my last year of school.) "I want you to make a decision that you will be happy with for the rest of your life. Maybe you could do a year studying law and then come back to me?" After some further conversation, he decided he would pray about it and would have an answer, yes or no, in two weeks' time.

I returned exactly two weeks later, expecting to receive the yes or the no. Neither came. "I still haven't decided", he said. "I need more time to think and pray about it. I want to make sure I'm doing what's best for you. So give me time and I'll contact you with an answer."

Several weeks passed until I finally received word: "You have bullied me into it." Bullying George Pell is not just another oxymoron. It is an ontological impossibility!

Upon reflection, this first encounter typified the genuine and ongoing interest the cardinal had in the happiness and welfare of seminarians and priests.

Another poignant example comes to mind. In my third year of formation I wanted to see him, as I was struggling with seminary life. I rang his secretary, Josie, and, as I expected, was told that a meeting was going to be a few weeks away, as the cardinal's appointment book was full. However, she said she would get back to me to confirm. A few minutes later, Josie rang and said, "The cardinal will see you at 4:00 P.M. today!"

As I sat in the reception area, I could hear the cardinal's loud, sonorous voice shout, "You better get his nibs a cup of tea and a few biscuits!" (I later had to google "his nibs".) At the end of our meeting he said, "Greg, I have one issue to raise with you. I am your bishop. My job is to look after you. So I am a bit disappointed you did not come and talk to me sooner. You can come and see me anytime you like. I hope you know that now?" My experience on this score was far from unique.

In virtually every encounter I had with the cardinal, he would ask two questions: "Are you happy?" and "What are you reading?" On one occasion at Domus Australia in Rome, the cardinal spotted me on the couch and my collection of books on the dining table. This time, he made a beeline for the books—a collection of Derrida, Heidegger, and Foucault—and then remarked, "Good Lord, Greg. I hope you remember how to say grace, let alone Mass!"

Despite accusations that Pell was an implacable, closed-minded conservative, he was actually very open-minded and eager to learn new things. A British philosopher once told me that the cardinal made him explain his rather esoteric metaphysical thesis and wouldn't let him leave until he felt he had started to understand it.

Of course, Pell made no secret that he wanted others, both inside and outside the Church, to understand the genius of the Catholic faith. His famously blunt or brute approach often made him a magnet for media attention. A memorable example of such magnetism occurred when I was having lunch with him in a hotel restaurant. Without warning, we were joined by a camera crew led by a member of the Chasers, a group of comedic journalists who once turned up at St Mary's Cathedral each dressed as George Pell, heralding "Look! A Pell for every parish" and suggesting to the cardinal that he should revise his attitudes towards cloning.

Although I don't remember all the details of the exchange, I know the interruption began with the journalist saying something about "dwarves", "lesbians", and the "Old Testament". Pell immediately asked them to identify themselves. "We are from the ABC", said the journalist.

"The ABC?" Pell responded. "You usually have a little more courtesy than this."

"No. We are from the lowest part of the ABC."

(In hindsight, this is a moot point.) To Pell's credit, he then began to answer the deliberately provocative questions, and I remember being quite impressed that he not only held his nerve (and temper) but also answered the questions so well. The fact that the footage was never used (as far as I know) is probably a sign that he answered the questions a little too well.

At my ordination to the priesthood I publicly expressed gratitude to the cardinal for his fatherly kindness and generosity. His response, delivered with characteristic wit, was that the panel beating in the seminary had done some good![1]

In hindsight I see a deeper side to this. The last time I saw the cardinal was the night before he left for his final trip to Rome. In the course of our conversation he said, "We will only begin to forestall decline in the Church if we start to acknowledge, honestly, the decline." This is not a one-sided issue. To do this, hearts need to be humbled and minds need to be sharpened. Whilst Pell's education may have made him insufferable to his adversaries, I am certainly one who gives great thanks to God for his legacy and his intellectual "panel beating".

—Rev. Dr. Gregory Morgan

[1] In Australia "panel beating" refers to repairing damaged panels on vehicles, and thus in the context of human relations, "panel beating" means removing the rough edges from a person's character. In other words, "panel beating" is shorthand for character development.—Editor's comment

25

Rowing Coach

I first caught sight of George Pell (or Dr. Pell, as most knew him at the time) at a St Patrick's College speech night held in the Ballarat Civic Centre nearly fifty years ago (1977 or 1978). As episcopal vicar for education for the Ballarat Diocese, he was a member of the official party. He was easy to remember: Tall and self-possessed, he cut a striking figure in the scarlet and dark blue academic dress of an Oxford doctor of philosophy.

A year or so later, I met Dr. Pell at the St Pat's rowing shed on Lake Wendouree. He was well-known around the shed, having coached various St Pat's crews since the mid-1970s. "What's a doctor of philosophy?" I asked him as he stood by the big green door. He told me of his studies in early Church history and the requirement, for any doctorate, to make a new and unique contribution to the chosen area of study. "What was your unique contribution?" He smiled self-deprecatingly. "I forget."

In 1980 George Pell became my rowing coach. We were the Sixth Crew—Bruce Ryan (a farmer's son from Edenhope), Darrell Akua (an athletic Nauruan), Richard Morris (from a well-known Ballarat hotel family), Brett Murphy (the cox), and me. George Pell was a terrific coach. He had an easy rapport with the crew, neither stern nor overly familiar. What he lacked in technical insight (after all, he once observed, his only qualification as a rowing coach was as a member of a "fat-boys crew" at Oxford), he more than made up in emotional intelligence and a capacity to engage and inspire. He was generous and good fun.

After training each night, George would give us a lift back to school. Once a week or thereabouts, he would first take us down to the local fish-and-chips shop, Mario's, and treat us to a milkshake (and an occasional hamburger). It might read as a modest treat, but for insatiable adolescents resigned to the meagre gruel of the boarding-house menu, it was like winning the lotto. George Pell understood this.

For the 1980 Labour Day long weekend we piled into the coach's car—in those days a Chrysler—three shoulder to shoulder in the front seat, the same in the back, and headed off to Mildura for regattas on the Murray and Darling Rivers. It was some adventure. We had barely reached Avoca when the police pulled us over for speeding. Happily, the copper was a good Catholic, and when he discovered it was a priest driving, he let us off. We stayed at the presbytery in Mildura, and on the first night George took us to the Grand Hotel for dinner. At that time the dining room at the Grand was an old-fashioned silver-service affair, and most of us were making our silver-service debut. In any event, George guided us through the cutlery selection and gently inducted us into a wider cultural world. That night was my first experience of oysters. Clearly the oysters were a long way from home, but for me it was like tasting another country.

The next day's rowing was unremarkable. That night George took us to the drive-in, another first for most of us, to see the original *Rocky*. We loved it. The following day, no doubt inspired by the Italian Stallion, we won our heat and final at the Wentworth Regatta.

I was blessed to be coached by George Pell again in 1982, this time as part of the First Crew—Bruce Ryan, Peter Leonard (from Simpson), Rick Murphy (from Maryborough), Johnny Walker (from Euroa), and me. Assisting George was Frank Ritchie, an urbane academic specialising in English literature from Aquinas Teaching College (where George was director).

That rowing season was rich, varied, and fun. The year began with a summer training camp at Torquay (where the Pell family had a holiday house), and for a few days we raced along the beach, charged up and down sand hills, and did hundreds of push-ups. Meals were big and basic; steak and veggies was the order of play each night. Any last skerrick[1] of youthful energy was used up visiting the Torquay waterslide, where—thanks be to God—we didn't injure ourselves or anyone else.

Back in Ballarat, we settled into a steady rhythm of training, regular treats at Mario's, and an occasional restaurant meal. After a poor row at the Scotch Mercantile Regatta in Melbourne, George took us to see the movie *Chariots of Fire*. He thought it might work on two accounts ... a little inspiration and a little culture. It was typical George.

Whilst being coached to row, in truth we were being mentored for life. George was interested in us: our studies, our families, our hopes for the future. Being an avid reader with a precocious interest in ideas, I naturally gravitated to George's learning. A couple of times each month, I'd wander down to Aquinas College after school and sit in his office for forty-five minutes and no doubt bore him to death with my ill-formed thoughts and opinions. But kindness

[1] "Skerrick" is used in Australian and New Zealand English to mean the smallest amount of something. It originated in the United Kingdom in the early 1820s as a slang term for half a penny.

and generosity were his markers. I'd always depart encouraged and with three or four books to keep me company.

Traditionally, sport and religion went together in Christian Brothers schools. It was no different at St Pat's. A week before our big race (the Head of the Lake), we had the annual rowing Mass at school. George preached, and the First Crew served and read the readings. As if this wasn't sufficient spiritual preparation, it was decided that on boat race eve, the crew would stay at the Bishop's Palace, across the road from the school, where George lived and assisted the very infirm retired Bishop James O'Collins. Such an arrangement would ensure a decent meal (steak and veggies), a good night's sleep, and one final Mass Saturday morning prior to the race.

The crew awoke in the Bishop's Palace on boat race morning. We enjoyed a traditional breakfast and then headed upstairs to the Bishop's Chapel. It was not your usual Mass: an ancient chapel (or so it seemed to us) adorned with reliquaries of dead saints; an ancient, incoherent bishop; George; and the First Crew. George led the Mass, and we all prayed fervently for rowing success. At the end of Mass just as we were about to leave, Rick Murphy—as fine a fellow as one could meet, but not especially renowned for his religious piety—spoke up: "I think we will now pray the rosary!" And we did. George would later remark, with just the barest glint in his eye, "It was one of the finest moments of my priestly life!"

We enjoyed no great success that day. A big-boned Ballarat grammar crew had our measure from the start. We were devastated. As we returned to the sheds and saw our parents, tears flowed. When my dad highlighted the depths of our disappointment, George was quick to remark, "Oh, for goodness' sake, Pat, the lads simply have to brace up!" It was another of life's lessons from George.

The 1982 St Pat's First Crew never forgot George Pell. The bonds of loyalty and friendship run deep.

When they packed up George Cardinal Pell's apartment in Rome after his death in January 2022, amongst the accoutrements from a lifetime of learning and service to the Church they found a remarkably well-preserved photograph. It was the 1982 St Pat's First Crew.

George Pell never forgot us.

—Tim O'Leary

26

"Mio Fratello, Cardinale!"

"Mio fratello, Cardinale!" It was after saying these words that I found out that our beloved George had died.

I had two missed messages from his phone at 7:23 A.M.: "Call me! Call me!" It took me twenty minutes and four tries before someone picked up. It was an Italian nurse, I presume, who answered. She was speaking a hundred miles an hour, and I gathered that he might have died. It was not until I said "Mio fratello, Cardinale!" that she realised who I was and said, "I sorry, but he dead." At that time Father Andrew had just walked back into the room, and she passed the phone to him.

Father Andrew Kwiatkowski is a young Melbourne priest studying in Rome. He was assigned to look after the cardinal. Father Andrew had messaged me at 3:40 in the morning our time to let me know that George was well and that the doctors were pleased with the surgery. He also said that he was in good spirits and seemed fine. That was around 6:00 P.M. Rome time, and I received the final call around 9:40 P.M. Rome time. Apparently, George had made a couple of calls, had eaten something, and had done a couple of leg exercises. Certainly, there was no indication of what was to happen.

I then had to let the world know that George had died. After telling my wife and then our four children, I called

Archbishop Denis Hart and Dr. Michael Casey, the executor of George's estate. His Grace was saying Mass with Bishop Les Tomlinson, and Michael was in Bologna with his wife on holiday. They were due to see George in the hospital that afternoon. Michael was in the right place at the right time to take command.

We are still devastated. We still can't believe that George and Margaret have both gone, in pretty quick succession. I am used to getting phone calls in the early morning: The nursing home rang me at 4:30 A.M. when Marg died. While Marg had been gradually deteriorating over a period of time—COVID lockdowns didn't help—George had appeared in top spirits, and his last interview on EWTN about his good friend Pope Benedict was the best I had heard him: no ums or ahs, right on the money.

We still expect the phone to ring with George calling to see how everyone is, especially the grandchildren. After that period of incarceration and his inability to visit Marg because of the border lockdowns, we were anticipating spending more time with him. We were so lucky that our grandkids were with us when he called as he was going into the hospital, and young Billie roared, "George, George!" when she heard his voice.

These insights are an offering of some facts from the family about George. Judy and I reckoned we knew about 10 percent of his life, but as time goes on, we reckon it would be lucky to be 1 percent.

His Early Life

George was born in 1941. Mum and Dad had lost twins a few years earlier: a little girl who was stillborn and a little boy who lived a few hours. Margaret arrived a couple of years after, and I was a little gift from Heaven nearly nine years later. We used to tease Marg—George and I were a great tag team—that dad did not know Marg had been born for three days after her arrival: He was cutting up the SS *Karariki*, which had collided and sunk in Hobsons Bay in 1937! Progress had to continue on the salvage of the ship. We frequently assured her that she was special and certainly the most wanted middle child.

Mum was one of twelve. Her father was of Irish descent with the name Paddy Burke. Except for the last couple of years of her life, she lived in Ballarat. She was a devout Catholic, and in my school days we always said a nightly Rosary, midweek novena, and benediction; we attended First Friday and First Saturday Mass and weekly 9:30 A.M. Sunday Mass.

Dad was a nonpractising Anglican and a fee-paying non-attending Mason. He was originally from Perth and came with his cousin to see a Melbourne Cup. His cousin was a Temby, a famous West Australian racing family—Jacky Purtell, the famous jockey, was apprenticed to the Temby stable. Dad was a former W.A. surf champion with belt and reel. He also won a series of elimination rounds to win the W.A. heavyweight championship. A newspaper article described his last fight as "the most gruesome and bloodiest fight seen in the West Perth Stadium". He won by a knockout in the twelfth round. He fought under the name of George Bell—his family never knew that he boxed!

Dad certainly had an interesting life. He was one of the last to evacuate Misima Island, in the Milne Bay Province of Papua New Guinea, during the Second World War. He was not military. The locals told him that the Japanese had been there during the night, so he was going, whether he had a boat ticket or not. No one dared to argue with him or tried to stop him from getting on. He sat up on deck for a couple of nights with Philip Strong, who was at that time the Anglican bishop of New Guinea and later archbishop of Brisbane. When they pulled into the Port of Townsville, there was no one to be seen. Then Dad saw a head pop around the corner of a shed, and he yelled out, "We are bloody Aussies!" and they came out from everywhere. They thought it was the Japanese. Mum did a fine job of curbing the adventure boy!

They were both very strong personalities, both straight shooters who were able to develop a "congregation" of regular customers at the Royal Oak—I reckon in many cases, far better than many priests develop a following. Their first sortie into pub life was at the Cattle Yards Inn, where they hosted regular cattle- and sheep-sale days. I think it was a baptism of fire for them. Things changed, however: George and Marg were charged with looking after me as a two- or three-year-old. They decided it was safe for the three of us to walk along the top on the six-foot-high railings over in the sale yards, across the road from the hotel. George dropped down and I followed, landing on my head. I blame them for my issues now! I brought this up frequently during our friendly banters. I also continued to remind them that I was the little gift from God—Mum was nearly forty-six when I was born.

They were at the Royal Oak for twenty-three years, providing a family home environment to bring up three kids. It was the only home that I knew. We all grew up with an appreciation that the customers allowed us to exist.

We were very fortunate to have Mum's sister Mollie living with us. She was my second mum and a special person. The pub could not have survived without her contribution to the team—looking after the kids, filling in during Dad's lunch times, and so on. Mum's youngest sister, Cele, described George as a "bugger of a kid, but the apple of his mother's eye", much to George's chagrin.

Our hotel customers were from a cross section of society, the majority working-class with a few suits. We had a couple of communist Railway Workers Union officials and shop stewards as nightly regulars, and they always brought their Melbourne seniors to the pub whenever they were in town. My mother was always a DLP Movement supporter and after the Split, anti-Labor.[1] She always went to bat whenever the Commos got a bit agitated; she was not frightened to pull them into line. Dad always backed her to the hilt. While always sympathetic to the working man and his rights, he believed in a fair go. A number of the regulars who were roped in as union stirrers could not read, and they were taken down to the Trades Hall to learn their lines by heart from the blackboard.

Our uncle was in charge of the office at the local Railway Workshops and was a staunch Movement/DLP member and activist. The unionists who came into the hotel knew of the relationship between brother and sister and were only too willing to stir things up a bit. Our uncle was a regular correspondent with the Ballarat *Courier*. One of his mates would lodge the letter to the editor with the pseudonym "Demos"—sound familiar?—with name and address supplied. George was very close to this uncle, and I am sure received a great understanding of the Split and the workings of the Catholic Church, Bob Santamaria, and Archbishop Mannix from him.[2]

[1] DLP stands for the Democratic Labor Party. The "Movement" refers to the political movement organized by the Catholic social action leader B. A. (Bartholomew Augustine) Santamaria. The "Split" refers to the division in the Australian Labor Party in 1955 that gave rise to the formation of the Democratic Labor Party. The DLP was formed and supported by Catholics who opposed the influence of Communist Party–controlled labor unions over the Australian Labor Party. This influence was far stronger in the state of Victoria than in the state of New South Wales. Many Catholics in New South Wales continued to support the ALP, while many Victorian Catholics supported the DLP.

[2] Archbishop Daniel Mannix was the archbishop of Melbourne for forty-six years, from 1917 to 1963.

I can remember, as an eight- and nine-year-old, George playing BPS footy.[3] I went to St Patrick's College straight after Loreto College and started in grade 3 in 1957—exactly the same process as George. For home games of footy, the entire college student body assembled in the grandstand and its foreground to watch the full game; we could not nick off early. We had to participate actively in the college war cries and encouragement for the First Eighteen team. After each Wednesday game there was always a summary of the game published on the school noticeboard. I can recall that after one game, there was a drawing of George with the football on a string—he had played well and kicked a few goals. In those years there was a fierce rivalry between SPC and Bendigo High School. I reckon Bendigo High School had beaten St Pat's for the first time, and at the repeat match at St Pat's, George got chopped in the throat at the first bounce, and it was on for one and all! He whacked everyone and anyone who dared to get near him. He played well and kicked a few goals. Our pub roof was bricked that night.[4]

My dad would always come up and watch his game on Wednesday afternoons. He would sit on the other side of the oval in his Ford Pilot. He was there when the Richmond Footy Club officials said, "That's the one we want", when the team first jogged out on the ground and around to the other side and then sprinted off together. After twenty-five meters George was five meters ahead of the rest of the players. I can remember when the sign-up team came home one Sunday to talk to Mum and Dad and to get George's signature—they all were big, broad-shouldered

[3] "Footy" is what Australians, especially Australian children, often call the game of football.

[4] "Bricked" as a verb in this context means had rocks thrown onto it.

men in gabardine overcoats, as was the fashion of the day. Much excitement. Then the letdown, as Mum told me that George was becoming a priest. I believe Dad said, "What a bloody waste." This certainly changed over the years, as Dad and Mum were his number one supporters.

In 1958 George matriculated and won a Newman College Exhibition after studying the sciences. He then went back in 1959, as a boarder in McCann House, basically to be sure of his calling. He again matriculated and won a Newman Exhibition for his arts study. During 1959, to keep his strength up—we can't have our little boy fading away to a shadow on college food—I would come home for lunch every day and take a pile of freshly baked goodies back to him. I am sure his roommates looked forward to those days as well.

I can't remember George doing much bar work, except for a couple of weeks during 1957 when George and Mollie looked after the pub while Mum, Dad, Margaret, and I went to Sydney. He boarded in 1959, and from 1956 onwards he went back to school for night study. His classmate Gerry Coffey, who lived around the corner, would accompany him to the night study.

I can remember during the summer holidays from the seminary, George would help out with the external painting of the hotel. He'd climb the ladder only to the top of the ground floor—he couldn't go up the extension ladder. He would work in the morning before it got too hot, especially if the side of the pub was in the shade, wearing khaki overalls and a white floppy hat.

I don't believe that he was ever domesticated—he had everything done for him while he was at home. More on this later.

In 1960, his first year at Corpus Christi College, Werribee, we were not allowed to see him until Easter Sunday, and after that on one Sunday a month, from 3:00 P.M. till 5:00 P.M. The bell would go, and out they would walk. That is a long time ago. The dual carriageway from Geelong to Werribee was being built, and on many trips we were on gravel and sand roads. These were great afternoons—the family, including Mollie, were thrilled to see him. Then during midyear, there was home time with a round of ordinations to attend. All the seminarians attended, so our pub was a hive of activity, with seminarians dropping in.

George left in September 1963 to go to Rome. I can still remember the breaking of the streamers as the ship moved off. I was thirteen years old. He thoroughly enjoyed the weeks of travel to Rome, stopping off at exciting ports and learning Italian.

He would write home every week. We eagerly awaited the blue aerograms, and I reckon we still have every one he wrote: fuel for a researcher! These were epic times—Vatican II was in full steam and seminarians and priests were reevaluating their vocations. I can remember one seminarian in Rome who wrote home to his family just weeks before his ordination to tell them he was not sure. I couldn't believe what I was hearing. He was ordained but resigned in later years.

By this time Margaret was in Rome studying the violin and was with her big brother. Mum and I went to Rome for his ordination in December 1966. I was sixteen years old and as big as I am now. It was a big difference from when he left! What great celebrations. Mum was in heaven: Her boy was a priest, having been ordained in the sanctuary in front of the Chair of Saint Peter, and she was reunited with her daughter and son.

A couple of days after his ordination the annual Propaganda Fide vs. North American College basketball game was on. I had never seen him play basketball, let alone give the

American captain a mouthful at every opportunity. Aussie cricketers could learn a thing or two that day! Talk about being competitive.

We went to Paris, Lourdes, London, and Ireland—Dublin, Cork, County Clare—and then back to Rome. We had an exciting trip. Mum twigged early on that when George suggested that we sit in front of a masterpiece in the Louvre "to absorb the painting and to ponder on it", he was actually having a rest! George was in great form and, I think, delighted that his brother had grown up—at least in size.

George and Margaret had a remarkable time together, taking many holiday jaunts, even into East Germany, where the apartment house offered them two squares of toilet paper each!

They would eagerly wait on the regular money sent over and have a steak at Scoglio's and then tea and scones at Babington's, near the Spanish Steps.[5] Plus, there were regular newspaper cuttings posted to them, as well as Christmas and birthday cakes sealed in large silver tins.

After George finished his studies in Rome, he went to Oxford University in England. There he became the

[5] Scoglio's refers to a restaurant in the Via Merulana in Rome. Following World War II, the restaurant was frequented by American military members, not only because of the good food but also because of the excellent English spoken by the owner and resistance fighter, Dr. Augusto Rossi. Then, with the whirlwind arrival of Hollywood film producers at Cinecittà, Lo Scoglio di Frisio became their favourite place to meet with friends. During the "La Dolce Vita" era, dinner at Lo Scoglio di Frisio meant that one could find a seat at a table near Liz Taylor, Richard Burton, Kirk Douglas, Burt Lancaster, and many others. Babington's Tea Room was founded late in the nineteenth century by Isabel Cargill, daughter of William Cargill, the founder of the city of Dunedin in New Zealand, and Anna Maria Babington, descendant of Anthony Babington, who was hanged in 1586 for conspiring against Elizabeth I. At that time in Rome tea was sold only in pharmacies, which made life difficult for British tourists.

chaplain to an American Air Force base near Campion Hall, where he was residing. From there, he was invited for summer holidays as a visiting priest to several American parishes. He met and made many lifetime friends in the States.

His Time in the Ballarat Diocese and in Melbourne

George's first post after arriving back from Rome was to Swan Hill under parish priest Father Bill Melican. He enjoyed his time there and had regular duties at Nyah West. One of the best George stories of this period is that when he was at Nyah West, he was given a present of some fish. Rather than leaving the fish on the front seat of his car while he played tennis, he put it under the car seat. Well, he forgot about the parcel! You can image the smell a week later—he had everyone checking his car out for the smell, but nobody could locate the problem. Some brain trust decided to look under the seat, and lo and behold, it was certainly moving. I don't know whether he was ever given any more fish.

He then came back to Ballarat and was stationed at a number of spots, including the nefarious parish house of St Alipius under parish priest Monsignor Bill McMahon. St Alipius Church was Mum's family church, and Mum and Dad were married in the sacristy, so it was a coming home for him. Little did he know what was ahead of him.

When he was appointed to head up Aquinas College (formerly Mercy Teachers' College), he resided at the Bishop's Palace along with Sir J. P. O'Collins, former bishop of Ballarat, and his housekeeper, Lady Nancy. Lady Nancy finally got her driver's licence later in life and would drive Sir James in his Benz to Aquinas every day to deliver George his sandwiches for lunch. When the bishop died, George, with Lady Nancy, set up camp at Bungaree as parish priest. He enjoyed his time there and made many friends.

His sortie into Melbourne began when he was appointed rector of Corpus Christi Seminary. It was apparent that he was appointed to do a job. Many of the staff moved on, not wanting to follow some Catholic fundamentals like daily prayer and Mass. He got very annoyed when there was not a daily Mass offered at churches where priests resided. He could not understand why a priest would not want to say a Mass every day.

When appointed archbishop of Melbourne, he faced a similar issue. He had two meetings of priests of the archdiocese. I believe that the treatment dealt out to him was appalling. He gave them the opportunity to toe the party line or leave. A number left. Several dissenters stayed and did not agree to uphold basic Catholic beliefs.

I believe his problems started in 1996 or before, with the issue of the coloured ribbon and not giving Holy Communion to those wearing it. Over many years, these like-minded people had formed an organisation, and its members refer to themselves as "soldiers". Membership extends across all walks of life and had a major influence on George's trial and his conviction in Victoria.

Rome

Prior to his appointment as cardinal in 2003 by Pope John Paul II, and over the years, he spent considerable time in Rome on various commissions and bodies, including the Justice and Peace Commission, the Congregation for the Doctrine of the Faith, and the Vox Clara Committee, which he chaired and which authorised the translation of liturgical texts into English. He also oversaw the renovation and establishment of the hotel Domus Australia, a home away from home for Australian pilgrims visiting Rome. His main man was Mr. Danny Casey, whose claim to fame is that the multi-million-euro project was delivered on time and *on budget*—something unheard of among Roman tradesmen. George's coup was to have Pope Benedict bless and open Domus Australia in October 2011—streets were blocked off, and the locals were very excited to have the pope visit.[6] This was the same friend and pope who had visited Sydney earlier for World Youth Day in 2008.

Pell and Casey, two big Australian thugs, as they would be classified by the Roman old school, were straight shooters who wanted action. They were a formidable pair when George was appointed prefect of the Secretariat for the Economy, effectively the number-three man in the Vatican.

Many issues were identified. For example, there are a couple of thousand Vatican employees, yet there were over forty thousand enrolled to receive benefits from the Vatican pharmacy. You can image the fuss when the rules were tightened. They initiated new accounting procedures—new for the Vatican, not new for the rest of the world—that initially identified 1.2 billion euros that had not been previously accounted for.

George's office and apartment were bugged, and so were his phone and Danny Casey's phone, as well as some of our family member's phones. As recently as November 2022, on two separate occasions when he was away in

[6] The hotel Domus Australia is located at 14/B Via Cernaia, not far from the central railway station in Rome. It is famous for the fact that its showers are big enough to accommodate a six-foot-plus Australian male, vegemite is available for breakfast, the day's front page of *The Australian* newspaper is available for guests to read over breakfast, and its chapel is the only place in the world where the ambo is supported by bronze kangaroos.

the States, his apartment was scanned by Polish specialists and bugs were found. This was well after his jail time and retirement as a voting cardinal, so who knows who was behind it and what they were hoping to find.

He told me during a trip to Rome that he had detected many serious fraud issues. I suggested that laypeople were involved. He said no, but clergy were. I expressed disbelief, and he added that it went as far up as the red hat!

Judy and I last visited George in Rome for Easter in 2017. We attended all the Holy Week activities with the Holy Father celebrating and had a special visit to Castel Gandolfo. We walked the historic grounds and had an enjoyable meal at the cliff-top restaurant overlooking Lake Albano, the site of the 1960 Olympics rowing course.

Before he came home in 2017 to defend himself, he gave the Holy Father a list of seven issues that he had identified and was asking the Holy Father to act on. It wasn't until Cardinal Becciu lost his rights as a cardinal in September 2020 that the Holy Father acted—some three years after receiving the advice. When that event occurred, George commented publicly that things happened slowly in Rome.

A lot has been written about funds being sent to Australia during Becciu's tenure—about how much and why. All we know is that there is $2 million unaccounted for and that George and his team were advised to stop their investigation!

During his trial he would come up for a weekend and stay with us. These were great family times, especially when young Sonny and his mother, Georgina, were living with us. After both his knees were replaced in Sydney, we had our own "last supper" before he headed off to Melbourne for sentencing. George enjoyed his meals with the family. He loved a roast lamb with all the trimmings and even a bowl of ice cream afterwards. He also specifically liked potatoes that had been wrapped in tinfoil and baked for fifty minutes or so. He did learn to use a microwave when he was in the Acacia Wing at Barwon and had to heat up his Saturday meat pie. That was as far as his culinary skills extended. He rang me up once and wanted to know how long he had to cook the tinfoiled spuds in the microwave! I told him oven only, but he went ahead because that would take too long. Just maybe he did not know how to turn the oven on! Della, his carer from the nearby seminary in Homebush, tells the story of receiving a phone call: "You had better come over to my house." He had put dishwashing liquid into the dishwasher, and the place was full of suds. Della was very good to him. She came to the house every day, brewed coffee, and sat in his garden to drink it with him. She wasn't, however, allowed to touch his desk. When we visited his house after the Sydney funeral, his desk was as he had left it over six months earlier. Even his toothbrush was still on the side of the sink in his bathroom.

The two trials, Victorian appeal, sentencing, incarceration, and then appeal to the High Court were certainly tumultuous times. I still can't believe how an accuser's statement can be changed twenty-four times from the first trial to the second trial and that he was not interrogated at the second trial. George did not want our family to attend court but phoned in at the end of every day. The team thought they were making progress. The final verdict did not line up with the evidence. Anecdotally, it seems that there was one dissenter in the first trial and that a couple of the female jury members openly wept at the verdict.

In direct contrast to the reporting of the ABC, I wish to thank Mr. Andrew Bolt for his courageous and consistent public support of George and for his reports on the implausibility of the accusations. I realise that there are many others who have publicly supported George over many years and continue to do so. I thank them as well.

The time in remand and in the Acacia Wing at Barwon prison must have been harrowing for George, although you would never have known it. His three magnificent volumes are testimony of that—no malice, no feeling sorry for himself. He was concerned about how we and others were coping. Sister Mary, the remand centre chaplain, said that when she visited him, he greeted her with a smile and a handshake, and this never varied.

We took Marg down a couple of times to visit him. Even Judy and Rebecca took her to Barwon. It was an ordeal, as she was wheelchair bound and immobile. It was even difficult just to get her in and out of the car. Her crowning moment was when she asked the warder if he was "behaving himself". We pushed the wheelchair even faster!

We know that he had many visitors and many letters—there are over four thousand that have not been answered. They will eventually end up in Sydney. We know that Pope Benedict corresponded via unsigned mail with him, as did Pope Francis.

The Rome Requiem

Thanks to the magic of Damian Quirk, our travel agent extraordinaire, we were able to attend George's funeral in Rome; the Vatican held up proceedings for a few hours, knowing that we were on our way. Our trip is still a bit of a blur. We were met by Father Robert McCulloch in a blackout Mercedes people mover and escorted to and from Saint Peter's and to Domus Australia, where the wake was held. We did not have to face the reporters.

Who would have thought that fifty-six years after his ordination he would have a Requiem Mass from the same altar at which he was ordained? I doubt whether anyone else attended both events.

It was commented that it was the biggest funeral for a cardinal in living memory, with the better part of seventy-five of his fellow prelates attending. Cardinal Re, dean of the cardinals, officiated at the Requiem Mass and spoke glowingly of George—at least that is what we were told, as it was in Italian. The ceremony was unbelievable, as some of the photos can attest. We did not know whether Pope Francis would officiate at the Rite of Commendation until just before he was wheeled in. His chair was strategically placed.

In Sydney, Sonny visited George for a minute or so to say goodbye. He was a bit disappointed that he was not allowed to speak at the funeral in Sydney, as he had a speech prepared and a drawing done. However, not to be outdone, he and his mother composed a note to George and another drawing of George in a Tigers jumper, and the funeral director poked it up inside George's sleeve. It did say that George liked ice cream!

The evening Vespers on Wednesday night was magnificent, with Father Joseph Hamiliton, his personal secretary at the time of his death, speaking so eloquently, especially about being greeted before their meeting with Pope Francis in October 2021 by the head of the papal household: He dropped to his knees and said, "Welcome! Welcome, confessor of our Church!"

I am sure that George was doted on by Father Joseph. He helped George work through some dark times. After George's incarceration, Father Joseph treated him like his grandfather, as I believe George might have told Joseph to just try it when he was making his mind up to become a priest. Just after George's funeral, Father Joseph visited family in South Africa and was involved in a car accident. He can still see the front of the car crumple, the flames, and the air bag going off and can hear George saying, "Joseph, get out of the car." The doctor who examined Joseph after the crash said that he had someone looking after him. Joseph knew who that was!

Father Joseph also told me that people in Rome are having dreams about George. His driver, Umberto, dreamt that George, dressed in white vestments, was speaking to him in English. Umberto told him to speak in Italian, and then a nun appeared and told him that George was very happy and was with God!

The Funeral Mass in Sydney was magnificent and just showed the world what Catholics can do. How could a state funeral compare to that! The procession of over 250 priests, bishops, and clergy; the music; the singing; the celebration of the Mass; the eulogies of Archbishop Fisher and Mr. Abbott; the procession down College Street; the greeting from the believers; the Ave Marias from the faithful Lebanon Christian Community; and then the Salve Regina in the crypt with over three hundred male voices as George was laid to rest: These are things I will always remember.

Conclusion

In George's final sermon, at a spiritual retreat in southern Italy three days before he died, he opened with the cry "Repent, because the Kingdom of God is near." And I quote further:

> [Pope Saint John Paul II and Pope Benedict XVI] were missionaries of the truth. We don't build the truth. We don't have the ability to change the truth. We can only

> acknowledge the truth, and sometimes the truth isn't all that pretty....
>
> These two Popes did not affirm that the teaching of Jesus was conditioned by the time.... They did not claim that the essential and central teaching should be updated, radically changed.... As for them, and also for us, Jesus remains the way, the truth and the life....
>
> These two Popes understood well that we are not the teachers of the apostolic doctrine, we are the defenders.... All Catholics, of any age, throughout the world, also have the right to receive the same teaching that Jesus and the apostles gave in the early years of Christianity—this is Catholic doctrine.[7]

His final message, delivered in his own handwriting, was engraved on his tomb—"Please Pray for Me"—along with a quote from Cardinal Ottaviani: "He Greatly Loved the Church!"

He was indeed a lion of the Church.

—David Pell

[7] Terry Mattingley, "The Haunting Final Sermon of Cardinal Pell", *The Other Cheek*, posted on May 2, 2023, https://theothercheek.com.au/the-haunting-final-sermon-of-cardinal-pell/.

27

A Promoter of Catholic Truths Rather than Gospel Values

I was privileged to be an auxiliary bishop to George Cardinal Pell for ten years, from 2003 to 2013. Prior to this I had been a parish priest and then rector of the Good Shepard Seminary in the Sydney Archdiocese. When I received the call from the apostolic nuncio to inform me that I had been appointed as an auxiliary bishop for the Sydney Archdiocese, I learnt that a young Dominican priest, Father Anthony Fisher, O.P., had also been appointed as an auxiliary bishop in Sydney. We had been ordained together by Cardinal Pell in St Mary's Cathedral, Sydney, on September 3, 2003.

Thus began a close association with the cardinal. He nurtured us both as bishops by both assigning us areas of responsibility and allowing us to develop our own areas of ministry.

Pastoral Leadership with Purpose

It was very evident to me that Cardinal Pell had a clear understanding of what was needed to strengthen and build up the life and mission of the Church in the Archdiocese of Sydney. He did not develop a formal pastoral plan, but he was very clear about his priorities. He went about his pastoral leadership with purpose and determination. He would simply summarise his purpose as "strengthening Catholic life".

His episcopal leadership had a deeply pastoral intent. He wanted to strengthen the faith of the people. To this end he was conscious of the need to provide sound presentation of the faith.

His preaching was grounded in this purpose. He sought to expound the essential elements of Catholic belief. His preaching was direct and clear. He was conscious of ordinary Catholics and wanted to engage with them and confirm their faith.

Cardinal Pell was a leader. He saw what was needed and set about meeting those needs. His episcopal motto, Be Not Afraid, truly reflected his approach to leadership. He was not one to be cowed by resistance or opposition. One important element of his leadership was the identification and engagement of people with whom he could work. He raised up other leaders and entrusted them with responsibilities. He showed faith in them and gave them room to develop their gifts. He was always on the lookout for people whom he would describe as "being with the program".

Reaching Out to the Young

One of his particular concerns was attracting men to the priesthood. He took a very close interest in the quality of seminary formation. During my time as rector, he would frequently visit the seminary. Without imposing himself, he made me aware of what he expected.

During his time as archbishop of Sydney the numbers and the quality of men attracted to the priesthood grew considerably. He himself was the drawing card. His confident understanding of the sort of priest needed for our times inspired many to join the seminary. He formed relationships with these men and followed their progress through the seminary with great interest. They looked up to him. They knew that he was interested in them. He was a model of priesthood to which they aspired.

He naturally looked to raise up young leaders within the archdiocese. He made a serious commitment to university ministry, especially at the University of Sydney. Putting strong leaders in place in the university chaplaincy team attracted many young men and women to the faith. The chaplaincy was dynamic and unapologetic about its Catholic identity.

In general, he enjoyed meeting with young people. He was always ready to engage with them and to challenge them to develop a deeper faith and more serious commitment to the Church. His crowning achievement in his work with young people was the World Youth Day held in Sydney in 2008. It was a watershed moment not only for the Archdiocese of Sydney but for the whole of the Catholic Church in Australia.

A Special Interest in Catholic Education

Cardinal Pell took a special interest in Catholic education and sought to strengthen the quality of teaching provided in Catholic schools. He had been responsible for teacher formation in his home diocese of Ballarat. While archbishop of Melbourne, he had overseen the development of a set of religious texts entitled *To Know, Worship and Love*. These were content rich and beautifully presented, with strong Catholic imagery throughout. He promoted their use in all the Catholic schools in Sydney. The cardinal believed in the need for a robust religious education curriculum.

In a time when the language of religious education often spoke of "Gospel values", the cardinal insisted on the importance of "Catholic truths". He wanted all students in Catholic schools to have a sound religious literacy. He used to say that if a student did not embrace the faith, at least he would know what he was rejecting.

He visited every Catholic school in the archdiocese and spoke to the students in the classrooms. He organised meetings with senior student leaders and sought to have open conversations with them on topics of importance. He was interested in hearing their views and engaging with them on issues of the moment.

The cardinal understood the importance of sound leadership in the schools. He introduced the practice of including an oath of fidelity when commissioning principals.

The Catholic Intellectual Tradition

The cardinal had strong intellectual gifts and was interested in the promotion of Catholic thought. He invited significant Catholic thinkers to Sydney and enjoyed having private Chatham House Rule dinners with a small group of invited guests. He kept himself well informed on matters in which religion intersected with culture and politics. His office at Cathedral House was strewn with books and magazines. The hallway outside groaned under his extensive library.

He wrote for magazines like *Quadrant* and *The Spectator*, as well as overseas publications. He was a close friend of Father Joseph Fessio, S.J., the founder of Ignatius Press, and he enjoyed close friendships with a number of prominent Catholic thinkers from around the world, including the commentator George Weigel. He was stimulated by intellectual arguments on matters of faith and morals and was happy to engage in debate with atheists like Richard Dawkins.

From very early on in his priestly life he understood the need for the Catholic intellectual tradition to engage the broader culture. He was a key figure in the foundation of the Australian Catholic University and later in establishing the Sydney campus of the University of Notre Dame Australia, based in Camperdown. He was also a great supporter of the founding of Campion College, a liberal arts college.

He wanted to have solid Catholic scholarship inspiring young tertiary students. The cardinal was particularly concerned to ensure that the new Sydney campus of Notre Dame had a medical school so that there was an option of receiving medical training informed by the Catholic moral tradition.

Love for the Liturgy

Cardinal Pell had a love for the sacred liturgy and took a special interest in the quality of the liturgy at St Mary's Cathedral. In particular, he wanted a high standard of music to accompany and enrich the Masses celebrated in the cathedral. He had a love for the liturgical tradition of the Church expressed in its rich repertoire of sacred music and encouraged its use at the cathedral. He took a special interest in the work undertaken by the director of music for the cathedral and the Cathedral Choir.

During his time there he implemented a refurbishment of the interior of St Mary's Cathedral. He understood that all elements of the adornment of a cathedral should have a didactic purpose. Furnishings and artwork were not only to be beautiful but also to teach about the faith. While he willingly went out to parishes to visit them, it was clear that he loved to preside over the High Mass each Sunday at St Mary's. He believed that a bishop should be in his cathedral.

Cardinal Pell considered nothing to be too good for God. Whenever there was an opportunity for him to be involved in the building or refurbishing of a church or chapel, he applied himself carefully to the selection of the architecture and furnishings. He especially took great interest in the art that adorned the church. We can see his clear influence in the chapel at the Benedict XVI Retreat Centre at Grose Vale and the refurbishing of the chapel in Domus Australia in Rome.

A People Person

His formidable personality and determination to advance the mission of the Church was not always well received. He was seen by many as a rather austere and distant man. This was the image presented in the media. The opposite was the case. He was great company around the dinner table. He had a light touch in conversation and enjoyed good meals and good company. He had a wide circle of friends.

The cardinal always had time for people. He would stand outside the cathedral after Sunday Mass and speak to anyone who approached him. He never rushed away but was content to listen to and engage with all who wanted to speak with him. When he celebrated the Sacrament of Confirmation in parishes, he was very happy to spend time with the people. He was interested in people, and people sensed that in him.

My Debt to Cardinal Pell

George Cardinal Pell formed me as a bishop. It was his vision for what was needed in our times and his example that inspired and shaped my own mission, now as archbishop of Hobart. I owe him much indeed. He was a giant of a man not only in physical stature but also in personality and vision. He will rank as one of the greatest churchmen Australia has produced.

—Most Rev. Julian Porteous

28

Too Real for the Bureaucrats and PR Strategists

The last time I saw the cardinal was in Rome just a few weeks before he upset us all so much by heading off on that last great journey. He was ebullient company at dinner. Outrageous, of course; concerned about me and keen to know what was going on; above all, alive with commentary on Church, world, and ideas. Dinner with +GP, at least for a layman like me, was far from an indulgence in the banalities of clerical gossip and scandal. Indeed, enjoying the cardinal's company felt like relishing a particularly fine after-dinner speech: He was learned, curious, witty, kindly. I now sit weekly at Sunday Mass in St Mary's Cathedral and cannot quite comprehend that he is lying below our feet at rest in the crypt.

I first met the cardinal in 1997. Previously, I knew of him as most others did—from media reports, TV interviews, homilies, and articles. As we all know, the disjunction between that public persona and the actual person, whether at table or at the altar, was so jarring that it would come like a crunch to hear him spoken of roughly or with hatred. From that first dinner until our last, I found the man great fun, open in thought, charitable, and warm to everyone he met.

I connected with the cardinal over our common love of philosophy in the service of faith and also because his

Irish/Ozzie blarney and my Scottish reticence pointed towards a shared love of irony. It's a fact that some people get through life by running a private interior monologue that they occasionally share with trusted others as an ironic comment on what is going on around them. Good friends get this and enjoy our irony. Strangers may not see (and enemies pretend not to see) that we are playfully saying what is *not* as if it *were*. They instead read this as "what he really thinks". Regularly, this habit of irony would get the cardinal into trouble. I've faced this myself on occasion and have come to the resolution that rather than change my personality and habits, I'll put up with being misjudged. I believe the cardinal made a similar decision—harder for a man of the cloth than for a man of the world, of course. But how I admire the fact that he stayed with irony even when the bureaucrats and PR strategists were pulling out their hair.

Talking of PR, shortly after his appointment as archbishop of Melbourne, the cardinal hired some PR experts for himself and the archdiocese. He was quite strongly criticised for this. I was unsure myself. There is humility and sense in consulting the best wisdom of the world, but risk, too, in letting it prompt you too often or too forcefully. The cardinal approached PR with his usual irony. He was not one to be easily squashed into shape and repackaged. I remember sitting in TV audiences where his agonised staff would adopt slow-breathing exercises as the cardinal warmed to themes no politician would dare touch. He was skilled in political contexts but immune to the control and suppression that lifestyle usually entails. His style of bishopping came from an older world than politics and spin—it was more to the point and more princely, despite his famous (unfortunate!) support for republicanism in Australia.

Early in my employment the cardinal sent me to teach a new philosophy program at the Melbourne seminary. The small class of seminarians refused to be taught by me—caught up in the backlash of His Eminence's attempts to stabilise their troubled seminary. I returned to the chancery and can still hear him roaring along the corridor, "Those b—— seminarians won't let Hayden teach them!" Those days were great fun, but there was a serious plan to put back in place a philosophical foundation and to adjust theological education so that it built on that philosophical understanding. It was always optimistic. I never thought it would really succeed. But indirectly, it did lead to improvements in seminary formation in much of Australia. The method, wonderfully affirmed by Pope Saint John Paul II in *Fides et ratio*, did work.

Later in my working life with the cardinal, I played a role in helping develop the University of Notre Dame Australia in Sydney. The cardinal visited the campus regularly, addressing students—particularly education students: He placed great importance on the formation of teachers and attended every book launch and ceremony. At the same time there was the small matter of hosting World Youth Day 2008 in Sydney. The cardinal was at his very best there, preaching at the opening Mass and invoking the Holy Spirit from the four corners of the land to breathe upon the young people gathered with Pope Benedict. The pope clearly—and perhaps to his surprise—had a wonderful week. The cardinal shone with enthusiasm for youth and for faith. And Sydney sparkled. It was the cardinal's greatest triumph.

Later years brought hard work in Rome and an increased role on the world stage. This suited him, but his friends saw the yearning for home. He could not have ended up anywhere but Rome, the city of the martyrs, but he needed Australia. The final events of arrest, trial, judgement, imprisonment, appeal, vindication, and release are still too close for many of us to explore and analyse in any detail.

Yet he stayed serene. Those who should feel most ashamed probably will not. These things are ultimately judged by a higher court. At least we all know now just how such terrible wrong can happen in a free and law-abiding society: It doesn't need a single leader; each person plays his own small part in the persecution and then melts off afterwards into the crowd.

But the final impression is far from bitterness. George Pell was a man steeped in his own time and in the faith. Sometimes I felt he could have been a religious—there was wisdom, compassionate acceptance of the world, and a love of company. Sometimes I felt he would have preferred the hands-on care of souls (think of those marvellous stories of him corresponding from jail with fellow prisoners). Sometimes we all wanted to scream at him to lighten up a bit for the cameras or to play it more safely. But he was himself—a very Australian take on an old European approach to living in the world by stepping aside daily from the world. Religion was the priority, but it crowned a life of investment in a full array of human goods. The Church will see his like again, but not soon.

—Professor Hayden Ramsay

29

The Rome Years

It would be hard to say whether the cardinal or Rome received the greater shock when he arrived in 2014 at Pope Francis' invitation to take up the care of the Vatican's finances. In many ways one could hardly have picked a more appropriate choice, nor a churchman more habituated to the Eternal City. Cardinal Pell had studied there at Propaganda Fide College in the 1960s, and he loved the city deeply. He had been ordained to the priesthood in Saint Peter's Basilica at the Altar of the Chair and retained ever afterwards a great affection for that church above all others. By his own count he had travelled to Rome over a hundred times as the years had passed, and he knew its characters and its methods of operation well. Nevertheless, although he had been a member of many different committees over the years, he had never actually worked in the Roman Curia, and it was quite another thing to see that venerable but mysterious institution from the inside.

His job was to be a most unconventional one in a city and a Church that depends to a large degree on convention. Most great churchmen called to service in Rome from the dioceses of the world find themselves at the head of a department that in some cases has been operating for centuries. It has its own staff, its ranged experts, its streamlined processes, and its own expectations. The new man inserts himself into a venerable stream, brings his own talents, of course, but always has to conform to the procedures in place.

Cardinal Pell instead was asked to do something extraordinary: to begin his working life in Rome by starting an entirely new dicastery (department) of the Roman Curia from scratch. It had not been done before, and many doubted that it was possible. Of course, new dicasteries had been created, even in recent years, but always with curial experts who were from within the system and understood how it worked. This was a double obstacle, and it was to prove a major difficulty for the cardinal in the years ahead. Nevertheless, he threw himself into the work with great enthusiasm. A staff was gathered from the rest of the Curia, people with sufficient expertise and often a little bit of English.

This dicastery would operate to international standards of efficiency and would need to engage with financial institutions and experts from around the world who might not speak the elegant, but parochial, Italian tongue. He found offices in the splendid historic Saint John's Tower, a medieval fortification on the grounds of the Vatican gardens. So began the happy days of his service there. How he loved inviting visitors to his tower and showing them the view! The splendid panorama of the exclusive Vatican gardens was intoxicating for his guests, and perhaps a little bit for him too. In those early days everything seemed exciting, and the tower was a hive of activity. Everyone cooperated with him and was deferential, for he clearly had the confidence of the pope, and that counted for a lot. Of course, things were to change, and the reasons for that are still not certain.

After a few months everyone noticed a distinct alteration. It baffled the cardinal that he seemed to be meeting resistance to perfectly sensible and straightforward requests for compliance and information. Before long, more sinister behaviours started to emerge.

When fitting out the tower, he found he had to make minor provisions for the chapel. Some low character in the administration got hold of the receipts for his vestments and spun an absurd story to a compliant press about the extravagant purchases of the new finance head. In fact, the vestments were both ugly and cheap, but a certain impression was being cultivated. It was the first attempt at discrediting a process of reform. The cardinal took note of the episode, perhaps not as much as he should have, and powered ahead.

When he held a press conference to announce that he had found over a billion euros of hidden cash and pointed the finger at the Secretariat of State, all hell broke loose. The SS personnel were outraged and defended themselves. In their view he was grandstanding and misrepresenting their intentions. The cardinal maintained that all he wanted was transparency and honest dealing with the faithful's donations. So began the story that continued ever afterwards.

Meanwhile, Cardinal Pell started to enjoy the life of the city and the country. A phenomenal number of people came to see him. Never for a lunch or dinner did he seem to be alone, for he had many friends and was in great demand in the city. A skilled raconteur, he provided witty and entertaining company and proved a popular guest at Roman soirees. Not all Roman potentates are quite so engaging.

Of course, the great question that dominates the attention of Roman cardinals is "Where will I live?" and he was no less prone to this crucial consideration. Various options were presented to him, and while he mulled over them, he had comfortable, if simple, accommodation of his own at hand in the Domus Australia, the hotel he had established in Rome, managed and largely owned by the Archdiocese of Sydney. There he held court, and to there a steady stream of visitors came to admire his splendid chapel and comfy hotel rooms and facilities. It was an ambitious project, but he enjoyed that sort of project.

But where would he live? There was a splendid opportunity that briefly appealed to him but that he decided against. The old apartment of Pope Alexander VI, the Borgia pope, was available. Cardinal Harvey, its former occupant, had moved to Saint Paul Outside-the-Walls, and this historic and evocative place was standing ready. What an opportunity! His friends begged him to take it. What a fun place it would be to visit, and how many entertaining jokes one might have about Borgia and Pell having the same quarters. Thank goodness he decided not to! The eventual newspaper references would have made life impossible for him when his troubles later began. In fact, the apartment had two major drawbacks. First, it had a profusion of stairs, which was an agony for a man with two bad hips and two bad knees. It would have been more trouble still for his sister, Margaret, who travelled to meet him each year and whose mobility was less than his. The poor woman would have been a prisoner in the pope's bedroom. Then there was the fact that no one could come and see him without being observed and recorded, and there was increasingly no guarantee that all the recording eyes were friendly. So it was that he passed up a historic residence where a former pope had kept a particularly good friend.

The cardinal opted instead for a more pedestrian cardinal's apartment, not exactly in the first rank, but more conventional, in the Piazza della Città Leonina, just outside St Anne's Gate, the main entrance to the Vatican. No red damask walls and fancy gilded furniture, I'm afraid, and no grand terrace for entertaining, but it had enough of the basics to be respectable and central. A small community of American Sisters of Mercy looked after him—highly educated women who had other jobs or studies in Rome and who took on domestic care as a sideline. They provided good company and enjoyed his good wit but were too respectful to engage in the banter he employed. The cardinal enjoyed entertaining enormously and preferred to chat over a good meal, putting his company at their ease and making the most of the resultant informality. He was rather good at serving the drinks too and particularly enjoyed pouring a beer. His offsiders who poured unsatisfactorily could expect a loud reproach. Some lessons of the Ballarat pub were learned well and could not be unlearned.

Nor was Rome the limit of his engagements. Invitations started to pour in from around Italy and beyond, and he found himself often scooting off to one of the many dazzling parts of Italy where he was in great demand. Both tall and relaxed, he spoke good Italian and enjoyed both a solemn ceremony and a good joke with the locals. They loved him and lined up for photos and handshakes. Sometimes his laid-back manner could be deceiving. On one occasion when visiting a historic abbey, he arrived slightly less formally dressed than his office might have suggested. The Italian *monsignori* with him were in various shades of grey as usual, and at the end was the struggling secretary in black, insufficiently senior to be dispensed of the conventions of dress. To his embarrassment the abbot raced towards him, knelt, and tried to kiss the nonexistent ring on his hand before he discreetly pointed to the cardinal (who enjoyed the display immensely). The abbot leapt to his feet and went to grovel before the right cardinal, and order was restored.

Cardinal Pell happily accepted modest invitations to parish anniversaries as well as simple occasions and gave everyone the same attention. Remarkably, all sorts of people write to Roman cardinals asking for jobs and favours, and while he could not help with jobs and the evasion of proper avenues, if there was an opportunity for charitable assistance, he would make use of it, occasionally even taking the letter of a correspondent to the pope to ask for an assurance of prayers or a blessing. People did matter to him, and he knew he was in a privileged position to do something for them and would if he could.

Back in the city of Rome, Cardinal Pell was often to be found on the weekend in a parish or helping the Neocatechumenate, who had in a way adopted him and gave him a lot of moral support. He was very loyal to his cardinalitial church of Santa Maria Mazzarello, in the outer suburbs, near Cinecittà Studios. This unfortunate structure, not quite redolent of Bernini or Borromini, was constructed in the 1980s and made no effort to conceal it. Nevertheless, it was a happy and well-run parish, and the parish priest was a good man. I'm not sure why he continually insisted on coming to collect the cardinal for visits in his tiny Fiat, squeezing the poor man into unnatural shapes and cutting off arteries as they sped through the traffic. The cardinal never complained (at the time) and always went along with the arrangements, no matter how slipshod they might be, for fear of giving offence. So it always was. Italy, of course, is a chaotic country, and foreign attitudes simply have to conform themselves to the pace and expectations of the locals. The cardinal was very good at this, and it was clear that many years of Roman visits had allowed him to develop that necessary *pazienza* that Italians value (by necessity) so highly.

He was courteous and kind to people of all backgrounds. I found it a bit baffling when his enemies—and even his friends—repeated the cliché that he was brusque and overly direct. He was certainly direct, but I never found him brusque or ill-mannered. Quite to the contrary, he showed great tact and sensitivity to every sort of person, perhaps a consequence of his early youth in the pub of his parents, or perhaps simply because of his innate kindness.

The homeless people who live around the Vatican know who their real friends are. He knew the names and lives of the people around the square where he lived and sincerely interested himself in them. His charitable offerings were discreet but significant. Once when his secretary misunderstood him and transferred 5,000 euros instead of 500 to a particular charity, he sighed and said, "Well, I'm sure they need it." Few would have shown such equanimity.

Who knows what successes and challenges might have been his to confront had he not been met with the famous false allegations of child sexual assault in 2016. Overnight, his world changed, and new preoccupations clouded his days. They would have been enough to crush any ordinary person, but the cardinal had broad shoulders and managed to carry on day by day with extraordinary courage and resilience. Once he was asked how he managed to do it. "Oh, I feel it," he said, "but I don't always show it." It was a rare view into the interior suffering that he went through and that he would never have referred to publicly, as he would have considered it unseemly and perhaps contrary to those notions of manly taciturn fortitude that he had acquired during his Australian country youth. Day by day, differing news reports would arrive from Australia as the sinister and incompetent authorities oscillated between abandoning the stitched-together case and doggedly pursuing it.

Different factions seemed to be arguing back and forth, and the cardinal's hopes rose and fell accordingly. It was a cruel and absurd position to be caught in, but he never fell into self-pity. This was a challenge, and it had to be dealt with in a no-nonsense manner. He found capable people to advise him, and he took their advice, adding the seasoning of his own considerable experience. So the months passed, with all the emotional turmoil and torment they involved.

Meanwhile, his work at the Secretariat for the Economy entered a new and delicate phase. More troubling events were being uncovered, and resistance was growing to the simplest requests for accountability. The cardinal had encountered deep resistance both from the Administration of the Patrimony of the Apostolic See (APSA), the Vatican department that managed the Holy See's investments and property holdings (under the guidance of Cardinal Calcagno), and from the Secretariat of State, where his nemesis Archbishop Becciu proved a determined foe of the cardinal's reforms.

Eventually and famously, Cardinal Pell's much vaunted external audit of the Vatican's finances by Price Waterhouse Coopers was cancelled by the Vatican, apparently on the authority of Archbishop Becciu and without Cardinal Pell even being informed. He learnt about it only when the media started calling, asking for his reaction. How did Archbishop Becciu get the authority to do such a thing? And was this really proper to conduct open war between government departments? The cardinal was astonished by this behaviour but was powerless. Meanwhile, the Vatican's auditor general, Libero Milone, started to find himself in increasing difficulties and sought support from Cardinal Pell. Their relationship had not always been quite so close, but they seemed to find themselves in a baffling environment of unresponsiveness and unenforceability with regard to their work. Most Vatican departments cooperated fully and willingly. Only a very few caused difficulties, but dealing with them was a great headache.

The staff of the Secretariat for the Economy were kind and competent people and, like many others in the Vatican and contrary to many stereotypes, were often men and women of high principle passionately convinced of the cause of reform and of the need to act honestly and conscientiously before the Lord. It was a bit of a surprise as time passed and the troubles deepened for the cardinal to see how many of them were personally devoted to him. When he went through the worst of his agonies, they were openly weeping for someone they had come to know and respect deeply. There had unquestionably been grave injustices, which they had silently observed for many years, and the thought of someone of incorruptible character being as determined as he was to correct them gave hope to these honest men and women. Even so, they watched his progress with trepidation and feared that the common fate of reformers might be his.

As June 2017 drew to a close, there was a sudden sensation. The Vatican gendarmerie under the control of their commandant had staged a raid on the offices of Libero Milone. It had been a shocking scene: doors broken down and the auditor general dragged off for many hours of interrogation. He had been forced to resign on threat of imprisonment. It was a blow to Cardinal Pell, who was stunned by the sudden removal of his ally and the savagery of the episode. How to respond? What could be done? In the midst of this turmoil the terrible news was received that the Victorian police had determined to bring charges against him. This was a dark moment and meant the end of the hopes he had had that the justice system in which he trusted could really be relied upon. Now he would have to leave his position quickly and return to fight these monstrous charges. And so there it was; in the space of only a handful of days both agents of the reform were definitively removed from the stage.

Cardinal Pell prepared a statement for the press and went to see Pope Francis to lay the situation before him. The pope was very kind and supportive, assured him of his confidence, and agreed that he should only take a leave of absence from his position. Hopefully it could all be dealt with quickly and he would be back at his desk soon. The pope would keep his position for him. There would be a locum tenens appointed from within the secretariat as acting leader while the prefect was away, and we would wait and see. Of course, the case was drawn out, as we know, and the cardinal's job was quietly shelved when he came to the end of his five-year term. A minor announcement in the Vatican Press reported that he had concluded his term of office.

Much water would flow under the bridge before he would see Rome again. After his release from prison he returned to his old haunts, perhaps expecting a triumphal exoneration in the eyes of his old enemies, but the world had moved on a bit and he was no longer an important figure on the Vatican scene. For some, his star had waned and he had become a mild embarrassment. For many, he was still a great defender of the faith and a pole of orthodoxy. People still sought his company and counsel, but increasingly they were those further from the centre of power, and not infrequently those worried by a perceived drift in the Roman centre. The same worries increasingly occupied him. He had no position and had perhaps hoped that something might come his way as a form of public rehabilitation, but it was not to be.

These last couple of years were a difficult time for him to process old wounds and at the same time reorient himself towards a future he was sure was coming. His friends were loyal and enjoyed his company, and he enjoyed seeing so many of them coming to the great crossroads of Rome. He also enjoyed the opportunity for travel that had been denied him so long. At the same time, a rather unexpected change came over him as he found himself less occupied with the cares of office and with a lot more spare time on his hands. He was giving himself over to prayer and the interior life far more and was increasingly in demand as a spiritual speaker. The great enforced retreat from the world that he had undertaken thanks to the Victorian courts had borne fruit in a soul ever closer to God. A new tenderness and gentleness was apparent in his character. It had always been there, but it had not had the opportunity to flourish, as his new circumstances now permitted. Of course, the old twinkle in the eye and irrepressible cheekiness were there as well. Nothing would have entertained and also baffled him as much as seeing the faithful who pray at his tomb in Sydney now.

—Rev. Fr. Anthony Robbie

30

"I Hope You and Your Ilk Can Liberate Danustan"

Turning up at the Melbourne airport, together with my twin brother and rightly anxious mother, for our first overseas trip is something that will always stick with me. We were there to catch an Alitalia plane to the Holy Land as part of the World Youth Day 2000 pilgrimage. Through the sea of two hundred or so other young pilgrims I saw the tall and somewhat imposing frame of Archbishop Pell, the pilgrimage leader.

At the age of fourteen, my brother Brendan and I were the youngest pilgrims on the trip, requiring special permission to attend. We were both young altar servers in our home parish of Stella Maris Beaumaris, and with the support of parishioners and the local community, we had raised sufficient funds to join the pilgrimage. Pell soon took us both under his wing and made an effort to include the youngest pilgrims in all the activities. He took a genuine interest in us and our well-being.

At every pilgrim site my brother and I served Mass. I can remember the spirit of the pilgrims, the camaraderie, the singing of hymns and chants at pilgrim sites significant to both history and religion: the place of the Annunciation; Bethlehem; Mount Tabor, the place of the Transfiguration;

the Jordan River; the Sea of Galilee; Jerusalem. At every point we traced the footsteps of Christ.

From the Holy Land we travelled to Rome. It was the peak of the European summer with consecutive days of 104 degrees Fahrenheit. But nothing was going to stop us! We were joined in Rome by more than two million young pilgrims from around the world. This was, at that point, the largest gathering of young people in continental Europe in history.

Reflecting upon this now, I think Pell so enthusiastically wanted to participate in World Youth Day for three reasons. First, it was an opportunity for Melbourne's young Catholics to experience their faith instead of just reading about things in the Bible. Second, Pell wanted the Melbourne pilgrims to experience the universal Church. And finally, perhaps most importantly to Pell, he wanted to foster the next generation of Church, faith, and community leaders. On that final point, Pell wasn't just interested in identifying and attracting future priests and religious—he recognised that the Church needed community leaders also, those prepared to step up and stand up for what is just and right and true.

For my part, World Youth Day was a large contributing factor in my decision to enter the Catholic seminary. The pilgrimage set me on a path of inquiry where I found in the other young pilgrims a place of comfort, acceptance, and community. Before I made the decision to enter the seminary, I remember speaking to Archbishop Pell and seeking his counsel. He took my call again when, after two and a half years at Corpus Christi College Seminary in Carlton, I decided that a priestly vocation was not for me. He was measured and generous in his advice, but never overbearing. I was aware that he provided moral support and counsel to other seminarians at the time. Even in the midst of his own troubles, he always generously had time for others.

On our return from World Youth Day, we invited him to share a family meal with us in our home in Beaumaris. I remember, even as a then-fifteen-year-old, being a bit cheeky—a cheek that could be matched only by Pell. When the then-archbishop was seated for dinner, I presented him with a platter of two fish and five bread rolls. I remember him saying, after a dry chuckle, "Sorry—I'm off duty tonight!" It was a pleasant evening of good company and conversation.

Some seven months after our return from World Youth Day, he was appointed archbishop of Sydney and installed at St Mary's Cathedral in March 2001. Together with a dedicated few from Melbourne, we visited Sydney for his installation. He had arranged reserved seats for us during the Mass and the following day took us for a tour around his new home and a small bite to eat.

I always felt like he had more work to do in Melbourne. I'd even go so far as to suggest that Pell was taken from Melbourne too soon. That was indeed the view of many at the time. His legacy during his five years as archbishop of Melbourne is enduring: the work of the graduates of the John Paul II Institute for Marriage and Family, the reform of the regional seminary and its relocation to Carlton, the new religious texts taught in Catholic schools, and the drive to take young people on World Youth Day pilgrimage. Of course, there is much more that could be added to this list. He certainly didn't waste any time in making an impact and getting things done.

Some years after his move to Sydney, I remember, together with my brother and our mum, Josephine, visiting the cardinal and his dear sister, Margaret, at his holiday flat in Terrigal on the Central Coast of New South Wales. Shortly after we arrived, I was tasked with cooking the barbecue. The unpretentious nature of our lunch spoke to the simple pleasures that underpinned the cardinal. He wasn't fancy and high-maintenance—far from it. He was a holy man and I suspect a deeply spiritual man, but entirely pragmatic—not pious in the slightest. He recognised that as a Church leader, he had a responsibility to the faithful to uphold the faith. He wasn't scared of a fight, and he wasn't scared to articulate his views—even in front of a hostile audience.

Cardinal Pell's motto, Be Not Afraid, was certainly worn on his sleeve—more than that, it was his shield, and he put forward his view in the battle of ideas. This in itself is an inspiration for others seeking to make a difference in the public square.

My last contact with the cardinal was when I was organising a hundredth birthday celebration for Brother Christian Moe, F.S.C. Brother Christian taught me in the seminary and was a great mate of Pell's. They worked together on a series of religious education textbooks that were mandated in Victorian Catholic schools. I thought Brother Christian would want to hear from Pell on the occasion of his birthday. And in true form Pell penned a note to Brother Christian with his usual flair and sense of occasion. Of course, he didn't miss the opportunity to give a bit of cheek either!

Pell wrote to me,

> Dear Brad,
>
> Thanks for the note. I hope you and your ilk can liberate Danustan.[1] I'm delighted you are where you are and paying tribute to C.M. [Brother Christian Moe].

[1] "Danustan" is a pejorative term used to describe the Australian state of Victoria under the leadership of Premier Dan Andrews.—Editor's comment

Love and best wishes to Kate, Abigail, and Charlie. What about one or two more for the country? (Cf. Pete Costello!)

Hope to see you later in the year.

Godspeed,
CGP

That email was received in February 2022, and he died some eleven months later. Sadly, we didn't catch up later that year.

I hope these few reflections paint a picture of the Pell that I knew: a good man whose impact will be remembered for generations to come.

—The Honourable Brad Rowswell, M.L.A.

31

Canon Law and Cuff Links

When I was growing up, there were a number of priests who were just part of our family. They came round for meals. They dropped in to say hello. They rang up to find out how things were going. Cardinal Pell was one such priest. He was a mainstay in my life. It was not uncommon for the phone to ring and one of my sisters to answer it and begin chatting. After a while, my mother would usually mouth, "Who is it?" "Oh, it's George", was a common response. He usually rang to speak to my father but would not miss the opportunity to chat with whoever picked up. He moved easily in our family and our extended family, knowing how our dinner table operated and how the conversation, stories, and jokes worked. He knew our family so well that one time when I visited him in jail, I began to relay a number of recent events in our family and some funny stories, and he began to grin: He had already heard about them. Other family members had already written to him, and so he proceeded to tell me other stories about my own relatives for good measure.

Cardinal Pell was very close to our family in part because of his close friendship with my grandfather. We were blessed to have him celebrate the funeral of my grandfather, and he travelled from Sydney to attend my ordination, I think, in large part to honour this friendship. (He also played a providential role in my vocation, writing the reference that helped me get my foot in the door of Newman House, the Catholic chaplaincy for University College, London, where another priest friend asked me whether I had ever considered the priesthood.)

Cardinal Pell also honoured my grandfather by accompanying our family and some friends on a trip to Salina, one of the Aeolian islands to the north of Sicily. This trip was for the opening of a museum about Aeolian migration, including that to Melbourne, using my grandfather's story as a lens through which to view that history. It was a great trip filled with many happy memories. That a cardinal would be attending the festival was also a real coup for the organisers. As we neared Salina on the ferry, my brother went to organise the luggage. One uncle shouted out, "There are no prizes for first place", to which my brother, on looking out at the approaching pier, responded, "I am not sure about that." Waiting for the ferry to dock was a brass band and the mayors of the three towns of Salina, all wearing their best satin sashes. (Actually, one of them was a deputy mayor, since the mayor was being investigated for corruption.) One of our friends, Father Kevin Flannery, S.J., a professor at the Gregorian University, disembarked first, whereupon the band struck up and the various dignitaries came forward to grab his hand. I think it was Father Kevin who quickly pointed out that he was simply a voice crying out "Make a clear path" and that the one they sought was coming after him. Cardinal Pell found all this highly amusing.

Another highlight of the trip was a visit to a church on the island that had family significance. The church was right next to a nursing home. When the staff found out that Cardinal Pell was there, they began introducing him to all the residents. He took the time to speak to each one of them. On a side note, I have to believe that this took a lot out of him because our next stop was Mass at another church where one of my great-grandparents had been baptised. Cardinal Pell presided and I preached. Afterwards, one of my sisters asked whether it was too soon to tell me that the cardinal had slept through my homily. Cardinal Pell loved this story, mostly for the way my sister conveyed the news, but also as a way of imploring me to make my homilies just a bit more interesting.

The generosity he showed in making time for this trip is but one example of his priestly nature. He would always say yes if he could. It also shows his ever-present sense of humour. When I was in Rome studying for my licentiate and doctorate, a few friends decided to start a discussion group. We would invite a speaker for dinner and a bunch of priests to discuss theology. Cardinal Pell agreed to be one of our first guest speakers. (Again, this was a major coup for the organisers—this time, some friends and me. Immediately, many wanted in on the dinner.) Most of the guests were American priests, so Cardinal Pell talked about the role of the American Church especially in the English-speaking world. He lauded various things about it and encouraged those present in their priesthood. One of the priests, a Cistercian, perceptively asked whether, in addition to the compliments, he had any criticisms. I can still remember the mischief in his eyes when he looked at me to see whether he had the green light to stir up trouble amongst my friends. "Too much canon law and cuff links", he replied. Quite a few wrists disappeared immediately from the table. That comment immediately passed into lore in our student house.

It was a great blessing to be in Rome at the same time as he was. It meant being able to have meals with him and being introduced to other guests, but also, again because of his generosity, being able to introduce him to my friends and colleagues. Each dinner was an occasion: One had to come prepared. What was I reading? What did I think about it? What was going on in my studies? What was happening back home in the Church? What did I think about various events?

Recently, as part of another discussion group, I read Saint John Henry Newman's sermon "Unreal Words", in which he exhorts us to mean what we say, to avoid loose speech, to preserve a certain asceticism when it comes to language. Cardinal Pell would make the same point repeatedly. As in the Rule of Saint Benedict, he would listen to everyone, but the bar was set appropriately high. He did not allow me to get away with cliché or store-bought opinion. Though intimidating at first, it was freeing because there was no guesswork. Truth makes demands on us all, but in the end it is the lightest of yokes: All others just get heavier. His dinners were a great lesson in this.

And he embodied that freedom. I saw it especially during his time in jail. I was blessed to be asked to celebrate Mass for him while he was in jail. I cannot remember whether it was before or after Mass, but we were with Sister Mary, the prison chaplain, who was an absolute pillar of support for Cardinal Pell. We were chatting about the doctrine of the Assumption, about whether Our Lady had died or not. I relayed something that I had heard, a brother priest saying that he thought she had died because "if it was good enough for her Son, then it was probably good enough for her." Pell took that on board and had a good think about it, making his own comments. I was struck by how free he was spiritually. Though in solitary confinement, an environment I found initially quite daunting, he wanted simply to know more about the Lord and the Church. One gets the same impression of this spiritual freedom in reading his prison journals.

One final thought: With Cardinal Pell, what you saw was what you got, but at the same time, what you saw barely scratched the surface of what he gave to so many people. I have met many other individuals, families, and groups, all who have similar stories of times with Cardinal Pell. For all the stories of his amazing contributions to the Australian Church, the international Church, and public life, anyone could get to know him: He had time for people of all walks of life. Whether amongst high-powered intellectuals or residents of a nursing home, having dinner with a family or chatting with someone visiting him in the high-security wing, he was tough, generous, principled, open-minded, funny, and caring. At a family dinner he once complimented a fellow cleric, who in the discussion was coming in for some criticism, by saying, "He did not undermine the faith of the faithful." The same and more could be said of Cardinal Pell. Not only did he uphold the faith like a true successor of the apostles, but he encouraged its spread and, more importantly, showed what that life, the life of Christ, looks like as a daily reality. As a true disciple, he went where he was sent and tried as best as he could to say what God gave him to say.

—Rev. Dr. Jerome Santamaria

32

Ezekiel 47

Then [the angel] showed me the river of the water of life, bright as crystal, flowing from the throne of God and of the Lamb. (Rev 22:1)

I met George Pell in Oxford on Easter in 1975. I was attending Sunday Mass in the Oxford chaplaincy, and he had come back to Oxford, accompanied by his sister, Margaret, to receive his degree. Thereafter, I was to attend many Masses celebrated by him.

I remember, several years later, him giving a lecture in the Thomas More Centre in Melbourne. What was very striking about his remarks was his public meditation on being a priest. It remained a source of wonder to him that he had been called to the priesthood and that being a priest had been the source of such fulfilment.

Over the years my wife and I attended several significant events. I will mention three: his installation as archbishop of Melbourne (which took place at the Melbourne Exhibition Buildings because the cathedral was still being renovated), the celebration of the fortieth anniversary of his ordination in December 2006, and a Mass he celebrated when he was in Rome to receive the red hat from John

Paul II. On each of those occasions he chose to read from Ezekiel 47:

> The angel brought me to the entrance of the Temple, where a stream came out from under the Temple threshold and flowed eastwards, since the Temple faced east. The water flowed from under the right side of the Temple, south of the altar. He took me out by the north gate and led me right round outside as far as the outer east gate where the water flowed out on the right-hand side. The man went to the east holding his measuring line and measured off a thousand cubits; he then made me wade across the stream; the water reached my ankles. He measured off another thousand and made me wade across the stream again; the water reached my knees. He measured off another thousand and made me wade across again; the water reached my waist. He measured off another thousand; it was now a river which I could not cross; the stream had swollen and was now deep water, a river impossible to cross. He then said, "Do you see, son of man?" He took me further, then brought me back to the bank of the river. When I got back, there were many trees on each bank of the river. He said, "This water flows east down to the Arabah and to the sea; and flowing into the sea it makes its waters wholesome. Wherever the river flows, all living creatures teeming in it will live. Fish will be very plentiful, for wherever the water goes it brings health, and life teems wherever the river flows....
>
> "Along the river, on either bank, will grow every kind of fruit tree with leaves that never wither and fruit that never fails; they will bear new fruit every month, because this water comes from the sanctuary. And their fruit will be good to eat and the leaves medicinal."[1]

[1] Liturgy of the Word, Solemn Celebration of the Liturgy on the Occasion of the Reception of Most Rev George Pell as Seventh Archbishop of Melbourne (Melbourne, August 16, 1996).

To a group of senior secondary students, George Pell explained how he understood this passage:

> We Australians understand the importance of water, the difference it makes. We stand in awe of the outback, a vast desert, usually bone-dry, relentless. But we also appreciate the other side of the coin. We have often seen how the brown, parched countryside greens up, responds to good rains; the dust settles and the bushfire danger recedes.
>
> The Old Testament prophet, Ezekiel, who wrote when the Jews were in exile in Babylon in the sixth century BC, also understood the difference water makes....
>
> Ezekiel spoke of a huge river coming out of the Jerusalem Temple, God's dwelling place at that time, teeming with fish and producing every type of fruit tree in the surrounding countryside. Good, faithful people have this sort of effect on their families, friends and their communities. Fountains of water are a symbol of what we all should be doing, of what you as young adults are now called to do.
>
> Ezekiel also knew that the effects of bad religion can be very different from streams of living water, which can become dangerously polluted. He also has another famous image of a valley full of dry bones; dead, without flesh or sinew or skin. Religiously, they were people whose hope was gone; they were as good as dead.
>
> These are the alternatives, which confront every adult. Not one of us can avoid choosing life or death, love or hate, good or evil, the waters of life or drought and the desert.[2]

His attachment to the powerful symbolism of water is also strikingly evident in his redesign of the gardens within the precinct of St Patrick's Cathedral. From the eastern transept of the cruciform cathedral, a fountain of water

[2] Cardinal George Pell, "The Faithful of Tomorrow", in *Be Not Afraid: Collected Writing*, ed. Tess Livingstone (Duffy & Snellgrove, 2004), 143–44.

runs down towards the east. At one level the fountain represents the water that flowed from the side of Christ. At the base of the watercourse he had engraved an extract from James McAuley's "A Letter to John Dryden":

> Incarnate Word, in whom all nature lives,
> Cast flame upon the earth: raise up contemplatives
> Among us, men who walk within the fire
> Of ceaseless prayer, impetuous desire.
> Set pools of silence in this thirsty land[3]

In December 2018, a County Court jury had found Pell guilty of several offences. He had been on bail since then, and on the day that he was sentenced, he was to be taken into custody. The verdict made a prison sentence inevitable. The cardinal had been staying with his friends the McFarlanes, and I, with my wife and one of my daughters, attended his morning Mass on March 13, 2019, celebrated in the McFarlanes' lounge room. He read what was written for him and performed the rites stipulated: "saying the black and doing the red". He did nothing to draw attention away from the sacred liturgy, particularly nothing to draw attention to himself or any part of his predicament. We left the McFarlanes' with heavy hearts, knowing the humiliation and degradation that awaited him.

The last Mass I attended that he celebrated was at St Kilian's Bendigo on December 31, 2021. It was the Requiem Mass for his sister, Margaret, whom, during the homily, he described as "not only my sister but my best friend". He concluded his homily with words from John Donne, which he enjoined us to make our own:

[3] James McAuley, "A Letter to John Dryden", in *Collected Poems: 1936–1970* (Angus and Robertson, 1971), 94.

All changing unchanged Ancient of days,
But do not, with a vile crown of frail bays,
Reward [our] muse's white sincerity,
But what thy thorny crown gained, that give [us],
A crown of glory, which doth flower always;
The ends crown our works, but thou crown'st our ends,
For, at our end begins our endless rest.[4]

—The Honourable Joseph Gerard Santamaria, K.C.

[4] John Donne, "La Corona", in *The Complete English Poems*, ed. A.J. Smith (Penguin, 1971), 306.

33

The Son of the Royal Oak Publican

One of the rites of passage for those cosseted by years of privilege some forty-five years ago was to be sent out on a gap year, to travel the world and perhaps get toughened up. These journeys were before the package industry of protected gap years common nowadays, skilfully sculptured by "educational trusts" that are for many the norm, whether to explore the rainforests of South America or the villas of Tuscany. In my case, almost as a Ten Pound Pom, I landed in Perth, Western Australia, with a little pocket money and no return ticket in the spring of 1977.[1] My trips to Australia over the years have always been marked by a penitential desire to watch England be thrashed by Australia at cricket. This first trip Down Under was no different in that we lost the Centenary Test in Melbourne by exactly the same margin as a hundred years before. After the defeat I continued hitchhiking around the country and picking up jobs where I could find them. At the time hitchhiking was pretty danger-free, and there were jobs aplenty. I also would find myself lodging in public houses,

[1] The expression "Ten Pound Pom" was used to describe British migrants to Australia after the Second World War who arrived under the Assisted Passage Migration Scheme of 1945. In return for paying an administration fee of ten British pounds, the Australian government would cover the travel expenses of British migrants to Australia.

as they were the only accommodation available in outback towns. Australian pubs then were of a particular flavour, for it was only ten years or so since the end of the "six o'clock swill". Such was the nature of Australian licensing laws that you had to drink as much as you could in those few minutes before returning to an often-irate household. The memories of that "swill" were still real on my arrival in Australia. My watering holes and dormitories were pubs, and although I couldn't confess to being an expert on them, I came to know something of their culture. You might well be thinking, What does this have to do with a remarkable, much loved and missed prince of the Church?

George Pell was brought up in the Royal Oak in Ballarat, where his father was the publican. Many times he spoke about pub life and painted perhaps a slightly romantic picture of it. Despite being wet behind the ears, as a Pom, I knew something of where he was coming from. These were places of extraordinary social interaction, honesty, misogyny, conviviality, and a certain robustness. They were like the refiner's fire for character formation. They were not places for the fainthearted, and as a son of a publican, you would have had to survive. Pell's athletic ability and fighting instinct were naturally honed in such a culture. It meant that you could or indeed had to be at ease with all—no airs or graces and a readiness to engage in combat, whatever was coming. This was the character of George Pell that I remember. He was at ease with all, interested, engaging, and combative. There was an instinctive kindness and generosity that knew no affectation. I never expected to become a priest or indeed count as a close personal friend the archbishop of Sydney. In a strange quirk of divine providence, when I did get to know him, I could understand his remarkable pastoral skills, whether in the privacy of confession, where he would judge and bestow mercy; in conversation, in which he would accompany and perhaps admonish; or in the public forum, where he would be unbending. His remarkable human qualities perhaps shone forth most in his prison cell. I wonder whether, had he not been the son of a publican, things might have turned out differently. As Archbishop Ullathorne, former missionary to Sydney and archbishop of Birmingham, went from cabin-boy to archbishop, so Pell went from pub-lad to cardinal.

In the intervening years after my first visit, I had passed through university, other activities, and seminary and now found myself a priest in Oxford, where the cardinal was speaking. In those years I had heard something about him and was drawn to him as a John Paul II bishop. Many may forget that in the late 1990s the Australian Catholic Church was meandering towards the waters of confusion and heterodoxy, and the Statement of Conclusions was a robust initiative on behalf of the Roman authorities to reaffirm Catholic teaching and practice.[2] Pell would have been no innocent bystander to these manoeuvres. He was clearly leading some kind of fight-back for the voice of orthodoxy and the joyful and life-giving proclamation of the faith.

Having asked a rather controversial question at the cardinal's Oxford lecture, later, when we were having dinner together, I rather tentatively said I was coming to Melbourne on another penitential pilgrimage. He kindly gave me his telephone number and said to ring when I was in town. This I did, and he asked simply what I was doing that evening and then came and picked me up and took me back to his residence for supper. There are few bishops, I suspect, who would have taken such a risk on a brief meeting, and

[2] The Statement of Conclusions was a document released in 1998 following the ad limina visit of Australian bishops and the Special Assembly of the Synod of Bishops for Oceania. It was critical of a number of practices, such as the so-called third rite of confession.

certainly as Australians, they would have been very wary of a crazed English cricketing fan priest.

That was the beginning of twenty-five years of friendship. He now has been taken into eternity and is no doubt at peace and rest after years of labour, in which he was misunderstood, maligned, and traduced but also through which he transformed the Church in Australia and beyond. How much we already miss him. In the same character demonstrated by that first meeting, he became a tremendous friend of the parish, so much so that we named one of our three bedrooms "the Cardinal's Room". How many times he visited and truly rejoiced in the young people who have been very much part of this parish (St Patrick's, Soho), and in particular our School of Evangelisation. An occasion I remember was going down the Thames to Greenwich, and one of the very cheeky students was making fun of me. The cardinal did not come to my defence, quietly chuckling as he took in the history of Father Thames. He may well have mused that cheekiness and robustness often end up in religious life or priesthood. That student is now a Sister of Life in Phoenix, Arizona.

We also have the Queen Catherine of Aragon vestments, protected by recusant families, fully restored thanks to the generosity of the Archdiocese of Sydney. There are so many stories and memories, but what always stands out was his incredible rapport with young people and families. It's difficult to explain how much people were drawn to this physical giant of a figure who could appear inquisitive, hard of hearing, incisive, and perhaps a little brusque. However, they knew that he was the real thing.

In that spirit of mischievousness he was drawn to the robustious foreign secretary of the time, Boris Johnson, and was struck by his book on Winston Churchill, such an emblematic figure for ANZAC Australians, despite the cardinal's republican tendencies. I was able to arrange a visit to the Foreign Office for what was to be no more than a ten-minute meeting. It lasted for an hour, and using one of the original Enigma decoding machines, the cardinal was to prise open Johnson's Catholic sacramental history. It was somewhat shrouded in his colourful life story, but he understood and spoke of his Baptism and First Holy Communion. Much has happened since, but the cardinal always had an affection and admiration for him, convinced he would embrace at some time in the future the fully lived sacramental reality. What is now true is that the cardinal's intercession will be invaluable.

As a parish community and a group of friends, we followed the accusations that were levelled against him and for which he received a sentence of six years. He was released after 404 days. How much people fasted, prayed, and did Eucharistic vigils for his release. Whatever social commentators might say, I knew it was a spiritual battle, and I think the cardinal, who was not given to supernatural language, acknowledged the dark arts. Indeed, after the second trial he spoke of a darkness that he felt in the courtroom in Melbourne. He could have easily avoided the whole turmoil, as some in Rome argued, by not going back to Australia, but he believed both in Australian justice (which in the state of Victoria was not an easy task!) and in the need to stare down the accusation. Despite knowing him well, I think what was particularly remarkable was how, in the spirit of Saint John Fisher, his cardinal's red realised its divine calling. He forgave and did not judge but prayed for his accusers and showed a serenity that surprised many.

It was such a joy to be able to speak to him in what was appropriately a Carmelite monastery, where he first touched base after his release, and I believe some very respectable wine was brought to the convent. The description "white martyr" is not often used; we think particularly of Saint Maximilian Kolbe, who prayed for both the white and the red rose of holiness. The cardinal was very unassuming and self-deprecating about matters of the supernatural, transcendent, or indeed diabolic infestation, but as he became, as some of his friends would say, more mellow and gentler after his release, his understanding of such realities was very real and pronounced—and he would speak of them.

Saint Philip Howard would have been another man after his heart, as we remember how he remained in the Tower of London and could have seen his beloved wife, thus compromising his Catholic faith, but refused to deny Christ and the truth of the Church, particularly in regard to marriage, fidelity, and the validity of the Sacrament of Holy Matrimony. Philip stands out amongst many of those brutally killed by Elizabeth I. His stand was much more about the unbreakable bond of Matrimony than it was about throwing himself into the political battles of the time.

So many stories about the cardinal's humour abound, but with them there was always the proclamation of truth. Saint Philip Howard was the occasion of one.[3] A dear cousin of mine arranged a visit to Arundel Castle, and we took Ambrose, my dog, who was normally confined to the concrete of the West End of London. We arrived at the castle, and Ambrose immediately fell into seventh heaven, as lawns and flower beds opened out in front of him. He found it difficult to distinguish, as he galloped into this enormous castle, the difference between lawns, flower beds, wooden passageways, and glorious woven carpets. We got to this very grand drawing room, and the cardinal was absorbing the hundreds of years of history portrayed on the walls. He then looked down at his size-thirteen feet and announced, somewhat matter-of-factly, that he had stepped in something. Ambrose saw no difference between the Ducal Gardens and carpets and had done his business. There was nothing else

[3] Saint Philip Howard was the 13th Earl of Arundel.

to do. I had to throw myself on the floor and start scrubbing those size-thirteen shoes and rather pathetically clean the carpet. The cardinal was naturally amused, and it gave him more ammunition for his invective against what he called "that b—— dog". He carried on quite happily, whereas I had to eat much humble pie. Cousin Mary assured us that this would not have been the first time for such a carpet, but the cardinal blamed me entirely, albeit with a wry smile—and he was right.

You would never believe that Margaret, his sister, was brought up in a pub, for she was refined, polished, and musical—indeed, a very fine violinist. Brother and sister were like Tweedledum and Tweedledee, often ribbing each other, quietly praying together, and deeply respectful of each other. I never had the chance to talk to the cardinal about Margaret's death a few years back, but how much he would have missed her. They both showed a love of life and a love of God. How much Margaret would have suffered from George's trial, imprisonment, and being cast aside by many. She would often talk of those poachers who had turned gamekeeper, both secular and ecclesiastical. She was truly a fierce and certain defender of her brother and, in some ways, the sorrowful mother that we meet at the foot of the Cross. One of the marks of our time for priests is the accusatory culture in which we live and a questioning trust in the episcopate. The cardinal was a countersign to both. Many clergy live today with a fear of an anonymous accusation that could lead to suspension, laicisation, or separation from parish, family, and flock. In addition, many can feel that clergy have somehow been abandoned. The cardinal would be a riposte to both. First, as has been proved, he was innocent, and he was fully exonerated. Second, he believed in Australian justice and went home to face the angry crowds and vilification heaped upon him. It was a decision totally in keeping with his character, his faith, and the centrality of his love of Christ and his Church. The humiliation of being segregated and strip-searched and not being able to celebrate Mass was terrible. He lived it with more than stoicism; he expressed deep faith, humility, and prayer for his accusers and the braying mob. What humility and holiness, and how he was, in many ways, "a white martyr". Second, he went into the cells as a successor of the apostles. We often forget how much evil rages when it confronts the humility of the priest, and even more so when it faces a faithful, courageous, and trusting bishop. As Henry VIII and his daughter wanted to break the resilience of John Fisher, the holiness of the Carthusian monks of Clerkenwell, and the fidelity to God's law of marriage as espoused by Philip Howard, so the Evil One wanted to break George Pell.

Much has been said and written about the most significant Australian churchman of the last fifty years, and there are plentiful achievements to speak of. In a delightful and playful way, how much the cardinal confessed to loving and collecting his "baubles", as he called them. However, this was a spiritual battle—no more and no less. He often accused me of being somewhat melodramatic in my language, but in that last, most serene chapter of his life, the words of Saint Paul VI of how the stench of Satan was at work in the Church were on his lips as well.

The words of a dying person carry a resonance and a wisdom, but the tragedy was that we didn't know he was dying. He had badgered me for a favour a few times on the phone before he left for the clinic and his hip replacement. He could be a little impatient! However, memorably, at the end of perhaps the fifth telephone call, he said, "Thank you very much for all you are doing." The pub and its eternal values in terms of civility and human respect never left him.

He had been in London for a week before Christmas escorting a large group of Australian high school students and introducing them to Western civilisation. Every day there was Mass and a purposeful sermon to lift them out of the miasma of contemporary culture to the greats of latter years and the critical interface with Christian revelation. How inspiring he was in his care and inspiration given to young people. Before anything else he was a spiritual father to many. He celebrated a solemn Mass in St Patrick's, Soho, for the Immaculate Conception, and they came in great numbers. Perhaps the Holy Spirit had been at work in social media, something about which the cardinal knew little; but somehow, God may have wanted them there to say goodbye to a great figure of our time. His following in "Mother England", as he called her, was considerable—whilst he remained (I think) a diehard republican.

The funeral in Rome was full of sadness and joy. How could he have left us? However, we are called to believe that he has gone home. The most abiding memory of those precious few hours for many was in the Church of Saint Stephen of the Abyssinians, where his body lay. A couple with some eight children came in, surrounded his body, prayed, and sang. He was truly a father, a lover of family and the Sacrament of Marriage, and the most resolute defender of Catholic orthodoxy. As Saint Monica said to her two sons, "When I die do not look to the things of an earthly and temporal nature, but look to Heaven and the communion of saints. I beg you remember me at the altar of God." That we must also do.

—Canon Alexander Sherbrooke[4]

[4] This memoir was first published in the journal *The Priest* of the Australian Confraternity of Catholic Clergy in March 2023.

34

A Great Man and Friend

George Cardinal Pell was my good friend for some forty years. He was an immensely good man, and I loved him. Yet perhaps the most striking memories I have of our long friendship were our arguments, which were mostly good-natured but often very vigorous.

To have been his friend is one of the great privileges of my life. He was not only the most important Catholic leader Australia has ever produced (just shading Daniel Mannix, I think), but he was also one of the most consequential cardinals from an English-speaking background in the history of the Catholic Church.

After Benedict XVI was elected pope in 2005, American cardinals were emerging from their Rome accommodation when some young seminarians thanked them for electing Benedict. "It's not us you should thank", one cardinal replied. "It's that Australian, George Pell. He convinced us to get behind Benedict." Pell is also a powerful symbol of the dystopian moment our culture has reached. Pell was wrongly convicted of child sexual abuse and spent more than a year in prison, most of it effectively in solitary confinement. The charges were absurd, fantastic, implausible from the start, as Justice Mark Weinberg demonstrated in his withering minority judgement in the Victorian Court of Appeal, and as the High Court showed in its crushing 7–0 verdict that Pell was innocent.

Pell was convicted because of anti-Catholic hysteria and because he was the designated conservative public villain in the culture wars. He had the temerity to speak back to the culture, to contest its assumptions seriously, systematically, and most maddening of all, often with humour, and good humour. It's also true that the Church's terrible past failings in dealing with clerical sexual abuse were the unavoidable context.

In a piercing essay Pope Benedict argued that such clerical abuse occurred when priests lost all sense of God. In the peak years of the abuse, roughly 1960 to 1980, many priests, much of the whole culture, did lose the sense of God.

Pell became the symbol of every failing, real and imagined, of the Catholic Church. The former prime minister John Howard told me that Pell was convicted because of who he was. This was an episode of terrible shame for the Australian legal system and most of the Australian media. Despite what the courts found as to fact, the passionate Pell haters succeeded in convincing millions of Australians that Pell was guilty—not only of abuse but also of covering up abuse.

But not everyone was convinced. Shortly before his trial began, I picked up the cardinal from the private home where he was staying in Melbourne. We went to dinner at an Indian restaurant in Camberwell. The cardinal, with his height and bulk and presence, was pretty unmissable. Australians are generally very good to public figures they come across in private moments. But three times that night our dinner was interrupted as people approached our table. Each of them wanted to wish the cardinal well. They could see a setup was in progress.

Over the years I went to a lot of restaurants and coffee shops with the cardinal. This was a pretty good policy on my part because on occasion the restaurateurs simply refused to accept any payment for the meal. On another occasion I went to pay, and some passerby had already paid. At every point of his long public life lots of people supported the cardinal.

Pell could not have been less like his public image. He was an exquisitely sophisticated and well-informed intellectual who nonetheless projected an earthy, sometimes rugged Australian manner. He was drolly humorous and routinely self-deprecating. Irony and wit sparkled out of him. But he was also a man of vigour and passionate engagement in the faith he believed in completely and in the world around him.

As you'd expect in a long friendship based on frank conversation involving a controversial Church leader and an especially opinionated opinion columnist, we had our share of rich and vigourous arguments. There was something complementary in the friendship. I was a professional foreign affairs journalist, greatly interested in theology and the Church. He was a great Church leader and intellectual, passionately fascinated by international affairs and global and domestic politics. He always wanted to talk to me about China, Asian politics, defence policy. And he was acutely smart about all this.

But I was able to converse on those subjects all the time. I always wanted to talk to him about theology, Church history, Biblical translation, the situation of the global Church, and the prospects of Christianity. But he routinely spoke to people who knew vastly more about these subjects than I did. You might classify our separate spheres as two nonoverlapping magisteriums. In fact, there was more than enough overlap for a lot of creative interaction.

Mostly I talked to him on my own. Sometimes there was a bigger dinner or a few other fellows. I think that like most men of his generation (and many of mine), he had two separate standards for what constituted appropriate language: one when women were present and something a little looser when it was just blokes. As I say, he was famously earthy. Talking to me about someone he'd helped get a job, he told me the fellow "was happy as a pig in shit".

Once, many years ago, I rightly felt I'd been much too aggressive in an argument with him. We didn't meet for a while. I rang and suggested lunch, to which he readily agreed. I'd rehearsed a pretty fulsome apology. But I didn't get far into it when he interrupted. "Don't give it another thought", he said with a laugh.

I used to ring the cardinal for advice, especially if I was writing about the Church. He never leaked any secrets to me, but I was never after secrets. I was always writing about matters in which the facts were public. What I was after from George was judgement, advice, context, evaluation, analysis pointing to the future. What I was really after, and what I always got from him, was wisdom.

Occasionally he'd ring me for advice, mainly related to politics in the broadest sense. Once I was able actually to be of some use. One day in 2013 I got a phone call from the cardinal. Pope Francis had asked him to clean up the Vatican's finances, which were opaque and, as it turned out, in part corrupt. To do this, Francis appointed Pell the secretary of finance for the Vatican. Pell, in turn, wanted to appoint a committee of the most financially literate and best Catholic laypeople from around the world to oversee the reform of Vatican finances.

Pell asked me whether I knew a Catholic in Asia who had serious financial background and high standing and who was a sufficiently devoted Catholic that he might be willing to do the job. He wanted a name quickly. Pell had a good knowledge of Asia and a deep sense of its importance.

He was always scandalized about the absence of Asian Catholics in the Vatican itself.

It took me only about thirty seconds to suggest George Yeo, the former Singapore foreign minister. He had also been trade minister and had some finance portfolio responsibilities. He was a typical Singapore overachiever, with high academic qualifications, great achievements in the air force, and a long and illustrious government career.

As I've written elsewhere, Yeo is one of the most intellectually gifted people I've met in a long career in journalism. He had been generous in the time he spent with me over the years. He had great technical competence in whatever he was doing, but a singular ability to place contemporary issues in a broad historical context. Pell kept questioning me: Was he a good man? Was I confident in his character? Did I think he'd do it if asked?

Although 90 percent of my conversations with Yeo concerned foreign policy, as two Catholics, we had occasionally discussed religious matters. I knew he was a profoundly believing Catholic.

The rest, as they say, is history. Pell got in touch with Yeo through his bishop. Yeo accepted the offer, which Pell gave him precisely forty-eight hours to consider. Yeo brought his forensic mind and his Singapore work ethic to the job. I'm delighted to say they became friends. Yeo steadfastly defended Pell all through the ridiculous trials.

Pell is rightly seen as a theological conservative. But this term is inadequate. Certainly he was no reactionary. He was always open to innovation and new ideas. Within the Australian Church he'd reached the position of wise pragmatic eclecticism. He would back any movement or person he thought was broadly in line with Church teaching and was having some success in attracting and caring for people.

When I wrote a memoir, and then when I started writing books about Christianity, he did me the great kindness of reading some chapters for me in advance to help me avoid mistakes and improve things stylistically. I didn't always follow his judgements. In my first Christian book, *God Is Good for You*, I labelled Saint Paul "Christ's Lenin". Obviously I wasn't comparing an apostle of peace with a communist tyrant. But in the combination of theoretical insight and operational genius, I thought the comparison useful. Pell strongly advised me against it. We had a lot of back-and-forth over it. I consulted a number of others. But I took the cardinal's advice on board and made the limits of the comparison much clearer. He went to the trouble of reviewing that book and recommending in particular the last chapter, where I tried to offer today's churches practical advice.

It was unbelievably kind of him to put this much time and effort into these matters, for Pell really was an intellectual superstar in global Catholicism. Even the most liberal redoubts wanted to hear from him. He told me of an interview with a German Catholic magazine. His interviewer was unhappy that Pell was insisting on the continuity of Christian teaching. "So you're saying to the modern person, 'Take it or leave it', are you?" his interviewer asked. "No," said Pell, "I'm saying, 'Come and join us in the truth.'"

Pell's point, and the profound centre of his view in all Christian controversies, was that Christ's own words in the Gospels were paramount. Christians believe Christ is the second Person in the Trinity of the Godhead, that he is God himself. If they believe that, it was Pell's view, they have no mandate to set up an authority that contradicts Christ's own words. If they believe the insights of secular society today are superior to Christ's own teachings, there's no reason to have a Christian church at all.

The modern temptation is to fudge things with equivocal words and weasel formulations. This was against Pell's nature. He was a mixture of singular courage, unbelievable energy, deep insight, clear thought, and occasional clumsiness in statements to the media. He was, after all, a human being.

The cardinal's legacy will be great. It resides in the institutions he founded and reformed, in the people he inspired, and in his prison diaries, which are a spiritual classic as well as often very funny. In them Pell is surprisingly and frequently grateful for the consolations in his life. The diaries sit honourably in the tradition of Christian prison writings going back to Saint Paul.

I will miss phone calls and meals that would typically begin with teasing words along the lines of "I noted with interest your wildly intemperate and misbegotten enthusiasm for Joe Biden's China policy." Our friendship was robust and vigourous. Just once or twice, he made some inquiry of me about spiritual matters and offered useful advice, without ever straying into presumption or pulling rank, though he had every right to.

Pell's humour and irony were great fun. He once told me how to become a saint: Found a religious institution that will pray for your canonisation, destroy all correspondence that is at all disobliging, and collect everything flattering and keep it in a box marked "to be destroyed on my death". This was a joke, of course. Pell revered the traditions of the Church. But even these did not compare for him with the actual words of Christ. The love of Christ was the heart of Pell's life. Like many others, I will miss him dearly.

—Gregory Sheridan

35

Red—the Only Appropriate Colour for a Cardinal!

It was a splendid late summer day in beautiful Melbourne, which, in retrospect, turned out to be one of the last weekends in lighthearted prepandemic times. The city was pulsing with joy and optimism as people strolled through the parks along the Yarra River, enjoying the gentle breeze that offers respite from the sun. Cafés spilled over onto the sidewalks, which were filled with people holding animated conversations; others sought shade under the sprawling trees.

One hour outside the city, the contrast could not have been any starker. It was Saturday—for the prisoners of Barwon Prison, the day on which they could receive visitors. Barwon is the only facility in the state of Victoria to be classified amongst the highest security prisons in Australia. And indeed, security protocols are impressive: With all personal items locked up, visitors—many of whom look as if they have just stepped out of a mafia movie—first proceed through a drug-testing machine and then undergo a search that is significantly more rigorous than one would experience at any airport in the world.

However, for visitors of the few prisoners held in solitary confinement in this maximum-security facility, this search is only the beginning of a process that overall takes more than half an hour. Having undergone the regular search and having been escorted by an officer to the solitary confinement section on the other side of the huge compound, the visitor is subjected to another pat-down search. From the moment one enters the building, there is no talking apart from the instructions given. In fact, as the only visitor to any of the solitary confinement prisoners on a particular day, one is completely alone with the law enforcement staff behind the many walls, pikes, and checkpoints. While staff are highly respectful, the procedure is overwhelming. When I visited and was eventually left alone to wait for George Pell, I was finally able to grasp fully how extreme a place this was, in every possible respect.

The cardinal's legal team had advised that the visit would be subject to several possible constraints, including potential disruptions and an unpredictable duration. They also let me know that our conversation could be monitored. Blogs around the world expressed outrage at how isolated the cardinal was, claiming that he was even living without access to the sacraments, and my first impressions of the visitors' room in Barwon's solitary confinement wing confirmed this isolation. It was made even more tangible by the thick wall of bullet-proof glass that separated the visitor from the prisoner.

In light of these conditions and all that the cardinal had experienced—imprisonment for over a year, the dismissal of an appeal before the Supreme Court of Victoria, a proceeding pending before the High Court of Australia, and the supposed denial of the sacraments—one would have rightly expected the worst in terms of George Pell's condition. Considering his previous eminence as one of the world's most prominent Catholic clerics and a chief adviser to the pope, one would have easily believed that visiting him in his current condition of solitary confinement was a true work of mercy and would require one to uplift his spirit.

But these assumptions could not have been further from the truth. This inmate was quite different from all the others, and so was the visit. Even before he entered the room, it was hard to miss the reality that George Pell was his usual self—his formidable voice could be heard down the hallway as he addressed the corrections officers, sounding just as it had when he had spoken with his staff at the Vatican. And when the cardinal entered his side of the room, it was also instantly noticeable that he was in top spirits: serene, calm, and greeting me happily. Lacking his pectoral cross and bishop's ring, he was wearing a prison jumpsuit—in red. He even joked that he was given the only appropriate colour for a cardinal. From the first moment it was clear that it was not I who was going to be lifting the prisoner's mood, but the prisoner who would be lightening mine from the feelings I had experienced while coming here. George Pell had remained unmistakably George Pell, the robust and confident former Australian Rules football player who, as the only cardinal on his continent, had fearlessly taken on public opinion on so many controversial topics and who later at the Vatican had fearlessly confronted the challenge to stamp out mismanagement and corruption.

And so we had, as surprising as it was to me, a completely normal conversation, not at all different (apart from the austere surroundings) from the last one we had had in his apartment in Rome, with my oldest daughter sitting at the coffee table with her modelling clay while we spoke, or from the lunch conversation my wife and I would have with the cardinal about a year after this visit at Barwon Prison. Thankfully, corrections staff were generous that day, allowing us over two hours to chat. The cardinal's serenity not only made it feel like any other meeting we had had, including a lot of laughter, but it also made the time seem so much shorter than it was.

Beyond his unruffled state of mind, it was astounding—and the basis for our animated exchange—how well informed he was about everything going on in the world and particularly in the Church. Supporters had been sending him clippings from media and blogs; friends wrote well-informed letters. So he was more than up-to-date on all things Catholic—so much so that even though our meeting occurred only days after a surprising decision by Pope Francis at the Vatican, the cardinal and I were already able to engage in a deep discussion of the background and various theories relating to that decision.

That the cardinal was anything but a broken person was evident not only from his mood and *how* he spoke (which could have been a facade) but also from the substance of *what* he shared. First, he offered a host of positive perspectives: praising the prison staff, who treated him so respectfully; commending the governor of Victoria, who had granted him a more comfortable chair for his cell; and appreciating Pope Francis, who intervened to ensure his Vatican apartment was not packed up. Most of all, he was grateful for the privilege he felt in having so much time to read and pray.

Second, the cardinal had very clear plans, especially for after his release, which he was nearly certain of (the only doubts he expressed arose from the dismissal of his previous appeal to the Supreme Court of Victoria, which, he shared with me, had shocked him). These plans included publications he had been preparing—very thoroughly, as it turned out later—while in prison.

Third, he was clearly in a good place spiritually. In response to my mentioning reports that he had been denied the sacraments, he detailed the real situation: He received Communion every week from a member of the Melbourne pastoral staff, and once a month a priest would come to celebrate Holy Mass for him since he could not celebrate himself given the strict alcohol ban by Corrections Victoria. The very essence of George Pell's unshakable character came out when I then expressed regret that despite all that, he could not go to confession. Initially he seemed puzzled by my concern, so I explained that his legal team had told me his conversations with visitors could be monitored, to which he responded, "Whatever—I don't care! I confess to the chaplain when he's here!"

Finally—and unsurprisingly to those who knew George Pell—even in the solitary confinement wing of Barwon Prison he found occasion to do pastoral work himself. The cardinal had three inmates who were also in solitary, and he explained that he could speak with them as we had been doing (referring to the separation by bullet-proof glass). He spent a reasonable amount of time with them. Two of them—one Catholic, one Muslim—had known Cardinal Pell well, having attended Catholic schools in Melbourne when he was the sitting archbishop. "I had a picture of you in my classroom", both of them had shared with him. While he was particularly sympathetic with one of them who equally maintained his innocence and had an appeal pending, he had taken all three of them into his heart.

And a mere thirty-eight days after our meeting under such memorable circumstances, the cardinal could hear in his cell the loud cheering of those three prisoners who likewise held him in their hearts. News had broken that the High Court of Australia had quashed all convictions against the cardinal. With the full bench ruling, the judgement unanimous, and the opinion of the court published in writing less than a month after the court hearings, the exoneration could not have been more comprehensive.

—Dr. Tassilo Wanner

36

The Pell Album of Memories

I first met then-Father George Pell in the summer of 1967, when, in between his Roman ordination the previous December and his Oxford studies that would begin in the fall, he spent several months "supplying" at the Cathedral of Mary Our Queen, my parish in Baltimore, Maryland. By the time the lanky young Australian left us, he and my family had become fast friends, although neither he nor I could have imagined in those days that our friendship would lead to working in harness during two papal interregnums and one synod. Fifty-five years of friendship inevitably include a large album of memories; two incidents will perhaps illustrate the texture of our collaboration and the character of a great churchman and wonderful human being.

At the first of two synods on marriage and the family in October 2014, Cardinal Pell, in league with Wilfrid Fox Cardinal Napier of South Africa, had made a decisive intervention, challenging the interim report prepared by Archbishop Bruno Forte as a distortion of what had actually been discussed in Synod-2014's first two weeks. Several weeks later, after the synod fathers had returned home, the cardinal called and asked—no, told—me to clear my calendar for October 2015. He wanted me in Rome that month, both as *consigliere* and to run a guerrilla media operation for the Anglosphere. Pell said that Synod-2014 had demonstrated that the Vatican Press Office couldn't be trusted to report accurately what was going on, so an alternative was imperative in 2015. Thus was born "Letters from the Synod-2015", which ran on the websites of the New York–based *First Things*, the London-based *Catholic Herald*, and the Sydney-based *Catholic Weekly*.

During the four weeks of Synod-2015 Pell and I met for breakfast every weekday morning to review the previous day's goings-on, to discuss strategy going forward, and to devise themes to be developed for discussion at the synod. The most memorable of those conversations took place when the cardinal told me what had happened when the synod's language-based discussion groups had first met. Pell had been swiftly elected chairman of the English-language group to which he had been assigned; Archbishop Joseph Kurtz of Louisville, Kentucky, had been chosen the group's secretary; and the first exchange at that first meeting had been one for the ages.

It will be remembered that Synod-2015's *Instrumentum laboris*, or working document, had been severely criticized for being Biblically anorexic: long on sociology and short on Scripture. Nonetheless, when Pell opened the floor for discussion, Blase Cardinal Cupich of Chicago displayed his striking inability to read a situation (like having just lost two elections decisively) by jumping right in and saying with some vehemence, "If we begin the [synod's] final report with Scripture, we're finished." This striking proclamation was met with dead silence for the better part of a minute. Then Cardinal Pell, who could be quite dry when he put his mind to it, lowered his head, looked through his half-moon glasses at his brother cardinal, and quietly replied, "A rather bleak view of the Word of God, wouldn't you say?"

Nothing else was heard from His Eminence of Chicago for some time.

And then there was what I call in my weekly column "The White-Martyr Cardinals' Dinner". A few days before the funeral of Benedict XVI, held on January 5, 2023, I suggested to Cardinal Pell that he should "host an Irish wake that evening", as both of us and others would likely need some cheering up after the man we had esteemed for decades was buried in the Vatican grottoes beneath Saint Peter's. The cardinal readily agreed and asked me to organize things.

By happy coincidence I received a message a day later indicating that Joseph Cardinal Zen, the heroic bishop emeritus of Hong Kong, had been allowed by the Chinese communist thugocracy to come to Rome for the Funeral Mass and wanted to see me. I got in touch with the cardinal's secretary, who was accompanying him, and invited them to Cardinal Pell's apartment for dinner the evening of the funeral. Thus, the company assembled at #1, Piazza della Città Leonina on the night of January 5 could marvel at being in the presence of two contemporary "white martyrs", men who had suffered greatly for the faith but had remained unbroken and full of the joy of the Lord.

As providence would have it, Cardinal Pell, in hosting that dinner, "provided his own Irish wake" (as one of those present remarked after Pell's unexpected death five days later). It was an apt description of a magical evening, in which the predominant mood of profound gratitude for Benedict XVI animated hours of robust conversation, full of wit and laughter. And as Cardinal Pell remarked afterwards to Father Raymond de Souza and me when we were sharing a nightcap after everyone else had left, "Well, the old boy [Cardinal Zen] really was the star tonight, wasn't he?" Indeed, he was.

At ninety-one years old and suffering irritating physical disabilities, the Shanghai-born Salesian cardinal remained incredibly energetic and eagerly spoke about his work in the Hong Kong jail where the great Jimmy Lai and other political prisoners were being held. The wardens, it seems, behaved decently with Zen, allowing him to stay as long as he liked and not (overtly) monitoring his conversations with the prisoners. The cardinal told of making several converts in the prison and was asked what he used for catechetical materials. The answers were striking: the Bible and the *Catechism of the Catholic Church*, of course, but also Dostoevsky's *The Brothers Karamazov*.

Perhaps the most remarkable moment of the evening came when, after Cardinal Pell offered a moving toast to his brother cardinal, the conversation turned to those times when the Lord seems to be deaf to the pleas of his people—times not unlike what many Catholics had been experiencing in recent years. Cardinal Zen reminded the group of the appropriate verse of Psalm 44 ("Rouse yourself! Why do you sleep, O Lord? Awake! Do not cast us off for ever!" [v. 23]); remembered that those verses had been part of the Introit for Sexagesima Sunday in the old Roman liturgical calendar; and then proceeded to chant, from memory and in impeccable Latin, that entire Introit![1]

The inscription on Pell's tomb in the Sydney cathedral reads *Christus Et Ecclesia Vehementer Dilexit* (He loved Christ and the Church vehemently). That George Pell certainly did. But this robust personality was also a man of great kindness, gentle with wayward souls, if also relentless in his criticism of untruths—theological and, latterly, financial. He was a happy warrior and a faithful friend, and I count our friendship as one of the great graces of my life.

—George Weigel

[1] The Introit can be heard at youtube.com/watch?v=b6gn-Gmj9tk.

Appendices

Homilies and a Eulogy Honoring George Cardinal Pell

I

First Anniversary of George Cardinal Pell's Death

Domus Australia, Rome
January 10, 2024

Just ten days after the death of Pope Benedict on New Year's Eve 2022, we were shocked by the news that Cardinal Pell, too, had preceded us into the house of the Heavenly Father. In the midst of the current battle for the "truth of the gospel" (Gal 2:14), as Paul boldly said to Peter's face, the pilgrim Church has lost two outstanding representatives of its sound apostolic doctrine. We grieve for them, but for those of us who do not think according to political categories, such as power and number of votes, but believe with Saint Augustine "that the Church advances safely on her pilgrimage between the persecutions of the world and the consolations of God" (De civ. Dei 18.51,2), we know that divine providence has given us both Pope Benedict and Cardinal Pell as role models of the true faith, and as powerful advocates with the Father.

As billions and billions of people come and go over the course of generations, the lasting importance of any individual man—most of whom will soon be forgotten—may seem doubtful. Those doubts are easily dispelled when we examine God's plan of salvation. God wants "all people to be saved and to come to the knowledge of the truth through the only mediator between God and men: the man Christ Jesus" (see 1 Tim 2:4–5). As we look forward in the hope of eternal life to come, we know from the outset that "[God] chose us in Christ before the world was made to be holy and faultless before him in love, marking us out for himself beforehand, to be adopted sons" (Eph 1:4–5, NJB). Theologically speaking, this means that we as creatures are not only determined by the contingency of our existence in the interplay of the finite world, but that our personhood is a parable of the aseity of God. God constituted us in the subsistence of our immortal soul. He called us by our name so that we could be counted as children and friends of God *and* actually be so in nature and grace. This dignity given to us by God is crowned in that he has made us co-workers in his universal plan of salvation—*cooperatores veritatis et gratiae*. In doing so, he enables us to participate in the actualisation of his kingdom in this world, and in the hearts of people. This is achieved through the specific grace given to each one of us according to the measure God has assigned to us (see 1 Pet 4:10).

One of these beloved sons whom God has called by his name is our brother George Pell. Born into a Christian family on June 8, 1941, he grew up in the Australian state of Victoria. With his athletic abilities and his high intellectual talent, which emerged during his school education, a brilliant career in the world would have been open to him. But he decided to follow Christ's call to the priestly service, which requires the dedication and willingness to sacrifice far beyond a mere philanthropic spirit. He crowned his studies at the world-famous Oxford, of which he was always very proud, with a dissertation. Its title is "The Exercise of Authority in Early Christianity from About 170 to 270". The young Father Pell's research included Irenaeus of Lyons, whom Pope Francis has declared to be a *Doctor Ecclesiae*. This greatest theologian of the second century established the valid hermeneutics of the Catholic faith against the manifold forms of Gnosticism and other heresies for all time, teaching that the one revelation of God in Christ has been handed down to us completely and unchangeably in the Church through Holy Scripture, the Apostolic Tradition, and the normative witness of the bishops in the Apostolic Succession. The teaching of the apostles can neither be expanded speculatively nor adapted in liturgical and pastoral practice to the changing spirit of the times nor sacrificed to the political and diplomatic constraints of Church politics.

With great boldness before the thrones of power and money, not to mention the arrogance of self-proclaimed but pseudointellectuals, Cardinal Pell faithfully and selflessly served the Church in Australia as a priest and then as bishop of Melbourne and Sydney. And finally, on October 21, 2003, John Paul II created him a cardinal of the Holy Roman Church. He was given special responsibility in the Roman Curia by Pope Francis, who appointed him to the newly created Council of Cardinals and appointed him prefect of the Vatican's Economic Council. Personally, I remember very well his commitment to marriage and family in the spirit of Christ's teachings—against their relativization by secularist-minded participants in the synod on this topic.

But the Enemy does not sleep. In the case of his faithful servant George Pell, Jesus' words were proved shockingly true: "If they have persecuted me, they will also persecute you.... They will do all this to you for my name's sake; for they do not know him who sent me" (see Jn 15:20–21). While Archbishop George Pell cared for victims of sexual abuse in an exemplary and compassionate manner during his time in Australia, he was relentlessly pursued by a blood-thirsty mob and made himself a victim of justice by anti-Catholic agitators in the media and in the police apparatus. He was held in solitary confinement for 404 days, a wrongfully convicted man, until he was finally released from prison by the High Court of Australia in a historic vote of 7 to 0.

With his three-volume *Prison Journal* (2019–2021) he has given us a great testimony of Christian patience in the midst of unjust suffering that, according to patristic standards, would have placed him, even during his lifetime, amongst the ranks of the confessors who immediately follow the martyrs in the *communio sanctorum*. This work is, to our mind, of comparable literary value to the work of Boethius, *De consolatione philosophiae*, which "the last Roman and first Scholastic" wrote in the dungeon of the Gothic king Theodoric. I also think of the Protestant pastor Dietrich Bonhoeffer, who wrote letters while imprisoned by the atheist German Nazi government. The persecution suffered by Cardinal Pell is the same persecution of Christians that recurs throughout history in different guises.

If you are looking for consolation in the distress of our time and want to assure yourself of Christ's word "Do not be afraid, I have overcome the world" (see Jn 16:33), then, in addition to the prison diary, you should read George Pell's last essay in the *Festschrift* for his friend and great Newman expert Ian Ker. Its significant and descriptive title is telling: "The Suffering Church in a Suffering World". Cardinal Pell's article concludes autobiographically with a memory of Gilbert Keith Chesterton, "who declared he was a pagan at the age of twelve, an agnostic at sixteen, became an Anglican at marriage, and was received into the Church in 1922 at the age of 48". And then Cardinal Pell continues, "In his best-known book *Orthodoxy* (1908), he writes of the 'thrilling romance of orthodoxy'. For him, it is easy to be a heretic, easy to let the age have its head. To have fallen into 'any of these open traps of error and exaggeration' would indeed have been simple, 'but to have avoided them all has been one whirling adventure; and in my vision the heavenly chariot flies thundering through the ages, the dull heresies sprawling and prostrate, the wild truth reeling but erect.'" And finally Cardinal Pell himself says at the end of his life and work in the vineyard of the Lord, "After eighty years of Catholic living, this is my vision."[1]

On January 10, 2023, here in Rome, the Lord told his faithful servant George Pell, "Well done, good and trustworthy servant, come and join in your master's happiness" (see Mt 25:23).

May he rest in peace.

—His Eminence Gerhard Cardinal Müller

[1] Cardinal George Pell, "The Suffering Church in a Suffering World", in *Lead Kindly Light: Essays for Ian Ker*, ed. Paul Shrimpton (Gracewing Publishing, 2022), 83.

11

Solemn Pontifical Funeral Mass of George Cardinal Pell, A.C.

St Mary's Cathedral, Sydney
Feast of the Presentation of the Lord
February 2, 2023

In 2007 Cardinal Pell issued guidelines reminding clergy that funeral homilies should focus on the Scriptures and the Catholic faith, especially regarding the Resurrection and God's mercy, and not be a eulogy or canonisation ceremony for the deceased. So, this one last time, Your Eminence, I will try to do as I'm told ...

In today's Gospel Jesus tells us to be ever-vigilant, like a householder on the lookout for a burglar, so that when the Lord comes we will be ready (see Lk 12:35–40). In the previous chapter Luke records another parable about determination, this time of a man banging on his neighbour's door in the middle of the night asking to borrow bread to entertain his guests (see Lk 11:5–8). The Greek word ἀναίδεια is rendered "persistence" in most translations,[1] since Jesus is commending perseverance in prayer and vigil. Yet "persistence" is a rather mild word for someone banging

[1] NRSVCE, ASV, GN, LB, NCB, etc.

on the door at 2:00 A.M. for party supplies! Ἀναίδεια was the Greek goddess of shamelessness or ruthlessness, and she lent her name to the quality of unembarrassed determination, regardless of circumstances.[2] In keeping vigil and persevering in prayer, in preaching the Gospel in season and out, and in pastoral outreach to every lost sheep, Christians should demonstrate an audacity that means they keep at it when others would give up.

It took more than a bit of Christian *shamelessness* for the son of a Ballarat publican to take a Roman monastery with a church, renovate it to Australian comfort standards, radically redecorate it, and so establish an Aussie watering hole—er, pilgrim house—in the heart of the Eternal City. It took *boldness* to get the bishops of Australia and the St Mary's Cathedral Choir there for the opening. And it took sheer *importunity* to bang on the door of the pope, asking him to bless and open the place—perhaps the only hotel ever opened by a pope! Yet ἀναίδεια was on-brand for Pell, and it enabled him to bring us not only Domus Australia but three good seminaries, four new Catholic tertiary institutions, the Benedict XVI Retreat Centre, the John Paul II Centre at Sydney Uni, several new institutes of consecrated women, a vastly expanded tertiary and youth apostolate, and World Youth Day—like the Domus opening, stuffed full of pope, bishops, and musicians, but with half a million idealistic young adults to boot!

Domus Australia is a high-standard hospitality centre for Aussie pilgrims in Rome. Yet to tour its chapel and public spaces is also to revisit the history and faith of the Church in Australia and to peer into the soul of George Pell.

[2] "Ἀναίδεια", Free Online Greek Dictionary, Bill Mounce, accessed January 7, 2025, https://billmounce.com/greek-dictionary/anaideia; Alan Johnson, "Assurance for Man: The Fallacy of Translating *Anaideia* by 'Persistence' in Luke 11:5–8'", *Journal of the Evangelical Theological Society* 22, no. 2 (1979): 123–31, and the sources therein.

The piety of earlier generations is told in the beautiful chapel architecture and in the rather sentimental paintings, inherited from the Marists, of *The Holy Family*, *Our Lady of the Rosary*, and the *Souls in Purgatory*. In his makeover the cardinal added altarpieces by Paul Newton of *Our Lady of the Southern Cross* and of the first Catholics praying before the Blessed Sacrament in 1818, as well as decorating the sanctuary with Australian emblems, flora, and fauna. Around the house we find images of the two Aboriginal novice monks who joined St. Paul's in Rome, and many items of indigenous Australian art.

So, while he rose to international prominence and roles, the cardinal remained very much an Australian to the end. As the Church had made enormous contributions to this great nation, he was convinced it has many strengths and will yet do much more good if it remains faithful to the Apostolic Tradition. So, all around Domus we see representations of Saint Mary MacKillop and Australia's first bishops, priests, nuns, and laity, of First Australians, convicts, and migrants, and what they built.

There are portraits also of contemplatives such as Brigid, Thérèse of Lisieux, and Bishop-Abbot Salvado—for Christians are people of prayer, and the cardinal drew from that well his composure amidst great challenges. Faithful to the Divine Office and mental prayer, he offered the Holy Sacrifice more than twenty thousand times.

On the walls of Domus there are also images of star pastors like Pius V, John Joseph Therry, Daniel Mannix, and John Paul—and for fifty-six years as a priest and thirty-five as a bishop, the cardinal's primary concerns were pastoral. Jesus told Peter to feed the sheep but also the lambs (see Jn 21:15), and George devoted much energy to building up young people through education, youth ministry, vocational discernment, and, of course, WYD-SYD08, the happiest and holiest week in the history of this nation.

There are paintings, too, of missionaries, preachers, and founders, such as Patrick, Dominic, and Francis Xavier—for the cardinal was an erudite preacher and public commentator, admired and hated for his willingness to contend with the culture on behalf of Christ and his Church. There are servants of the poor represented also, such as Mother Teresa with a beggar, and the first nuns who built so much of Australia's health and welfare infrastructure—as the cardinal knew weak humanity needs the Church's works of mercy.

There are educationalists, too, such as Mary Ward, Newman, and MacKillop—for the cardinal's great passion for truth and the life of the mind led him to create, defend, and strengthen Catholic education at every level.

There are also several martyrs portrayed: Fisher, More and Campion, Paul Miki, Andrew Kim, and Peter Chanel. But the most powerful portrait is that of the *white martyr* Cardinal Francis-Xavier Nguyen Van Thuan with his arms outstretched, kneeling in prayer in his prison cell. Little did Cardinal Pell know when he commissioned this work that his turn would come to spend 404 days in solitary confinement on what he good-humouredly called his "extended spiritual retreat". But then, John the Baptist, the apostles, and Jesus himself all had their prison time.[3]

Jesus told his disciples not to be surprised if the world hated them, as it had hated him first.[4] Persecution and suffering would be their opportunity to give witness.[5] And so, the cardinal accepted his fate with equanimity and forgiveness. Forbidden even to say Mass privately in his cell,

[3] Imprisonment of John the Baptist (Mt 11:2; 14:3–12), Peter (Acts 12:3–19), Paul (Acts 16:19–40; 22:24–28; 2 Tim 2:8–9; cf. Acts 21:11; 2 Cor 11:24–27), and other apostles (Acts 5:18–42) and Jesus himself (Mt 27:1–26).

[4] See Jn 15:18; 1 Jn 3:13.

[5] See Mt 5:10–12; 16:24–26; Mk 10:29–30; Lk 21:12–19; Jn 15:19–20.

he found a new apostolate fulfilling Jesus' call to visit and proclaim mercy to prisoners, as he corresponded with inmates from his cell.[6] He could say with Paul, "For your sake we are massacred daily and reckoned as sheep for the slaughter. These are the trials through which we triumph, by the power of Him who loves us" (see Rom 8:36).

Each painted hero in our Aussie pilgrim house gives us a peek into what drove George Pell the man and the priest: his passions for evangelisation, education, welfare, worship, and witness. But they also remind us of the many ways we can be saints—virtuous souls who ultimately abide safely in God's hands (see Wis 3:19). It is their company that the cardinal hoped to join in Heaven and their communion in which he strived to live on earth. Pope Francis recently called George "a great guy" to whom "we owe so much". Not everyone agrees. But if some experienced him as demanding, pugilistic, and polarising, and others as faithful, hospitable, and witty, it's now the turn of the saints to endure his teasing, lecturing, or commands ...

What all these saints and heroes had in common, of course, is faith in Jesus Christ. They spent their lives conforming themselves to his teachings and graces, above all to his life, death, and Resurrection. And so, in the courtyard at the heart of the Domus Australia complex stands a life-sized bronze of the Risen Christ.

George Pell's name saint was the rather martial Saint George. He was popularized as patron of England by Richard I (1157–1199), the king of England at the end of the twelfth century who wore the cross of Saint George on his chest. Six feet five inches tall, striking, and athletic, Richard dominated every room he entered. He was a far from perfect prince, but the calumnies of his enemies were baseless

[6] See Mt 25:36–45; Lk 4:18; 23:42–43.

and his imprisonment wrongful, and he is remembered by history as Cœur de Lion—the Lionheart—because of his courage. George Pell was also a giant of a man with a big vision who looms large in the history of the Church in Australia and amongst churchmen internationally. He had a big heart too, strong enough to fight for the faith and endure persecution but soft enough to care for priests, youth, the homeless, prisoners, and imperfect Christians. Ultimately that heart gave out, but only after more than eighty years of being gradually transformed to the heart of Jesus.

Twenty-three days ago the lion's roar was unexpectedly silenced. But George the Lionheart was dressed with the cross on his chest and ready, awaiting his Master's return. His influence has been far-reaching, and we can be confident it will long continue. He may even be more effective from his new address! Only yesterday I celebrated Mass to welcome seventeen new admissions to Sydney's Seminary of the Good Shepherd. That's the largest intake in the history of Good Shepherd Seminary. You have to go back thirty-seven years to 1986 since that many entered its predecessor seminary of St Patrick's, Manly. For our family to receive seventeen newcomers as it loses one leonine old-timer is a great grace!

I know that Cardinal Pell, such a great friend of seminarians and young priests and such a believer in the good that priests do, was interceding for this. At this news I expect he is doing cartwheels with his new hips and heart in Heaven! God grant an eternal reward to this man of ἀυαίδέια, who loved his Lord and served his Church shamelessly, vehemently, courageously to the end.

—Most Rev. Anthony C. Fisher, O.P.

III

Requiem Mass for George Cardinal Pell

St Mary MacKillop Church, Keilor Downs
January 23, 2023

Readings: Isaiah 40:1–11; Psalm 23; 1 Peter 5:1–10; Matthew 5:1–12

Cardinal Pell once observed that it's easy to talk about a good man at his funeral but that it's difficult to preach over a bad man. One might be tempted to fill tonight's homily with anecdotes about his colourful and often undiplomatic turns of phrase, and there were many of those. I remember at a Mass for Mother Teresa in 1997, that when the archbishop was presented with the prayers for the repose of the dead, he said, in a stage whisper that was heard around the cathedral, "I'm not reading that. Listen, Portelli, if Mother Teresa isn't in Heaven, then I, and most certainly you, have absolutely no chance of getting there. Find something else!" Perhaps this approach would work better if we were standing around the public bar of the Royal Oak Hotel in South Street Ballarat, where George Pell Senior was the publican. We could reflect on the cardinal's prodigious achievements, the buildings and institutions he founded both north and south of the

Murray River and over the equator. He was, for instance, immodestly proud of his rendition of Pooh-Bah, the Lord High Everything Else, from Gilbert and Sullivan's *Mikado*, which was acclaimed on two continents.

We might reflect on his talents or his erudition, both equally impressive. He was the embodiment of the motto of one of his boyhood heroes whose successor he would become: Archbishop Daniel Mannix. His motto was taken from Saint Paul's Letter to the Corinthians, where the Apostle says that he has made himself all things to all to save some at any cost. *Omnia Omnibus* (1 Cor 9:22) was as true of Archbishop Mannix as it was of Cardinal Pell.

I think that the cardinal would direct me to spend few words on his achievements and instead reflect on the faith that he professed and taught, as Saint Paul advised Timothy: "Preach the word; be prepared in season and out of season; correct, rebuke and encourage—with great patience and careful instruction" (2 Tim 4:2, NIV).

In an interview with the cardinal published on the day of his death, he repeated a phrase that I believe was the informing principle of all he achieved in nearly sixty years of priesthood and thirty-five years of episcopal leadership and service. I first heard him say the same thing in 1985 when he became rector of Corpus Christi College. He said, "We stand under the Word of God. We are the defenders and the servants of the Apostolic Tradition, not its masters."

His Eminence was not shy of repeating this to anyone, whatever their rank within the Church or the wider society, believer and unbeliever alike. He was absolutely convinced that it is only the truth that liberates and completes a person. And truth is to be found in the person and mission of the Only Son of God and in his Body, the Church. Saint Cyprian of Carthage, about whom the young Father Pell wrote his doctoral thesis at Oxford, said that "one cannot have God as his Father if he does not have the Church as his Mother."

So then, what we should do is to listen carefully to the Word we have heard and to find there and understand something of what was in the mind and heart of our dear friend.

When the prophet Isaiah was sent to a struggling and dispirited Israel, he began by urging them to repent and prepare the way for the Lord. Since the beginning of the Christian tradition these words have been also ascribed to John the Baptist. He was another of the cardinal's heroes. More than once he said that if John were to appear today, the clarion call of his message "Repent and believe" would remain exactly the same because faith can never take root in a divided heart.

"Be not afraid", the prophet cries. When Archbishop Pell adopted this as his motto, he was making a resolution to live out his vocation as a bishop in the light of John Paul the Great's appeal to the world at the beginning of his pontificate: "Do not be afraid! Open wide the doors for Christ!"

John Paul was addressing the mighty, the powerful of this world, who feared that Christ might take away something of their power if they were to let him in, if they were to allow the faith to be free. He was speaking to the young and the old, the poor and the rich, people of faith and those who are seeking the truth.

The cardinal's concern for the wider Church, especially the Church of silence, is best exemplified by his many visits to the oppressed and poor churches of China, Cambodia, the Ukraine, and India over a tenure of ten years as chairman of Caritas Australia. He visited them usually disguised as a teacher, dressed in a bad suit and collar and tie. He was given plenipotentiary powers by the Holy See so that he could reconcile to full communion with the Church those who had been separated from it. Only rarely would he speak of the living martyrs, especially those in the Chinese underground Church—bishops, priests, religious, and laity who in some cases endured years of imprisonment for the sake of their profession of the one, holy, apostolic, and catholic faith. I think that here he learnt how to remain constant in his faith, regardless of the prevailing wind.

Isaiah imagines the infinite Creator as a shepherd cradling the wounded lambs in his arms. I think that this image was at the heart of George Pell, the pastor.

In 1996 Archbishop Pell, as he was then, went to Rome to receive the pallium for Melbourne from Pope Saint John Paul II. He received another for Sydney in 2001. The pallium is a narrow band of lambswool embroidered with black crosses worn around the shoulders by an archbishop in his province. Both palliums will be buried with him.

When the pallium was imposed, this is what the Holy Father said to the new archbishop: "On the day of the coming and manifestation of our great God and chief shepherd, Jesus Christ, may you and the flock entrusted to you be clothed with immortality and glory."

A number of family and friends had travelled to Rome in 1996, and the archbishop organised various events for his visitors. One such event was a visit to the Catacomb of Callixtus. Many popes and martyrs were buried there. Some of the earliest Christian artworks can still be seen there, including the first image of the Good Shepherd. I can still see the archbishop in the dim light pointing out the almost spectral figure of the young man carrying the lost sheep to green pastures and the restful waters of eternity.

In his homily (which he said was the most important one he ever delivered) at Barangaroo the day before the pope's arrival for World Youth Day, the cardinal had this to say about the Good Shepherd:

> In developing this image on one occasion, Jesus explained that such a shepherd was prepared to leave the ninety-nine sheep to search out the one who was lost....
>
> Jesus was saying that both He and His Father are ... like this, because He knows each one of His sheep and like a good father he goes searching for the lost one he loves, particularly if he is sick, or in trouble, or unable to help himself....
>
> I begin by welcoming and encouraging anyone, anywhere who regards himself or herself as lost, in deep distress, with hope diminished or even exhausted.
>
> Young or old, woman or man, Christ is still calling those who are suffering to come to him for healing, as he has for two thousand years. The causes of the wounds are quite secondary, whether they be drugs or alcohol, family breakups, the lusts of the flesh, loneliness or a death. Perhaps even the emptiness of success.[1]

Few people were ever aware of the cardinal's genuine empathy and concern for those who were in trouble or in need. These encounters were never recorded or the subject of commentary. Like most men of his background and generation, he did not wear his heart on his sleeve. I remember being with him when he visited a facility for severely disabled children. A suitable speech had been prepared for the occasion, but when he saw his congregation, he put the speech aside and spoke very tenderly to the children and their families about the Good Shepherd. He was genuinely and deeply moved not because of the appalling disabilities they endured but because he could see in their faces a profound joy that suffering could not destroy.

[1] Cardinal George Pell, Homily for World Youth Day 2008 Opening Mass (Barangaroo, July 15, 2008), https://www.ewtn.com/catholicism/library/homily-for-world-youth-day-2008-opening-mass-3817.

We turn now to the second reading from the Letter of Saint Peter. Like the man himself, it is direct, almost blunt in its message. Peter is no Paul, but the urgency of his appeal is still apparent after nineteen centuries. The letter was written to Christians in Asia Minor who were beginning to experience the contempt of a society who preferred that this minority and their inconvenient Gospel should disappear without trace. Peter urges the elders to be genuine, consistent, and authentic in their governance. He urges the juniors to clothe themselves in humility.

Even though Nero had not yet released his lions—his persecution would begin about three years later—Peter can hear them roar. Paul uses the same image in his last letter to Timothy where he waits, like Peter, with quiet confidence for the crown of victory. In our time the lion roars on X, which is no less effective in drowning the voice of faith.

Should we be surprised that the lions are still roaring and looking for someone to eat? Life would have been far easier for Peter if, as legend has it, he had not met Christ carrying his Cross along the Appian Way to Rome, even as Peter was on the same road escaping the fury of Nero and the mob. "Quo vadis, Domine?" (Where are you going, Lord?) "To Rome to be crucified again", the Lord answered. Peter was once told by the Risen Lord that in his old age someone would tie a belt around him and take him where he would rather not go. This all came to pass for Peter and again for many confessors of the faith through the ages.

Another of the cardinal's heroes was the archbishop of Zagreb, Blessed Aloysius Stepinac. He endured and to some extent still endures unjust condemnation for the faith he professed and for his desire for justice for his country. He endured years of solitary confinement and then eleven years of house arrest in his home parish as the assistant priest even though he was created a cardinal in 1953. He managed to maintain a lively correspondence, sending letters hidden in hollowed-out vegetables from his garden. He wrote in one of his journals, "I know what my duty is. With the grace of God I will carry it out to the end, without hatred towards anyone and without fear for anyone."

These were the same attitudes that Cardinal Pell demonstrated in his observance of the long Good Friday of these latter years. He once quipped that prison was ten Lents in succession, which he hoped would make up in some way for Lents not well observed. Shortly before his sentencing we were able to meet for the first time in three years. He showed me letters he had received from both Francis and Benedict. Both encouraged him to carry the cross that had come his way. The cardinal said to me that he accepted the ordeal ahead as God's will for him. He said this without any trace of recrimination or bitterness. He remained the same, maybe even more so, after the spectacular decision of the High Court.

In his prison diaries the cardinal detailed the course of each day: regular prayer, although without Mass; exercise, which included sweeping the corridors and playing table tennis by himself; reading and reflecting on the four thousand letters that came in from every part of the world; writing in his journals—the text eventually ran to over half a million words. Tolstoy's *War and Peace* is only slightly longer. Reading his journals is a bit like sitting down with him at dinner—titbits of domestic news, a commentary on current affairs, and always a moment of reflection on an aspect of faith. We should note that he wrote very few letters to people outside the prison. Always the pastor, most of his letters were to other prisoners, encouraging them, answering their questions, and assuring them of his prayers. He maintained this correspondence even after his release.

Once inside he soon came to understand that as a prisoner in solitary confinement, he was now the lowest of the low, the bottom of the pile, as he put it. He found the regular strip searches especially humiliating. He was advised that the days would pass more easily if he allowed himself one small treat. He decided that it would be two squares of chocolate each night. It's hard to reconcile how the person the media labelled as "the third most important and powerful Catholic in the world" would have to count the squares in a bar of chocolate to make it last until he could afford to replace it. Last summer (2022) he stayed with me here at Keilor Downs. One night he settled down to watch television. He said it was a vice he only acquired whilst inside. We watched the Nicolas Cage and John Malkovich film *Con Air*—a film about escaping convicts—which he rather enjoyed. At eleven o'clock I asked if he wanted anything else, as the kitchen was closing. Rather timidly he asked if there were any Magnum[2] ice creams in the freezer. I asked whether he had ever had ice cream whilst inside. He said no, sadly. Praise the Lord for 7-Eleven stores. The next night we watched *The Two Popes* in reparation for *Con Air* and ate the rest of the Magnums.

Finally, we turn to the Gospel of the Beatitudes—the text His Eminence usually chose when he celebrated funerals. In the Gospel, Jesus, the New Moses, climbs a hill—a reference to Sinai—and summons his disciples. Here he gives the New Law. Pope Saint John Paul said this in his homily on the Mount of the Beatitudes in 2000, the Year of the Great Jubilee: "These two mountains—Sinai and the Mount of the Beatitudes—offer us the roadmap of our Christian life and a summary of our responsibilities to God and neighbour. The Law and the Beatitudes together

[2] Magnum is a brand of ice cream.

mark the path of the following of Christ and the royal road to spiritual maturity and freedom."[3]

The Catholic thinker G.K. Chesterton, whose common-sense approach resonated with the cardinal, wrote a short book on Saint Francis of Assisi. He said that the way Saint Francis viewed the world was as if it was upside-down. That is to say, the whole world is hanging and depending upon God. He continued, "On first reading the Sermon on the Mount, you feel as if it turns everything upside down, but on the second reading you realise that it turns everything right side up. The first time you read it you feel that it is impossible; the second time you feel that nothing else is possible."

Cardinal Pell understood this challenge to the wisdom of this world. Recently he wrote, "Are the teachings of Christ—and especially Catholic ideas on sacrifice and sexuality, on the need for prayer and repentance—simply outdated, superseded just like the belief the sun revolves around the earth? Has the theory of evolution and millions of years of dinosaurs knocked Judeo-Christian revelation off its perch? ... [Has] the age of religion ... passed so that it is no longer possible to keep Christianity up to date?"[4]

True wealth is found in poverty; mercy is born of forgiveness; meekness is real power; the vision of divinity begins with purity of heart. Most disconcertingly, peace is found in calumny and eternal life in persecution. Cardinal Pell lived and preached this paradox in season and out of season. Some listened; many would not. He remained

[3]John Paul II, Jubilee Pilgrimage of His Holiness John Paul II to the Holy Land (homily, Mount of the Beatitudes, Korazim, Israel, March 24, 2000), 2, https://www.vatican.va/content/john-paul-ii/en/travels/2000/documents/hf_jp-ii_hom_20000324_korazim-israel.html.

[4]George Cardinal Pell, "Standing with the Word of God", *First Things*, September 22, 2022, https://www.firstthings.com/web-exclusives/2022/09/standing-with-the-word-of-god.

undaunted by the judgement of this world. There was only one judge that he feared, and he hoped that he would face him with confidence in the next world.

We shall not see the cardinal's like again in our lifetime. His legacy will be both praised and denigrated. So how would he like to be remembered? Perhaps we should let him tell us. The last entries in his journal were written in the peaceful calm of the Kew Carmel and the Sydney Seminary. His journey there included a spectacular chase by two helicopters. A posse of reporters tailed him all the way to Sydney. He was mildly amused by all the fuss. He says,

> For seventy years, I have been writing and often found it hard work, a bit like prayer. But I didn't find it difficult to write this long journal; words flowed regularly, and on some occasions I suspected this might be providential for some, perhaps many, so I hope that these pages will be helpful religiously and socially to more than a few adults, be they Catholic or non-Catholic, believer or agnostic. After all, Christ rode into Jerusalem on his donkey.
>
> In a few days on Holy Saturday night during the Easter Vigil, the Paschal Candle will again be blessed and dedicated to the man-God, whom I love and serve, whom I have followed for all my life, just as saints and sinners, firebrands and the lukewarm have done for nearly two thousand years.
>
> Christ yesterday and today.
> The beginning and the end.
> The Alpha and the Omega.
> All time belongs to Him,
> And all the ages.[5]

—Monsignor Charles Portelli

[5] George Cardinal Pell, *Prison Journal*, vol. 3, *The High Court Frees an Innocent Man* (Ignatius Press, 2021), 333.

IV

Eulogy for His Eminence George Cardinal Pell

St Mary's Cathedral, Sydney
February 2, 2023

This funeral is less a sad farewell to a great friend and more a joyous tribute to a great hero.

It's the celebration of a wonderful life, a once-in-a-generation gathering of the people of faith to rededicate ourselves to the ideals George Pell lived for and to draw strength from one another for the struggles ahead.

He was a priest, a bishop, and the prefect of a Vatican secretariat, but he was never a mere functionary; in each of these roles he was a thinker, a leader, a Christian warrior, and a proud Australian who wanted our country and our civilisation to succeed.

In the pulpit, from the lectern, on television, in the Opinion pages, across the dinner table, after Mass, in the confessional—as everyone here would know—he was always thoughtful, often charismatic, occasionally imperious, constantly concerned for the well-being of others, and a pastoral priest who could find an echo of Christ even in the worst sinner.

In short, he's the greatest Catholic Australia has produced, and one of our country's greatest sons.

No one else has been both archbishop of Melbourne and archbishop of Sydney. No other Australian has been as senior in the leadership of the Roman Church or as influential in its conclaves.

He was instrumental in the foundation of three centres of higher learning: the Australian Catholic University; the University of Notre Dame, here in Australia; and Campion College—perhaps his favourite—named for the Jesuit martyr, which was our first liberal arts school, dedicated to giving its students a good grounding in the great books and the great debates that have shaped our civilisation and made it man's finest social and cultural achievement so far.

And far from being an apologist, or a dissembler about the sins of the Church—personal, financial, or intellectual—he was their hammer. As he knew, *eccelesia semper reformanda*—the Church is always in need of reform.

Here in Australia he was the first archbishop to sack misbehaving clergy and report them to the police, rather than hide them in another parish. In Rome he tried to ensure that the collections from the faithful were used for the glory of God, rather than the indulgence of the higher clergy. Most recently, he called a draft of a Vatican document further eroding the Apostolic Tradition a "toxic nightmare". He was never one to mince his words.

To the smug, to the venal, to the lazy, to the wayward, and to the intellectually sloppy, he was an existential reproach—and because that's all of us, in some way, it's hardly surprising that he became a target.

For all his presence and his natural authority, he was personally humble and never fell for the modern conceit, that he was bigger than that which had shaped him: faith, Church, and country.

In his celebrated eulogy for another Catholic hero, B. A. Santamaria, he declared that it was "the mark of the false prophet that all men speak well of him", before observing that Bob had "triumphantly avoided this fate". And so it was, even more, with the cardinal himself.

His recent observation that the climate change movement, quote, had "some of the characteristics of a low-level, not-too-demanding pseudo religion" was the kind of comment that enraged its adherents, precisely because it was true.

Throughout history that's what people have been martyred for—for telling the unpopular, unpalatable truth—and it's not possible to honour the cardinal without some reference to his persecution.

He was made a scapegoat for the Church itself. He should never have been investigated in the absence of a complaint. He should never have been charged in the absence of corroborating evidence. And he should never have been convicted in the absence of a plausible case—as the High Court so resoundingly made plain.

Had he died in jail, without the High Court's vindication, this—today—would have been a very different event, even though his innocence would have been no less had it been known only to God.

Still, the presence of so many here, from all walks and stations of life—many not Catholic, some not Christian, a few without any religious faith at all—is an overdue tribute and perhaps an admission that we should strive to do right in death to those who've been wronged in life.

His greatest triumph, in fact, was not to have held the highest ecclesiastical offices of any Australian but to have kept his faith in circumstances that must have screamed, "My God, my God, why hast thou forsaken me?" Not to succumb to anger, self-pity, or despair—when almost any other human would—but instead to accept this modern-day crucifixion, walking humbly in the footsteps of Our

Lord, is the heroic virtue that makes him, to my mind, a saint for our times.

And as I heard the chant "Cardinal Pell should go to Hell", I thought, Aha! At least they now believe in the afterlife! Perhaps this is Saint George Pell's first miracle.

Indeed, the ultimately triumphant life of this soldier for truth, to advance through smear and doubt to victory, should drive a renewal of confidence throughout the universal Church.

If character means "to trust yourself when all men doubt you but make allowance for their doubting too"; if it means bearing "to hear the truth you've spoken twisted by knaves to make a trap for fools", George Pell was the greatest man I've ever known. And if faith means the ability to endure crushing adversity, no one could be a better advertisement for it—especially for those of us for whom it often remains tantalisingly out of reach. As a centurion in the Gospel said, "Lord, I believe; help my unbelief!"

So I will hold on to him in my heart, from love of a friend and mentor, and as a gentle chide for virtues sought but not yet attained.

And in these times, when it's more needful than ever to fight the good fight, to stay the course, and to keep the faith, it's surely now for the Australian Church to trumpet the cause of its greatest champion. There should be Pell study courses, Pell spirituality courses, Pell lectures, Pell high schools, and Pell university colleges, just as there are for the other saints. If we can direct our prayers to Mother Teresa, Thomas à Becket, and Saint Augustine, why not the late cardinal too, who's been just as pleasing to God, I'm sure, and has the added virtue of being the very best of us.

—The Honourable Anthony John (Tony) Abbott

CONTRIBUTORS

The Honourable Anthony John (Tony) Abbott was educated at Saint Ignatius' College Riverview and then studied economics and law at the University of Sydney before attending Queen's College, Oxford, as a Rhodes scholar, studying philosophy, politics, and economics. While a student at Oxford, Abbott earned two blues for boxing. He became Australia's twenty-eighth prime minister, and since September 2020 he has been an adviser to the British government's Board of Trade.

Dame Joanna Bogle is a writer, lecturer, and historian and author of over twenty books, including a biography of the Australian pioneer heroine Caroline Chisholm. She lectures for the Maryvale Institute based at St Mary's University, Twickenham. After helping establish a British branch of the international Catholic charity Aid to the Church in Need, she was active with it for over forty years. In 2013 she was honoured by Pope Benedict XVI as a Dame of the Order of Saint Gregory the Great.

Andrew Bolt is Australia's most read columnist, writing for News Corp newspapers, including Melbourne's *Herald Sun* and Sydney's *Daily Telegraph*. He presents his weekday opinion show *The Bolt Report* on Sky News Australia. His books include *Still Not Sorry* and *Worth Fighting For*, and his evening radio show on 2GB with Steve Price led the ratings in Melbourne, Sydney, and Brisbane. He has three children and a very old dog and lives like a hermit outside Melbourne, where he cooks and reads.

The Honourable Jacinta **Collins** is a former Australian parliamentary leader and Labor senator for Victoria who served over a twenty-five-year period in a number of portfolios, including deputy leader in the Senate, parliamentary secretary for School Education and Workplace Relations, and minister for Mental Health and Aging. She was also the first woman to be appointed manager of Government Business in the Senate. Before entering Parliament, Jacinta was a social worker and union official and was educated at Monash and La Trobe Universities. On her retirement from Parliament, Jacinta was appointed executive director of the National Catholic Education Commission in February 2019. In 2023 she was awarded an honorary doctorate of letters from the University of Notre Dame Australia for her contribution to public life and education.

His Eminence Thomas Christopher Cardinal **Collins** was the bishop of Saint Paul in Alberta from 1997 to 1999, archbishop of Edmonton from 1999 to 2006, and archbishop of Toronto from 2007 to 2023. He holds a bachelor of arts in English from St. Jerome's University, Waterloo, a master of arts in English from the University of Western Ontario, a bachelor of theology from St. Peter's Seminary in London, Ontario, and a doctorate in sacred theology from the Pontifical Gregorian University.

His Eminence Timothy Michael Cardinal **Dolan** is the archbishop of New York. From 1994 to 2001 he was the rector of the Pontifical North American College; from 2001 to 2002, auxiliary bishop of St. Louis; and from 2002 to 2009, archbishop of Milwaukee. He holds a licentiate in sacred theology from the Angelicum and a doctorate in Church history from the Catholic University of America.

Monica **Doumit** is the director of public affairs and engagement for the Catholic Archdiocese of Sydney. She is an adjunct senior lecturer in law at the University of Notre Dame Australia and a regular columnist for *The Catholic Weekly*. Prior to working for the archdiocese, Monica worked as a corporate lawyer in Sydney and London, and she holds degrees in law and medical science, a diploma in finance, and a master's degree in bioethics.

Mary Julian **Ekman** works at the chancery of the Archdiocese of Sydney. She has a Ph.D. from the Catholic University of America, Washington, D.C., and is an adjunct lecturer at the University of Notre Dame Australia.

Most Rev. Peter J. **Elliott** is an auxiliary bishop emeritus of the Archdiocese of Melbourne. He was educated at Melbourne Grammar and then earned an honours degree in history from the University of Melbourne, where he was a resident student at Trinity College. He later read theology at the University of Oxford and obtained a doctorate in sacred theology from the Pontifical Lateran University's Institute for Studies on Marriage and Family in Rome. Bishop Elliott has also served in the Roman Curia as an official of the Pontifical Council for the Family, as a consultor for the Congregation for Divine Worship and the Discipline of the Sacraments, and as a member of Anglicanae Traditiones, the interdicasterial commission charged with preparing the liturgical books to be used by the personal ordinariates that Pope Benedict XVI established for Anglican converts to Catholicism.

Most Rev. Anthony C. Fisher, O.P., is the archbishop of Sydney. He was educated at Saint Ignatius' College Riverview; the University of Sydney, where he obtained degrees in arts and law; the Yarra Theological Union, where he obtained an honours degree in theology; and the University of Oxford, where he completed his doctorate in bioethics. He is a Dominican and moral theologian and the author of numerous books and articles. He presently serves on five Vatican bodies: the Pontifical Academy for Life, the Dicastery for the Doctrine of the Faith, the Dicastery for the Oriental Churches, the Council of the Synod of Bishops, and the Pontifical Academy of St. Thomas. He was a member of the Synod of Bishops on Youth in 2018 and the Synod on Synodality in 2023–2024.

Jean-Baptiste Douville de Franssu is a French investment management and banking professional. He has been the chairman of the supervisory board of the *Istituto per le Opere di Religione* (IOR)—the Institute for the Works of Religion, more commonly known as the Vatican Bank—since July 2014.

Clara Geoghegan, B.A. (Monash), B. Theol. (C.T.C.), Grad.Dip.Ed, is the executive secretary of two commissions at the Australian Catholic Bishops Conference: the Bishops Commission for Evangelisation, Laity and Ministry and the Bishops Commission for Life, Family and Public Engagement. She taught Church history at the Catholic Theological College, Melbourne (2004–2018). A research interest for Clara is promoting the canonisation of Caroline Chisholm. She has worked throughout Australia helping adults discern their spiritual gifts to animate the lay vocation. Clara has three adult children: Caroline, Dominic, and Timothy.

Professor Ashley Goldsworthy, A.O., O.B.E., K.S.S., K.M., K.S.C., F.T.S.E., F.C.I.E., is an Australian computer scientist and business executive. He was federal president of the Liberal Party of Australia from 1990 to 1993. He holds numerous academic qualifications across the fields of business, science (especially computer science), leadership studies, theology, and law, including canon law, as well as civil honours in the Order of Australia and the Order of the British Empire, and he is a papal knight in the Order of St. Sylvester, Pope.

Sister Mary Helen Hill, O.P., hails from Melbourne, where she pursued studies in science and chemical engineering when George Pell was the archbishop of Melbourne. She later joined the Dominican Sisters of Saint Cecilia, who were invited to serve in Australia by Cardinal Pell. Subsequently, she was assigned to work in the fields of the education and evangelisation of young people in schools and university chaplaincies in both Sydney and Melbourne. In her ongoing studies she has completed various graduate degrees in theology and education.

Rev. Dr. Peter Joseph is parish priest of St. Mel's in the Archdiocese of Sydney. He was educated at Saint Ignatius' College Riverview and then studied in Rome at the Pontificio Collegio Urbano de Propaganda Fide. He holds a doctorate in sacred theology from the Pontifical Gregorian University and lectures in dogmatic theology at the Catholic Institute of Sydney.

Paul Kelly is editor-at-large at *The Australian*. He is a former editor-in-chief of the paper. He writes on Australian politics, public policy, and international relations. He has covered the political careers of every Australian prime minister from Gough Whitlam to Anthony Albanese. He holds a bachelor of arts and diploma of education from the University of Sydney and a doctor of letters from the University of Melbourne. He also holds honorary doctorates from the University of New South Wales and Griffith University and is a fellow of the Academy of Social Sciences in Australia. He has been a Shorenstein Fellow at the Kennedy School at Harvard University and a visiting lecturer at the Weatherhead Center for International Affairs at Harvard.

Rev. Fr. Roberto Joseph **Keryakos** was born in Sydney to parents of Italian and Lebanese heritage. He entered St Mary's Cathedral Choir as a chorister in 2001, the year George Cardinal Pell was appointed eighth archbishop of Sydney. He remained in the choir during his school years and into his university studies at the University of New South Wales, where he graduated in 2013 with bachelor of music and bachelor of education degrees. In 2013 he joined the Seminary of the Good Shepherd, Homebush, and was ordained to the diaconate on December 15, 2019, in his home parish of St Raphael's, South Hurstville, by Bishop Anthony Randazzo. By then Cardinal Pell was in jail but was present at his ordination to the priesthood on September 19, 2020, by Archbishop Anthony Fisher, O.P. in St Mary's Cathedral. Father Roberto is a priest for the Archdiocese of Sydney, and his appointments have included assistant priest at All Saints', Liverpool; Sacred Heart, Cabramatta; and now full circle at St Mary's Cathedral. He has also served as chaplain to the Cathedral Choir and Cathedral College.

Anna Maria **Krohn**, O.A.M. is the executive director of the Thomas More Centre, the national convener of the Anima

Women's Organisation, chair of the Life Council of the Australian Catholic Bishops Conference, and board member of the Caroline Chisholm Catholic Library. She teaches in various settings and is a sessional lecturer at the University of Notre Dame Australia. She holds a bachelor of theology degree from the Catholic Theological College (now the University of Divinity) in the Archdiocese of Melbourne.

Stephen (Steve) **Lawrence** was a professional Australian Football Premiership player with Hawthorn (1991). He has vast experience working with young people, teachers, and leaders in education and ministry, as well as married people and families. His missionary adventures include serving as director of Emmanuel School of Mission in Rome (2000–2003) and as director of the World Youth Day in Sydney (2008). He is an entrepreneur, leadership speaker, executive coach, and mentor with Altum Leadership Group. He has a degree in humanities, a graduate diploma in education, and a master of arts degree from the John Paul II Institute for Marriage and Family (Melbourne). His third book, *The Tiny Book for Giant Men*, was published by Parousia Media in 2023. He and his wife, Annie, have six children.

Sister **Mary Grace**, S.V., grew up on the shores of Sydney and graduated from the University of Notre Dame Australia with a degree in theology. She then entered the Sisters of Life in New York in 2013 and made her final vows in 2023. During this time she has been missioned in Canada, offering retreats, serving vulnerable women and their children, born and unborn, and inviting those wounded by abortion into the healing mercy of Jesus. Sister has also served in her order's evangelisation mission that fosters a culture of life throughout the world.

John McCarthy, K.C., G.C.P.O., K.C.S.G., is a Sydney barrister who served as Australia's ambassador to the Holy See from 2012 to 2016. He graduated from the University of Sydney with degrees in arts and law and holds a master of laws degree from the University of Virginia. From 2005 to 2010 he was prochancellor of the University of Sydney, and he has held various positions on the boards of governance of ecclesial organisations. These include president of the St Thomas More Society of New South Wales (1993–2005) and member of the Australian board of Aid to the Church in Need (1994–2012). He currently serves as chairman of the Archdiocese of Sydney's Anti-Slavery Taskforce. While serving as Australia's ambassador to the Holy See, he founded the Vatican Cricket Club, whose members famously beat the Queen's Cricket Club at Windsor in 2018. He and his late wife, Christine, a renowned concert pianist, share six children and nine grandchildren.

Rev. Fr. Josh Miechels is a priest of the Emmanuel Community for the Archdiocese of Sydney. He holds a pontifical licentiate in theology from the Institut Catholique de Paris and is currently the administrator of St Peter Chanel and St Joseph Parish, Berala, New South Wales.

Rev. Dr. Wilson D. (Bill) Miscamble, C.S.C., is a priest in the Congregation of Holy Cross and a professor of history at the University of Notre Dame (Indiana). The Australian native was educated at the University of Queensland and then at Notre Dame (Indiana). He was ordained a priest on April 9, 1988. Father Miscamble's primary research interests are American foreign policy since World War II and the role of Catholics in twentieth-century U.S. politics and foreign policy. He has published a number of books and articles in these areas. Father Miscamble also has notable interests in the areas of Catholic higher education and Catholics and public life, and he lectures and writes on these topics. His study *American Priest: The Ambitious Life and Conflicted Legacy of Notre Dame's Father Ted Hesburgh* was published by Image in 2019. He is a member of the Notre Dame chapter of University Faculty for Life.

Rev. Dr. Gregory **Morgan** is the parish priest of St. Catherine Labouré, Gymea, in the Archdiocese of Sydney. He holds an M.Phil. from the University of Cambridge and a D.Phil. from the University of Oxford. Father Gregory teaches philosophy and ethics at the University of Notre Dame Australia and the Catholic Institute of Sydney. He is the author of *Natural Law and the Secular Mythos* (Bloomsbury, 2024).

His Eminence Gerhard Cardinal **Müller** served as the cardinal-prefect of the Congregation for the Doctrine of the Faith (CDF) from his appointment by Pope Benedict XVI in 2012 until 2017. In 1986 Cardinal Müller was appointed to the chair of dogmatic theology of the Ludwig Maximilian University of Munich, where he remains an honorary professor.

Tim **O'Leary** is executive director of stewardship at the Archdiocese of Melbourne. He has extensive corporate experience in the oil, banking, and telecommunications industries and holds an honours degree in arts and a graduate diploma in philosophy from the University of Melbourne.

David **Pell** is the younger brother of Cardinal Pell. He has been a practising public accountant for over fifty years, with a brief sortie into hospitality ownership. He still provides accounting and management advice to hospitality venues. He lives in Central Victoria and is married with four children and a grandson, Sonny, and granddaughter, Billie.

Monsignor Charles **Portelli** is the parish priest of St Mary MacKillop Church in Keilor Downs, Melbourne. He was master of ceremonies to Cardinal Pell whilst he was archbishop of Melbourne. He collaborated with Cardinal Pell on the restoration of St. Patrick's Cathedral and Corpus Christi College in Melbourne and in the development of Domus Australia in Rome and the Benedict XVI Centre in Sydney.

Most Rev. Julian **Porteous** was ordained a priest for the Archdiocese of Sydney in 1974. After serving in a number of parishes in the greater Sydney area, he was appointed rector of the Seminary of the Good Shepherd in 2002. In 2003 he was ordained auxiliary bishop of Sydney along with now-Archbishop Anthony Fisher, O.P. For ten years he served as auxiliary bishop under Cardinal Pell. In 2013 he was appointed archbishop of Hobart, Tasmania.

Professor Hayden **Ramsay** is the president of the Catholic Institute of Sydney. He has over thirty years' experience in speaking, publishing, advising on ethical issues, and teaching philosophy. He is regularly consulted by educational, health, business, faith, and community organisations on strengthening their ethical capacities and seeking guidance from philosophical questioning. He holds a Ph.D. in philosophy and a master's in mental philosophy from the University of Edinburgh.

Rev. Fr. Anthony **Robbie** is the parish priest of St Anne's and St Patrick's in the beachside suburb of Bondi in the

Archdiocese of Sydney. He attended Saint Ignatius' College Riverview and then Sydney University, where he attained degrees in arts and law, specialising in history. He also holds licentiates in ecclesiastical history and sacred theology from the Gregorian University. He lectures widely in the fields of Church history and doctrine. He is a conventual chaplain *ad honorem* of the Sovereign Military Order of St John of Jerusalem, Rhodes, and Malta, and he worked in the Roman Curia as private secretary to Cardinal Pell when Pell was the prefect of the Secretariat for the Economy. He currently serves as postulator of the cause for the canonisation of Eileen O'Connor.

The Honourable Brad Rowswell, M.L.A., is currently the Shadow Minister for Digital Transformation and Public Service Innovation in the state of Victoria. He is a member of the Australian Liberal Party representing the seat of Sandringham. He and his wife, Kate, have two children, Abigail and Charles.

Rev. Dr. Jerome Santamaria is the parish priest of the parishes of St Kilda East and Balaclava in the Archdiocese of Melbourne, and he lectures in systematic theology at the Catholic Theological College, Melbourne. He holds B.Sc./ LL.B. (hon) degrees from the University of Melbourne and an LL.M. from University College, London. He also has an M.Theol. from Catholic Theological College, Melbourne, and a licentiate in patristics and historical theology from the Pontifical Gregorian University, Rome, where he was also awarded his doctorate in sacred theology (summa cum laude) for research on the theology of revelation.

The Honourable Joseph Gerard Santamaria, K.C, is an Australian jurist and former judge of the Court of Appeal of the Supreme Court of Victoria. He is a senior fellow in the Juris Doctor program at the Melbourne Law School. He graduated with a bachelor of arts and a bachelor of laws with honours from the University of Melbourne and later attended University College, Oxford, where he graduated with a bachelor of civil law and a bachelor of letters.

Canon Alexander Sherbrooke is a priest of the Archdiocese of Westminster and canon of Westminster Cathedral. He has served the parish of St Patrick's in Soho Square since 2001. The parish runs various evangelisation courses and a soup kitchen and does tireless work amongst the poor in Soho. A monthly night fever event sees the church open all night for confession, counselling, and adoration. Father Alexander was educated at Eton, Oxford, and the University of Edinburgh.

Gregory (Greg) Sheridan, A.O., is an Australian foreign affairs journalist, author, and commentator. He has written eight books on politics, religion, and international affairs and has been the foreign editor of the newspaper *The Australian* since 1992. He is a regular commentator on Australian television and radio, including ABC and Sky News Australia. The ABC describes Sheridan as "one of Australia's most respected and influential analysts of domestic and international politics".

Dr. Tassilo Wanner is a German entrepreneur. During the first years of Pope Francis' pontificate, he advised the Holy Father and George Cardinal Pell on the financial and administrational reform of the Roman Curia.

George Weigel, the biographer of Pope Saint John Paul II, is distinguished senior fellow of Washington's Ethics and

Public Policy Center, where he holds the William E. Simon Chair in Catholic Studies. He also holds a master of arts degree from the University of St. Michael's College of the University of Toronto and eighteen honorary doctorate degrees, as well as the papal cross Pro Ecclesia et Pontifice and the Gloria Artis Gold Medal from the Polish Ministry of Culture.

The Compiler

Professor Tracey Rowland, O.D.M. (Poland), holds the Saint John Paul II Chair of Theology at the University of Notre Dame Australia. She also holds degrees in law and government from the University of Queensland and in philosophy and German language from the University of Melbourne, along with a doctorate from the Divinity School of the University of Cambridge and licentiate and doctor of sacred theology degrees from the Pontifical Lateran University. From 2014 to 2019 she was a member of the International Theological Commission. In 2020 she won the Ratzinger Prize for Theology, and in 2023 she was appointed to the Pontifical Academy of the Social Sciences. In 2024 she was awarded an honorary doctorate *litteris humanioribus* by Christendom College in Front Royal, Virginia. She is a patron of the Australian Catholic Students Association.